D0627312

COME WHAT MAY

COME WHAT MAY

AN AUTOBIOGRAPHY

Arnold Lunn

BOSTON

LITTLE, BROWN AND COMPANY · 1941

FIRST EDITION

Published February 1941

PRINTED IN THE UNITED STATES OF AMERICA

To

SOPHIE AND ETTA

Contents

COME WHAT MAY

CHAPTER I

Background

WHEN I was young life was simple," said my father. "I used to calculate the number of Liberals present at a political meeting by looking at the hats on the pegs outside. The big hats belonged to Liberals, because Liberals had big brains; the small hats to the unintelligent Tory champions of privilege. Of course there were still unsolved problems, but Liberals, at least, knew how to solve them. All that the world needed, so far as secular remedies were concerned, was Democracy, Free Trade and Education. There were still clouds on the horizon, still barriers to be overcome, but the final end was inevitable. Garibaldi was one of my boyhood's heroes; Garibaldi, who was fighting to introduce the British Parliamentary system into Italy. And that, of course, was all that Italy needed to ensure her prosperity. Tennyson was my favourite poet. I loved to flavour my political speeches with quotations from Tennyson. 'Freedom broadening down from precedent to precedent' . . ."

"Until we got to Stalin and Hitler."

"I know," said my father sadly. "That's just what we did not foresee. What inspired us was the Tennysonian future.

"Till the war-drum throbb'd no longer, and the battle flags were
furled
In the Parliament of Man, the Federation of the World."

"Well, at least," I said consolingly, "Tennyson's vision has come true at Geneva."

My father looked wistful, for he had spent much time and money campaigning for the League of Nations. He had lived, indeed, to see many, perhaps most, of the causes in which he believed go down to defeat, and yet to the end he retained his gallant belief in the greatest of all Victorian myths, the belief in inevitable progress. It was impossible to convince him that there is no predestined bias towards improvement, that progress is varied by regress and that civilisations are born and grow to maturity only to decay and die. He would have none of this. "No, what we are seeing to-day is just a temporary set-back. The causes for which I fought as a young man will eventually triumph. I shall live and die an impenitent Liberal."

My father's youth was passed in West Ashby, a little village near Horncastle in Lincolnshire. His home, a rambling house near the parish church, was surrounded by a small farm. My grandfather had deserted farming for trade, but the old instinct was still strong, and he was happier, I think, inspecting his pigs and cows than arranging for the display of groceries in his shops at Horncastle and at Louth. But the absorbing passion of my grandfather's life was neither business nor the farm, but his apostolate as a Methodist lay preacher. For seventy years my grandfather was a Wesleyan Methodist local preacher, a term used to differentiate the lay preachers of Methodism from its ordained clergy. The twenty villages round Horncastle constituted a circuit, and the twenty chapels were supplied by two ministers and some forty lay preachers, whose services were, of course, unpaid.

My grandfather and father had a great affection for the Church of Wesley's baptism and a hatred of the sectarian spirit of partisan Dissent. My grandfather's parents were Anglicans.

He had a pew in the village church and was appointed by the vicar as the treasurer of a church charity.

Had the bishops of Wesley's day been men of vision Wesley's followers would never have been forced into schism, and the Wesleyans would have developed into a religious order within the Anglican Church; their position would have been in some respects not unlike that of the Dominicans or Franciscans in the Church of Rome. Both my grandfather and my father would have welcomed reunion with the Church of England on these terms. Holding such views, my father was consistent in accepting, as he did late in life, Confirmation in the Church of England while remaining a Wesleyan lay preacher.

The eighteenth-century bishops, with a few outstanding exceptions, were curiously detached from their flock. John Wesley was a man sent from God to a very arid land, "for in the wilderness shall waters break out, and streams in the desert." Wesley's revival would have been impossible without the cooperation of the lay preachers. The system of course attracted not only the ardent evangelist, but also men to whom it offered the only hope of a platform and an audience. My grandfather, whose early training in the Church of England gave him a bias in favour of dignity and reverence, was distressed by the tub-thumping methods employed by one or two, but only by one or two, of the preachers on the Horncastle circuit. He lived, indeed, to curb the exuberance of a particular preacher who specialised in humorous interpretation of the Old Testament, for he was not at all amused by this preacher's rendering of the story of Jonah. " 'Come in out of the wet, Jonah,' said the whale. 'We don't often have a travelling preacher in these parts.' "

I was fond of my grandfather, though we had little in common. I could not interest him in the books I was reading or indeed convince him that Thackeray, Jane Austen, the Brontës and Dickens were worth reading. I soon tired of his only epigram: "When I have read all the facts, it will be time to begin with the fiction." He contented himself, however, with defining his own position and made no attempt to force his views upon me, or to insist that I should read St. Paul, his favourite author, instead of Dickens, who was mine. We liked each other, for affection can exist without many common tastes. He often drove me into Louth or Horncastle, and, by tacit consent, we talked neither of St. Paul nor of Dickens. He was my favourite lay preacher, for he never ranted or raised his voice, and I had no difficulty in not listening to his sermons, whereas most of his colleagues disturbed the privacy of my meditations by sudden fluctuations of voice. My grandfather possessed that breeding which you so often find, irrespective of class, among those who meditate on ultimate mysteries. I should not describe him as cultured, but his rudimentary schooling included some study of Latin, a reasonable deduction from the fact that he replied at once, "*Rudis indigestaque moles*," to a clergyman in his shop who – with Ovid's words in his mind – had pointed to a lump of cheese and remarked, "A rough and decomposing mass." I wonder how many modern products of Eton or of Harrow could have translated those words back into Ovid's Latin.

In the ordinary course of events my father would, I suppose, have joined my grandfather in his business. The foundation-stone of his enterprising career was laid by three gentlemen who travelled with him from Warwick to Birmingham. I would gladly record the names of his unknown benefactors if I knew them, but they were philanthropists of the old school who do good by stealth. They ignored the young man in the corner until they were sure that they had attracted his attention, and then one of the philanthropists produced three cards. It seemed an easy trick, and my father was invited to try his luck, an invitation which he could not refuse. My father never played cards for money, but he had the gambling temperament. He had the gambler's faith in his star and the gambler's readiness to back his luck. He accepted the invitation and lost three pounds.

This worried him. He had to account for his petty cash monthly to his father, and he determined to replace the missing three pounds before submitting his account. As a small boy he had begun by breeding mice and had gone on to breeding poultry. He supplemented his pocket money by advertising his mice and poultry in the *Exchange and Mart*, but he soon discovered that there were quicker methods of making money than exchanging Brahmapootras.

He observed that a wholesaler who supplied my grandfather with goods continued to advertise the implements of a new game, called "Sphairistike." My father – who was a boy of seventeen at the time – saw that this new game was beginning to catch on. His instinct did not betray him. Sphairistike is still played, though it is perhaps better known to-day as lawn tennis.

As a business man my father possessed the most important of all qualifications, a capacity for anticipating success. In the eighteen-nineties, when the winter Alps were deserted by all save consumptives, my father foresaw a boom in winter sports. In the eighteen-seventies he foresaw the immense popularity of Sphairistike. He began to sell racquets through the *Exchange and Mart*, and he replenished the petty cash before submitting his accounts to audit. In the year after the first Wimbledon, which was won by Spencer Gore from an entry of twenty-two, and was played before a mere handful of spectators, my father sent out his first circular to a list partly made up of his own clients and partly of people whose addresses he had collected in various ways. The exploitation of the eminent for the sale of anything from a tennis racquet to Pond's cold cream is a commonplace of modern advertising, but my father had few, if any, such precedents to guide him when he approached the eminent Mr. Harry Jones – or, to give him his *nom de plume*,

Cavendish – the secretary of the All-England Club. He offered this man twenty guineas to write an article on lawn tennis for a booklet which my father was publishing, a booklet which contained, among other valuable items, the rules for this new game, for which my father was proposing to sell the necessary implements.

In the year after the first Wimbledon my father patented a scoring dial which was affixed to the racquet just below the strings. People were complaining that scoring was so confusing. Why not, "one, two, three, four," instead of "fifteen, thirty, forty" ? The dials made things easy for the unmathematical; the Prince of Wales made things easy for my father. He ordered one of these dials, and his brother, the Duke of Edinburgh, not only bought a scoring dial, but also a number of articles of tennis equipment from my father's catalogue. From what I know of my father's methods I am quite sure that he exploited with consummate success these strokes of luck.

My grandfather was impressed. He decided that the time had come to put this business on a proper footing. He suggested taking my father into partnership. My father agreed, subject to one slight modification. He was prepared to offer his own father a junior partnership, and at the age of eighteen my father became the senior partner in a firm which was already distributing his goods all over the English-speaking world. One of the devices which my father acquired and patented is in use to-day: the system of marking pins, corners and cross-lines of the tennis court. F. H. Ayres, wholesale manufacturers, supplied my father with goods for his rapidly increasing business. In those days Ayres was unknown and my father was beginning to develop a big business. He was selling, not only tennis racquets, but footballs and cricket bats, and was developing a flourishing business in our leading national sports. He would, I am convinced, have founded a second Lillywhites and made a fortune, had not a dream changed the course of his life. In this dream he was walking with a friend past a large house, his own, with a lawn-tennis court on which young men and girls were playing. In his dream he turned to his friend and said: "That is my home. Those are my children. I have had a great success, but there is not a spark of religion in the place." He accepted the omen and decided to withdraw from business and become a medical missionary in India.

In order to obtain the necessary funds for a university education he sold the business to my grandfather. Unfortunately the "junior partner," though a sound business man in his own field, lacked my father's genius for exploiting a new development. The link between tennis and the Lunns disappeared.

My father was in residence at Trinity College from 1883 to 1887. He read arts, divinity and medicine simultaneously and he was a doctor of medicine before leaving for India. He was awarded the Oratory Medal of the Theological Society and the President's medal for the Prize Essay. He was elected secretary of the Historical Society, which corresponds to the Oxford and Cambridge Union Societies. My father lost the chairmanship of the Historical Society in consequence of his impassioned defence of Home Rule. Trinity College was a citadel of Irish Unionism and the Protestant Home Ruler was regarded with peculiar venom. Nothing better could be expected, of course, from Irish Catholics, but no condemnation was too severe for a man who advocated handing over his Irish co-religionists to the Catholic majority. My father's rooms were wrecked and he was beaten for the chairmanship by a man whom he had defeated for the secretaryship the previous year.

At the end of his university career he met his wife. On July 12th, 1887, he married Ethel, eldest daughter of Canon Moore, rector of Midleton in the county of Cork, and head master of Midleton College.

Temperamentally my father and mother were very different. My mother is shy and reserved to the point of morbidity; my father was expansive, and was never happier than when presiding over committee meetings or reunion conferences. He was a born politician, and would have loved the atmosphere of Westminster, and was disappointed by his two failures to secure election. But my mother, with the deep insight of love, knew from the first that these innocent, and on the whole praiseworthy, activities were little more than superficial interests, however engrossing. She divined that the dominant theme of my father's life was his devotion to Christ, a devotion which had to struggle, but which did not struggle in vain, against the cares of this world and against the standards of the market-place. As a young man my father was offered a safe seat in Parliament by Parnell. The offer was tempting. He was an impassioned Home Ruler, and to the son of a small tradesman a seat in Parliament must have seemed a glittering prize. But he never gave the offer a moment's consideration. He had dedicated himself to the mission field and he was incapable of deserting his post.

As a boy I spent my summer and winter holidays in the Alps and alternate Easter holidays with my Irish and English grandparents.

My grandmother, a Kingsmill, was a gifted woman, from whom my mother inherited her love of beauty in art and in literature. She died before I was born. My grandfather was a distinguished scholar with a passion for teaching. He introduced me to the beauties of the Hebrew tongue. At the age of seven I learned the alphabet and discovered that the Jews wrote from right to left, but I made little progress. My grandfather's sanguine beliefs in the possibilities of imparting knowledge remind me of Milton, who remarks in his tract on education that Hebrew can be studied on Sundays and the Syriac and Chaldaic dialects may be learned by a promising boy "at any odd hour." My grandfather was more successful with Shakespeare, for here at least he succeeded in kindling in me his own enthusiasm. He had a genius for teaching, but the successful head of a struggling school must be something more than a scholar. If a boy was clever he was ready to educate him for nothing. If the parents of any boy, clever or not, were remiss in paying their bills, my grandfather was no less remiss in reminding them. He hated thinking about money, and regarded all discussion of money matters as slightly indecent. Bank balances were not unlike those digestive organs which, at that period, were never mentioned in polite society. If anyone had presented him with a thousand pounds to ease the school finances he would have been grateful, just as he would have been grateful to a doctor who introduced him to a new and useful kind of pill. But in his eyes the only value of money (and pills) was to leave him free to do the things which he thought worth doing and to think about the things which he thought worth thinking about. He left just enough at his death to pay his bills, and his will, which disposed of his personal effects, was accidentally discovered in an obscure corner of the loft.

My mother, though methodical where he had been casual, inherited his hatred of mentioning money. I well remember her rebuke when I innocently asked, as a small boy, whether a certain friend of ours was rich.

Irish Protestantism gave many great leaders to Irish Nationalism, Parnell among them. Few Irish Protestants can have loved Ireland more passionately than did my mother. She was one of the first enthusiasts for Sinn Fein, the ultimate heresy in the eyes of most Irish Protestants. I had the distinction of being the first to introduce this heresy to the attention of the Oxford Union. I had been asked to second a motion in favour of Home Rule. The proposer, an orthodox English Liberal, laboriously proved that the Irish deserved Home Rule. I developed the thesis that Home Rule was not enough. The indignant cries of protest from my side of the house drowned the murmurs of dissent from the opposition. I was not, of course, a very impassioned Sinn Feiner, for my only knowledge of this subject was derived from my mother, but I was enough of an Irishman to enjoy uniting my supporters and my opponents in a solid block of outraged indignation. The mover of the motion, which, thanks to my efforts on its behalf, was decisively defeated, would not speak to me as he left the hall.

My mother's passionate love for Ireland disintegrated her inherited prejudices against the Catholic Church, for the divisions between Irish Protestants and Catholics were not only religious but also racial and social. "To think that my son should go to church with the cook," was Mrs. Tyrrell's outraged comment when her brilliant boy, one of my grandfather's pupils, became a Jesuit. There was little or no social contact between Catholics and Protestants apart from the few representatives of the landed gentry who had remained Catholic through the persecutions and who atoned for this offence by the ardour of their devotion to the union with England. But my mother was on the friendliest of terms with many of the nuns at Midleton and often found her way into Catholic churches, the atmosphere of which she felt was congenial to prayer.

It was this ability to transcend the taboos of her social environment which alone made possible her marriage with my father. That the daughter of an Irish manse should pray in Catholic churches was an odd performance which need not necessarily have any permanent effect; but that she should marry a Dissenter and the son of a tradesman was far more serious, and might well seem an irretrievable blunder. My grandfather was fond of his children, but his attitude to them was detached. He generally read a book at meals and seldom offered them any advice. When my mother announced her betrothal to a Dissenter she expected some protests. All my grandfather said was, "Well, my dear, I'm sure you wouldn't marry any man you did not love." After which he returned to his Tertullian. He was a distinguished theologian, and Tertullian raised many interesting problems. But my mother's engagement was not a problem; it was a fact.

I was born in India on April 18th, 1888. My father remained only one year in India because his health failed. On his return to England he was involved in an unfortunate controversy over the policy of the missionaries, and, as a result of this controversy, he left the Methodist ministry but refused, with reluctance, Bishop Temple's offer to ordain him. Instead he went into journalism and founded *The Review of the Churches* to promote Christian unity. In 1892 he summoned a conference at Grindelwald to discuss Reunion. The conference, which was attended by an Anglican bishop and many leading Nonconformist divines, was destined to change the course of his life – and mine. He had made the travel arrangements for this conference, and drifted gradually into the travel business. I should never have seen the Alps, as a boy, but for his enthusiastic interest in Reunion.

My mother used to take me to the Anglican Church in the morning, and my father to the Methodist chapel in the evening. Perceiving that two forms of the same faith doubled my church attendance, I naturally followed with sympathy his endeavours to merge all Churches into one.

My first clear memory is of Grindelwald in flames in the summer of 1892. The Baer Hotel was the first to catch fire, and our little chalet just below the Baer began to burn a few minutes later. My brother and I were enjoying a siesta when our German nurse rushed into the room and threw open the windows. She was in love with the cook at the Baer Hotel, and, such is the dramatic power of love, she was firmly persuaded that he was sticking faithfully to the spit, continuing to roast beef while he himself was being transformed into roast man. In fact, he was quietly watching the flames from the village street while our nurse called on the population to save him. We met him next day, in the best of health, the first big disillusion of my life.

CHAPTER II

Harrow

THE Victorian Age had only just ended when I entered Harrow in the late spring of 1902. England was still undisturbed in her supremacy and unperturbed by the symptoms which suggested the decline of that Victorian prosperity which was a product of the Industrial Revolution. Socialism was not yet fashionable, and the upper and upper-middle classes were solidly Conservative. The public-school system was still accepted with unquestioning faith as an integral part of the English way of life. Eton and Harrow still contributed the majority of Cabinet Ministers between them. The serene self-confidence of the public-school caste was undisturbed by the dawn of doubt. The criticisms of Left Wing products of secondary schools could be dismissed as unimportant because ill-informed. Until my book, *The Harrovians*, appeared there was no effective criticism from within. Many modern Harrovians have expressed to me their surprise that my story of Harrow life, which was a very mild essay in the now fashionable art of debunking, and was certainly not unfriendly, should have provoked such a violent storm of protest.

In the Harrow of my youth there were no clever young

iconoclasts to undermine our faith in the public-school code. The public-school boy, whether he was the son of a duke or a successful tradesman, was encouraged to regard himself as a member of Samurai, a governing caste trained for positions of responsibility in England and in the Empire. "Some of you," said a famous preacher at Eton, "will be great statesmen. Some of you great ecclesiastics. Some of you will serve your King with distinction in the Army, and some of you" – here his voice dropped – "will be only engineers." He did not, of course, say that "some of you will be only artists," for the public schools made little pretence to be concerned with culture as such, save, of course, with the classical culture which was still the traditional education of an English gentleman. From platforms and pulpits on speech days I heard many variations on a familiar theme, the general effect of which was that Harrow might not produce men as cultured as the French or as learned as the Germans, but it did produce men who could be entrusted with positions of great responsibility. "As monitors or as house prefects you have learned to exercise authority. You have acquired a sense of responsibility to something greater than yourself. The lessons which you have learnt at Harrow will be invaluable when Fate calls you to positions of responsibility at home or abroad." Though I found this reiterated theme a little tedious, I am inclined to think that these complacent remarks were justified. The success of our Imperial administration is not a little due to the training which our administrators have received in the public schools of Great Britain.

It is also only just to remember that, though culture was not the principal objective of a Harrow education, a boy with cultured taste received every encouragement. I can conceive of no finer training for a young writer than to read his immature essays, as I did, to the late George Townsend Warner, a Harrow master who was the author of a brilliant book on the writing of English, and who was, in some ways, the most inspiring teacher that I have ever met.

Matthew Arnold divided contemporary England into the populace, the Philistines, by which he meant the middle class, and the Barbarians, which was his designation for the aristocracy. "The Barbarians," so he wrote, "again, had the passion for field sports; and they have handed it on to our aristocratic class, who of this passion too, as of the passion for asserting one's personal liberty, are the great natural stronghold. The care of the Barbarians for the body, and for all manly exercises; the vigour, good looks, and fine complexion which they acquired and perpetuated in their families by these means – all this may be observed still in our aristocratic class. The chivalry of the Barbarians, with its characteristics of high spirit, choice manners, and distinguished bearing, what is this but the attractive commencement of the politeness of our aristocratic class? In some Barbarian noble, no doubt, one would have admired, if one could have been then alive to see it, the rudiments of our politest peer. Only, all this culture (to call it by that name) of the Barbarians was an exterior culture mainly. It consisted principally in outward gifts and graces, in looks, manners, accomplishments, prowess."

The typical Harrovian of my youth, like Matthew Arnold's Barbarians, was "a very passable child of the established fact, of commendable spirit and politeness, and, at the same time, a little inaccessible to ideas and light."

Precedence in the little world of Harrow was determined by the possession of those virtues which qualify for leadership in military feudal society, physical courage and athletic talent. The aristocracy of Harrow was an athletocracy. Even the head of the school would never have dared to appear in a fancy waistcoat or to walk down the middle of the road, reserved for "Bloods," unless he had achieved some distinction as an athlete. The intellectual, though he could never be a Blood, was not necessarily a useless member of society. In Homeric Greece the intellectual had his own modest position in society, as priest or soothsayer, bard or entertainer. In my house, "The Knoll," the Homeric heroes who led our cohorts to battle on the playing-fields of Harrow disported themselves at ease during the hours set apart for homework, while the local intelligentsia did their homework for them. Cadby, an excellent cricketer, raffled his homework for the week every Saturday evening. He would walk round the house with a bag from which the intelligentsia would be invited to draw a ticket. If a classical scholar drew "mathematics" he could easily trade it to a mathematician who had drawn "Greek prose." This system would seem to have been known in the Harrow of Mr. Winston Churchill's youth. "Poetry is the gilt on the gingerbread of life." This phrase found its way into an essay which purported to have been written by one of the more illiterate members of the school football eleven, but was in fact written for him by the youthful Churchill.

I participated mildly in the athletics which were so important a part of school life, though you might say that my activities were chiefly passive. It was at squash racquets that I achieved my greatest triumph. Cadby and I were drawn together in the house squash doubles which was played in the house yard. There was a gap in the left-hand wall by which it was easy to escape from the field of action and join the spectators. Cadby was school racquets player, and, though I enjoyed squash, I was perhaps the worst player entered for that particular tournament.

"All I ask you to do," said Cadby, "is to serve when it's your turn to serve, and to make an effort to return the service when they're serving. After which, for God's sake, hop out of the court. The sight of your ugly face puts me off."

I did what I was told. I hopped out of the court at the earliest possible moment, and left Cadby to play a spirited solo against the opposing pair. "Pass it another to win," is the refrain of one of our more moving school songs, a song which might have been written for me. No man ever played a less selfish game; no man subordinated himself more completely to the good of the side; no man ever gave a finer display of team spirit.

We won the house squash tie – a great triumph.

A few days later Cadby came into my room. "Let me see, Sally," he began, "I should say that I must have hit the ball at least forty times as often as you did?"

"Oh, yes, Cadby," I said, "I don't think that's an exaggeration."

"Yes," said Cadby pensively, "one shot in forty. That makes one bob in forty. Here's your share of the prize money."

And he threw me a shilling.

I entered the school as a home boarder in 1902, but an epidemic of measles at the school which my younger brother was attending exiled me from home and I spent most of my first term in the house which I entered a little later when I ceased to be a home boarder. The Boer War was drawing to a close, and my father was a notorious pro-Boer. I might have disowned this heritage, but I was convinced by his arguments and did my best to convert my room-mate and other friends to his views. This was most unwise. But I am glad that I had the courage of my father's convictions. All that I have since read about this war has confirmed my belief in the essential justice of the pro-Boer case.

The house I went to was called "The Knoll"; it had just been taken over by the Reverend E. C. E. Owen. It was the worst house in the school when he took charge, and perhaps the best house when he handed it over many years later to his successor. It had a bad name for bullying, and one of those, now dead, who helped to create a veritable reign of terror among the small fry figured later in a German report compiled by way of retort to the Bryce report on atrocities. He was accused by the Germans of ill-treating their prisoners. Whether the accusation was just I cannot tell.

I was not one of his victims. Though I was classified as mad, I was supposed to be amusing, a distinction of some importance. My experiences as a boy have given me a certain insight into the privileges and penalties attached to the position of the mediæval jester. Like him, I was expected to amuse the great, and because I sometimes succeeded I enjoyed immunity from persecution, which provoked much envy among my contemporaries. The position of court jester is precarious, for when the great are in ill humour the fool must walk delicately. The professional risks inherent in the jester's career may be deduced from the circumstances in which I made my *début* as a public speaker. The captain of the house Eleven had invited me to attend his leaving supper. A compliment, for only those who moved in the upper ranks of house society were invited to such functions. I blushed and murmured my thanks. "Take that grin off," said my courteous host. "There is no reason either to grin or to swank. I have asked you because you are a funny little madder, and you've got to make a speech, and, my Lord, if you don't make us laugh you're for it!"

This was not mere badinage. If my speech had been a failure I should have been lucky to escape a summary beating.

I slunk into supper feeling unhappy, for I knew that my presence lowered the social tone of the party and provoked the resentment of those who had only just scraped an invitation, the value of which was clearly discounted by the fact that I was included among the guests. I sat at the end of a long bench. My nearest neighbour edged away from me and ostentatiously addressed all his remarks to his other neighbour. Nobody addressed a word to me throughout this cheerful function. I was left to my thoughts, and these were by no means reassuring. I had never spoken in public, and I had no reason to suppose that I would speak well. And if I did not earn my dinner by making my host laugh there would be trouble – grave trouble. Seldom can a maiden speech have been delivered under more trying circumstances.

"Now then, Sally," said my host genially, "get on with it, and remember what I told you."

I did remember what he told me only too clearly. Fortunately my first joke, a pretty poor one, was a success. From that moment public speaking had no terrors for me. There is something to be said for teaching boys to swim by throwing them in at the deep end. By this method I was inoculated for life against hostile reviewing, for it was during my Harrow career that a premature publication exposed me to a very primitive form of "reviewing." The work thus reviewed was a journal in which I was collecting materials for *The Harrovians*. I had begun to keep my diary because I had come to the considered conclusion that oblivion descended on people when they left school. The cleric who addressed us from the school pulpit, the layman who lectured to us in the speech room, seemed to be separated from the school life by an insurmountable barrier. We lived in one world, they lived in another. Even the masters in close contact with us seemed remote from actuality.

Take, for example, this nonsensical business of "house games." Among the smaller boys in my house there were none who would not have preferred two hours' school work to one hour of a house game. It was not only that we loathed the game itself and the constant shouts of abuse, but we dreaded the aftermath. For those who were inefficient, or on other grounds unpopular, were frequently flogged for "slacking."

I was puzzled by the fact that the authorities tolerated house games. Football was theoretically a relaxation, and was not, I suppose, intended to be a grim ordeal designed to break the spirit of all save the most Spartan. Were the authorities naïve enough to believe that small boys enjoyed house games? Or were they really deceived by the sentimentalism of our football songs? Boys were crude realists who lived in a world of fact. Our elders were sentimentalists who lived in a world of fiction. What was the clue to this mystery? Did people begin to forget not only the trivial incidents but the basic point of view of a boy the moment they left school? It would seem so. But why were men so different from boys? What was the explanation of this strange myopia, this bewildering oblivion of their youth? How could grown men, in all sincerity, produce those extraordinary school stories, so fantastically remote from life as we knew it? Should I be like them one day? I hoped not. There was something, I felt, rather nauseating about the slushy indifference to uncomfortable facts. But would I too forget? If one kept a journal one would have at least no excuse for self-deception. And a journal might serve another purpose. The realistic school story had yet to be written. I decided to write it.

The industry with which I wrote up my journal attracted attention. One evening Cadby came into my room as I was at work on the journal and removed it in order to study its contents at his leisure. Seldom has an author had such good reason to hope that his work would be deemed worthy of only the most superficial examination. In due course I was summoned to a room which seemed to me, as I entered, uncomfortably full of characters who had featured in my Harrow scenario. I was invited to occupy a central position while selected passages from my journal were read aloud. The characters in my scenario then proceeded to review me – with a boot.

I did not resume my entries until my father had secured me a new journal duly protected with a Yale lock.

Bolshevism is a revolutionary movement, the unavowed object of which is to replace the dictatorship of the Barbarians by the dictatorship of the intellectuals, and my own boyish reverence for the Barbarians was qualified by a Bolshie streak of incipient revolt against the standards of a society which relegated me to the lowest ranks of the social hierarchy.

There was nothing heroic about my occasional deflections, impulsive rather than reasoned, from respectful orthodoxy. It was like a small terrier who cannot resist snapping at a tempting calf, but who whimpers ignominiously when he is kicked. Here is a case in point. I had just collected a peculiarly noisy alarm clock from the watchmaker who had repaired it, and was returning to my house, when I met the School Corps marching up the hill to the strains of the Corps band. The charming daughter of a house master stopped to watch them as they passed. In those days the chief attraction of the School

Chapel was that from my pew I commanded an excellent view of this young woman's fascinating profile. As the Corps approached I noted with irritation her complete surrender to that ancient spell which uniform and military music exercises over the feminine mind. At all costs that expression had to be removed from the much-admired face. Invoking the intercession of the Comic Muse, I wound up my alarm, and released it as the Corps approached. It was a powerful machine and it emitted a noise which combined the screech of a factory siren with the rumble of a tube train emerging from a tunnel. An officer shouted at me, two non-commissioned officers abused me as they passed, but the Comic Muse had not been invoked in vain. A ripple of delighted laughter blended deliciously with the enraged rumble of the retreating army. A good moment, and I could have done with more of them. Then suddenly I remembered – oh, horror of horrors! – that the head of my own house was an officer in the Corps. The Comic Muse, I realised all too late, was having her little joke not only at the expense of the Corps, but at my own expense. My sombreness at supper provoked comment. I tried to reassure myself by recounting the story of the alarm with assumed jauntiness. "Phew! You're for it!" said my young friends. I went up to my room.

"Bo-o-y!" The head of my house was shouting for a fag. I heard the scurry of feet past my door and desperately clung to the hope that the fag was wanted for some harmless errand. A few seconds later the messenger of doom thrust his head round my door. "Better ram a towel down your bags," he remarked slowly; "he looks sick as hell."

Never again, I vowed, as I crept miserably along the passage, would I yield to impulse. I would walk delicately, like Agag, all the days of my life. In a Barbarian milieu the artist had to pay too heavily for his creative impulses. *Qualis artifex pereo.*

"*Bend over.*"

I bent.

* * *

"Six of the best" had a taming effect upon the embryo Bolshevik and were responsible for a long period of eager subservience to the dictatorship of the Barbarians. My nonconformity, indeed, was fitful and intermittent, but it is only just to recall that this inconsequent streak of heterodoxy, though it involved occasional floggings, was also indirectly responsible for a change of fortune which was to have a decisive influence on my career.

In my third term at Harrow I found myself in a form with its own peculiar variety of co-operative tradition. Proceedings usually opened with questions on our homework. Slips of paper were handed round while the master read out a dozen questions, and we did our best to answer them. We then exchanged papers with our neighbours, after which the form master read out the correct replies, and we corrected our neighbours' papers. "Corrected" was indeed the operative word, for if Jones had written *dixerint* instead of *dixerunt*, Smith, who was "correcting" Jones's paper, was expected, in accordance with our tradition of courteous socialism, to change *dixerint* into *dixerunt*. "From every man according to his capacity, to every man according to his needs." We certainly did our best to translate into practice this basic principle of the Marxist creed. None of us would have cribbed in a competitive examination for a prize or a scholarship. Cribbing was regarded as contemptible if used to gain an advantage over another boy, but legitimate and even honourable as a communal scheme to outwit the authorities. I should probably have raised no objection to this co-operative scheme for reducing the tedium of homework had the scheme been explained to me, but it was in happy ignorance of this convention that I began to correct my first paper at the beginning of the term. Unfortunately I allotted marks to Jones, whose paper I was correcting, not in accordance with his needs, but in accordance with his work, with the unhappy result that he was required to write out the two pages of Latin grammar which he had insufficiently prepared. Jones was extremely indignant, and so was I. My objection was that it was unfair to kick me for failing to comply with requirements which had never been stated. If he wanted me to help him out he could jolly well ask me politely. Jones replied that he was not going to ask me politely, but that he would knock hell out of me if my textual emendation of his work did not meet with his full approval. As it happened it was Jones's paper which I had to correct next day, and Jones paid the penalty for his incivility, and I subsequently paid the penalty for trying to improve his manners. From that moment there was no turning back, for I felt myself committed to a policy of "no surrender." Actually Jones and my other victims avenged themselves by falsifying such correct answers as they discovered in my own papers, with the result that I sank to the bottom of the form, to the bewilderment of my form master, for I had attained double remove at the end of the summer term. Suspicions were aroused, and the form master began to submit the papers to a critical examination and soon discovered the truth. Meanwhile I was tolerably unhappy. Even in the warm spring weather I continued to wear the thickest of underclothes and a winter overcoat as a buffer against reprisals. It would, of course, never have occurred to me to discuss my worries with my father, for the public-school system had, at least, the virtue of compelling unquestioning loyalty to its own somewhat barbaric code of honour.

The facts which emerged from my form master's detective work seemed to compel the conclusion that I alone of all the form had a holy horror of cribbing. My form master was impressed and offered generous terms to my father (who was finding even the home boarder's fee rather a strain) if he would send me to his house with a view to becoming eventually his head boy. I had already spent most of my first term in this house, and in spite of its toughness I was anxious to return, if only to escape the ignominy attached to the home boarder's state. But I have often wondered if I should not have made some effort to undeceive my form master. I doubt if, at the time,

I could have analysed my own motives, and in any case it would be a dull world if we only got our deserts and nothing more than our deserts. The Comic Muse had intervened again. Because Jones had not couched his request for co-operation in courteous terms I had been forced into the rôle of a boy who would not crib; because I played this rôle with sullen obstinacy I ceased to be a home boarder; and because I spent nearly four years in a Harrow house I collected the raw material for a book which was the only best seller that I have ever written. All thanks to Jones.

When I eventually became head of the house I did my best to carry out the implied bargain, because my house master had inspired not only my gratitude but my affection. I claim to have been responsible for one solid and valuable reform. I deprived the house prefects of the right to flog and left them only the poor consolation of reporting offenders to me for execution.

A head of the house, if he was not himself a member of the athletocracy, was expected to content himself with the appearance of power and the control of the house. In my first week as head of the house I was, in a sense, accorded the same sort of terms as Hitler accorded to the Prime Minister of Czechoslovakia. I was not attracted by the rôle which the Bloods assigned to me, and a trial of strength was therefore inevitable. The opposition played into my hands and forced me into the rôle of a reformer determined to suppress smoking and other abuses. The campaign ended when the Captain of the House Eleven, convicted of a customary but unconstitutional assumption of authority, complied with my request to bend over and "take six." Public opinion was deeply shocked that a "Blood" should be forced to submit to such an indignity at the hands of a mere monitor such as myself. My own motives, as usual, were mixed. I was anxious to suppress certain abuses and I was still more anxious to suppress certain abusive critics. I did well to refuse to allow others to exercise the powers of the position to which I had been appointed, and I dare say that my action may have helped to improve, however slightly, the position of the unathletic monitor *vis-à-vis* the Blood. But when I re-read my journal record of those days I found myself sympathising instinctively with the liquidated athletocracy and faintly repelled by the outlook of Commissar Lunn.

CHAPTER III

The Evolution of a Radical

I ENTERED Oxford in the Michaelmas term of 1907. The status of a Harrovian is (or was) mainly determined by brawn, of a Balliol undergraduate by brain. Harrow was a feudal society, but the atmosphere of Balliol had something in common with Periclean Athens. "We have no sour looks for our neighbour even if he enjoys himself in his own way." Balliol, as Cyril Joad somewhere remarks, was the most tolerant of institutions, more tolerant perhaps of intellectual eccentricity than of undistinguished mediocrity.

As editor of *Isis* and secretary of the Oxford Union, my status in Balliol was much the same as that of a Harrovian on the edge of the Cricket Eleven, and *therefore* I enjoyed Balliol more than Harrow; but I should be very sorry if Harrow adopted the standards of Balliol, or *vice versa.* The intellectual receives quite as much flattery as is good for him in later life, and is all the better for spending a few years of his youth in a feudal climate.

In the course of a review of one of my books, Mr. Neville

Lytton wrote, if I remember aright, something to the following effect: "When I read Arnold Lunn's *The Harrovians* I was impressed by his spirited attack on the Harrovian worship of brawn, but when I visited Mürren I discovered that he had created a ski-ing athletocracy, and that by concealing the fact that he wrote books on anything but ski-ing he was treated with as much deference as the Captain of the Boats in my Eton youth. And I perceived that Arnold Lunn attacked the worship of games at Harrow because he wasn't good at games."

Neville Lytton's criticism is unanswerable. Vanity is the most potent of forces in the shaping of life and in the choice of political creeds. We tend to think well of institutions which think well of us. The man who is born into a family with a long tradition of distinguished service to the State derives some reflected glory from England's greatness, and tends to be a conservative. His instinct is to conserve a state of affairs which assigns to him high rank in the social hierarchy. And if, as a boy, he has reverently fingered an old sword hanging in the hall, if one of his uncles was a V.C., and one of his grandfathers a famous general, he will naturally accept without question the feudal scale of values which holds in high honour physical courage and the military virtues. If, on the other hand, your grandfather entered England in the fifties as an immigrant from South-Eastern Europe, if you yourself are an intellectual with more brain than brawn, if you were kicked about at school by embryo Blimps, if you have no stomach for fighting and, in consequence, a detestation of war, you will naturally resent a criterion of values which assigns to you a low place at life's table. There are two kinds of pacifists – those who think that it is wrong to kill, and those who know that it is unpleasant to be killed; and pacificism owes more than pacifists are willing to admit to the bias of the unwarlike against a system which honours the fighting man and despises the conscientious objector.

Though I was never a Methodist, I come of Methodist stock, and therefore acquired in my youth the traditional Radical anti-militaristic bias of my background. The rivalry between Church and Chapel reflects the rivalry between the landed gentry which provided the officers of the fighting services and the rising class of tradesmen from which Radicalism and Nonconformity were recruited.

My father was a pro-Boer, and my mother an ardent Sinn Feiner. As a boy I heard much of the injustices to the Boers and of Ireland's wrongs, but nothing of England's rights. I believe that the Boer War was one of the few occasions which justified a man in opposing his country's policy during war, and I have discovered no reason to change my views on Ireland, but I regret that pride of country which is normal and instinctive in most people is, in my case, a characteristic acquired partly by reading history, and partly by living abroad, which has enabled me to compare the English way of life with rival systems. It was a tradition, a bad tradition, of English Radicalism always to put the worst possible construction on anything which England did. It was, I think, the Frenchman Sorel who remarked that English Liberals in attacking their own country believed that they rendered themselves very sympathetic, but that this was by no means the case. The instinctive reaction "My Country, right or wrong" is open to criticism, but it is, in some respects, saner and sounder than the Radical tradition, which was inspired less by sympathy with foreign peoples than by envy of the class which governed England and waged her wars.

I remember the first occasion on which I felt a sudden and instinctive emotion of patriotism. I had spent, as a young man, some weeks in Palestine, which was then under Turkish rule, and on reaching Cairo I saw a battalion of an English regiment marching through the streets. I was surprised by, and slightly ashamed of, my sudden sense of Imperial pride—*Civis Ro-*

manus sum translated into modern terms. Race and inherited tradition had triumphed over the concepts of intellectual Radicalism.

Those who were educated in the old Liberal tradition were peculiarly exposed to the temptations of complacency and selfishness, for Radicalism encourages people to believe that altruism is displayed not by giving away one's own money to the poor, but by supporting political measures for the expropriation of the rich.

I entered Balliol a convinced Radical and began my career at the Union by eloquent attacks on the rich and demands for justice to the poor. A Balliol undergraduate who had heard me speak asked me if I would care to spend two or three evenings a week working among the poor. Balliol ran a Boys' Club in the poorer parts of Oxford. An embarrassing request, which I had not the courage to evade. I drifted down to the Club once or twice, played billiards with the boys, and was invariably beaten, but made no effort to emulate the more muscular Christians who took them on at boxing. I was not a success, and soon discovered that it was more amusing to defend the poor at the Union Debating Society than to amuse them in the Boys' Club. I had been slightly disconcerted to discover that all those who worked in the Club were either mildly conservative or uninterested in politics. There were many Radicals and Socialists in Balliol, but one and all they affected to despise the Boys' Club as an attempt to bluff the poor out of their legitimate rights by offering them the "opium of the people." Even in those days Marx's shallow definition of religion was popular among the irreligious. I was also uneasily conscious of the fact that these young proletarians disliked and distrusted Radical doctrinaires but admired and envied the typical "Bullingdon Blood" who rode to hounds, spent money like water, and drank anything but water. The failure of Socialism in England is due to the fact that the working man genuinely admires a sporting Conservative peer such as Lord Derby and neither admires nor believes in the Left-Wing intellectual. The trade-union leader retains these instinctive sympathies and antipathies, and is more concerned to prevent the capture of the movement by the intellectuals than to eject the Conservative Opposition.

But for the grace of God, and the Alps, I might have remained a doctrinaire Radical all my days. Fortunately the summer and winter holidays which I spent in the Alps provided a useful corrective. Among the mountains I came into contact with reality. The Radical thinks in abstractions, and his enthusiasm for the working classes is often qualified by his uneasiness when he comes into contact with individual members of those classes. I was never interested in the status of the Alpine peasantry, but my best friends have been Alpine peasants. As a boy I spent long hours playing with Hans, whose father owned the chalet where we lived. We quarrelled and fought, and experimented in rock climbing on a rocky boulder near the chalet. I respected him because he could lead up the steepest face of that boulder, a face which had defeated all my attempts. Few men in later life have inspired as genuine a reverence as that which I felt for Christian Almer, the great Grindelwald guide, who led Whymper on many of his most famous climbs.

The Alps helped to correct the inferiority complex which I had acquired at Harrow. My melancholy display at Harrow football convinced me that I was a coward. Intellectuals are sometimes heroic, but as a class they are less courageous than other men. My mountain passion helped to overcome my natural infirmities. I was reassured by the discovery that in moments of peril I could behave with that bare modicum of self-control which decency demands. And because I instinctively admired (and envied) the courage of the great mountaineers, I felt no temptation to applaud that belittlement of military gallantry which was one of the more nauseating symptoms of the post-war literature of the Left, a symptom which disguised that envy of courage which is nowhere greater than among intellectuals.

II

I am told that the Oxford Union Society has lost prestige in recent years. Certainly its notorious motion, "That this House refuses to fight for King and Country," impaired the reputation of what was, and perhaps still is, the most famous debating society in Europe. In my day the presidency of the Union was one of the great prizes of undergraduate life. It was the best possible introduction to a political career. The elections for the offices of the Union were by ballot of the members, and canvassing was forbidden. Merit as a speaker was not, of course, the only factor in success. Politics played a part, but as evidence of the greater tolerance of Conservatives it is worth nothing that it was far easier for a Radical to be elected in my youth, when the Union was preponderatingly Conservative, than for a Conservative to be elected in recent years when the Union was dominated by the Left. In those days religious affiliations were as important as political. An active member of the Oxford University Church Union, a prominent Methodist or Congregationalist, was almost sure to defeat an equally good speaker who had no religious backing. When I stood for the secretaryship, the Christian vote was split, and I was elected, but in a straight fight against a distinguished Congregationalist I was decisively beaten. "Christianity, a profitable superstition for Presidents" was the theme of one of my editorials in *Isis*, but all efforts to organise a free-thinkers' vote failed. Canvassing, though forbidden, proved impossible to control, and there was one unsuccessful canvassing petition after I went down.

Of the Union Presidents in my day, Ronald Knox was outstandingly the most brilliant speaker. His wit always seemed spontaneous, however carefully he had prepared his speeches, whereas Guedalla, the historian, was less successful in concealing the mechanism of his Art. Guedalla, a contemporary of mine at Balliol, was one of the more famous Presidents of my day. He was famous not only for his epigrams, but for the care with which he tried them out before debates on friend after friend, until they had been polished to perfection. He was alleged to keep a notebook so as to avoid imposing the same epigram more than once on the same audience. His reputation in this respect provided me with an escape from a difficult situation. Private business at the Union opened with questions, allegedly humorous, to the officers "relative to the discharge of their official duties." I had asked Guedalla two questions which I thought rather funny, but his brilliant and spontaneous retorts captured the house. The score was forty love in his favour, but the game was not yet lost. "And what was the third question," I asked, "which you told me to ask you?"

Guedalla was one of the brilliant young men of Balliol, and we all prophesied for him a great career at the Bar and in politics. In which we were mistaken. After various unsuccessful attempts to enter the House of Commons, he devoted himself to history. The late Lytton Strachey once described Guedalla to a friend of mine as one of his imitators, a bumptious remark for which there was no justification whatever. Guedalla's style has matured, but has not radically altered since his undergraduate articles appeared in *Isis*. And in those days Lytton Strachey was unknown. Guedalla's prestige as a historian would be greater in academic circles if he were less readable, but he has been guilty of achieving big sales, and is therefore classified as a "popular historian." Critics are always inclined to suspect that paradoxes are a substitute for research, but Guedalla is not only an entertaining writer, but erudite and hard-working. Like other historians, he writes in the style which is the natural expression of his personality, and it is not his fault that his style happens to be lively.

When I first called on Guedalla I was on the point of withdrawing, for I assumed that I had blundered by mistake into the room of some scion of a great military family. I have a confused recollection of cannon balls on the floor, a musket beside the fireplace, and innumerable prints of Napoleon, Wellington, and famous battles. Guedalla's interest in war is, of course, purely academic. He has no taste for violence, even for the modified violence of sport. Sorel somewhere remarks that Liberalism is founded on the repudiation of the feudal conception of personal honour and on the determination to substitute dialectics for violence in the struggle for power. Guedalla is a Liberal and an intellectual, and if Sorel be right Guedalla's choice of subjects for his biographies – Wellington, Napoleon III, and Palmerston – is intriguing as evidence of the triumph of feudal values over Liberal prejudices. Palmerston was a Liberal, but he had more in common with Tory squires than with the Radical intellectuals of his day. He rode to hounds and he loved hard sports. He was happiest in a setting in which Guedalla would be supremely miserable. I cannot see Guedalla following the hounds. Even his choicest epigrams would not be an asset in the hunting field. We all tend to cherish a romantic admiration for the qualities in which we ourselves are defective, and I suspect that if the Creator were to offer Guedalla a choice of careers in a second reincarnation, he would not choose to be an historian but would opt for the career of a modern Wellington or Palmerston. In deference to Liberal tradition he is, of course, careful to conceal his romantic affection for Wellington and Palmerston under a mask of humorous condescension and affectionate patronage, but the disguise will deceive only the undiscerning.

III

As a young man, I should have been flattered to have been described as an intellectual, a label which I accept to-day with resignation. The word does not imply the possession of a great intellect, but merely an interest in the things of the mind. An intellectual might indeed be defined as a man who is more interested in universals than in particulars. In my youth I was passionately anxious to achieve literary fame, and it is amusing to reflect that if I am remembered at all, after I die, I shall be remembered, not as a writer, but as the founder of the Arlberg–Kandahar and as the inventor of the Slalom Race, both of which will, I believe, survive for many years and perhaps for many centuries. *The Harrovians* will be consulted by an occasional social historian, concerned to contrast the extinct feudal system of education with the standardised State-controlled education which will be universal in the dreary world of the future. Ski-ers will turn to my *History of Ski-ing* as a work of reference; but the only book of mine which will, perhaps, be read for its own sake fifty years hence is *The Mountains of Youth*. Among mountaineers *pietas* is as common as it is rare in this irreverent age, in which almost the one thing which has not been de-bunked is the tradition of the Alpine Club. My own favourite escapist literature in these distracted times is the works of the Alpine pioneers. There is something solidly reassuring in the climate of Victorian security which dominates these records of an escape into a world of artificial danger. I am vain enough to hope that, in the next war to destroy Prussianism, an occasional mountain-lover may turn to *The Mountains of Youth* for consolation and distraction. Nothing, of course, is so ephemeral as controversial writing. The Catholic apologist can add little of value to the old arguments for the old Faith. His principal concern is with the fashionable heresy of the moment, and there is nothing as dead as a dead fashion, and few forms of literature as uninteresting, save to specialists, as the refutation of extinct heresies.

In 1909 I still cherished illusions, and I regarded my appoint-ment as editor of *Isis* as the first step in a distinguished literary career. My predecessor had been forced to resign in order to placate an indignant writer who had threatened a libel action. The writer had been a friend of Oscar Wilde, and my prede-cessor, stung by some insult to *Isis*, had referred to his "no-toriously wilde manner." Shallow people sometimes remark that the Catholics and Arians parted company over a single letter in one word, but one letter may, as my predecessor discovered, make all the difference. The proprietors were anxious to discover a safe, responsible, and cautious candidate for the vacant post. Hence my appointment.

Humility is not unknown among intellectuals, but is perhaps more common among geniuses than in the rank and file. Vanity is, of course, a universal failing, but it is a failing to which intellectuals are particularly prone. We do not write for ourselves alone, nor for ourselves and God; we express ourselves because we are anxious to influence other people, and we starve for want of recognition. Like Guedalla, we often secretly admire those whose code and whose ideals we profess to despise, and would be charmed if we could win their admiration in return. As this is not easy, we are content if we can attract their indignant attention.

I began cautiously, for I had been appointed as a "safe man" and did not wish to follow my predecessor into obscurity. My first experiment in the now fashionable art of debunking was a leading article in the Michaelmas term of 1909: "Play the Game. A Straight Talk to Freshmen." "If ever you feel tempted to an action which might bring discredit on your College, turn your gaze to the College Arms on your tobacco jar and murmur to yourself, 'It's not cricket.' " Heavy irony, but subtle enough to deceive the principal of one of the ladies' colleges, who summoned the freshmen and read my leading article for their spiritual guidance.

I followed up this experiment in irony by a succession of overt attacks on conservative traditions. In those days Oxford was predominantly conservative. The public schools were still sacrosanct, and the "old school tie" was still serenely secure from criticism. My attack on the public-school tradition provoked some indignant protests and inspired Keble Howard – in *The Sketch*, I think – to pay an undeserved compliment to the alleged courage of a man who could risk the displeasure of an Oxford recruited in the main from public schools. But it calls for far more courage to defend the public-school tradition to-day than it did to attack it in 1910. My friends were amused by my inconoclasm, and those who were not amused were not my friends. So I had nothing to lose.

From the universal I descended to the particular. My next target was the Annandale Society of Balliol, an exclusive club which consisted in the main of old Etonians. "Its atmosphere," writes Ronald Knox, "was one of energetic rowing, hard drinking, plain dressing, occasional gambling, and unexpected because apparently unmerited academic triumphs." The "Anner" of my day revived the old Elizabethan tradition of the scholar-athlete. They drank hard, and then beat the sober intellectuals at their own game, for many of the University prizes were captured by members of the "Anner." They filled the Quad with the echoes of their exuberant feasts, and then proceeded to prove their physical fitness by collecting Blues in addition to scholarships. Julian Grenfell and his brother were scholars of Balliol and distinguished athletes. Julian wrote the noblest poem inspired by the war a few weeks before he fell in action. Almost every member of this brilliant group fell in the war. Many of them refused staff appointments, for which they were eminently fitted. Charles Lister, an attaché at Rome when the war broke out, pestered the authorities until they released him for military service, and was killed a few months later at Gallipoli.

Had I been a member of the "Anner" I should have been as noisy as the noisiest, but like other members of the Balliol bourgeoisie I resented these periodic advertisements of exclusiveness, and as an Harrovian I was glad of a chance to have a dig at Eton. The necessary pretext was provided by the coincidence of an "Anner" dinner and a concert in Balliol Hall. As the audience (of both sexes) came out of Hall, the members of the "Anner" were serenading Trinity College, our neighbour, in a song which theologians would describe as "offensive to pious ears." In those days I assumed that all feminine ears were pious, and in the next issue of the *Isis* I made some tart comments on the "ungentlemanly" behaviour of the "Anner," most of whom, as I was careful to point out, had been educated at Eton. It was a silly article, for I confused two different codes. The opposite poles of the Christian code are represented by the saint and the sinner, of the feudal code by the gentleman and the bounder. It is not "ungentlemanly" to commit adultery or to get drunk or to sing Rabelaisian songs. It is both ungentlemanly and unchristian to cheat at cards or to display fear in the face of danger.

In this connection I may refer the reader to a conversation, in Philip Gibbs's *Blood Relations*, between a Balliol undergraduate and a German aristocrat. " 'My dear Fritz,' said Edward Middleton, 'in England, the aristocracy and landed gentry pride themselves on behaving like grooms and ostlers. It is one of our finest traditions. After all, grooms and ostlers have much in common with us in their love of horses and their stable language. Also, we do not despise vulgarity. On the contrary we admire it. It is only the upstart middle class, not sure of themselves, who despise those whom you are pleased to call the lower orders. The English gentleman has certain qualities of the peasant, and is very much at ease with that class to which originally, in many cases, he belonged.' "

My article on the "Anner" provoked an immediate response. A group of Etonians, of different colleges, called upon the assistant editor, my brother, to demand an explanation. My brother is not a horsy man. "I have heard," he remarked to me after this interview, "of people being horse-whipped, but I had never seen a horse-whip till my uninvited guests brought one to my room. I was glad to discover what a horse-whip looks like, but I should have preferred to have acquired this information in the course of private research."

Mr. Duff Cooper, of New College, was one of the party. He had his own reasons for disliking the Lunn brothers, for Hugh reported the Union debates for the *Isis* and, an inverted Dr.

Johnson, he took care that the Tory dogs, of whom Duff Cooper was one, got the worst of it.

Duff Cooper had much in common with the Elizabethans of the "Anner." He was a good scholar – his study of Talleyrand is one of the most illuminating biographies of that cryptic diplomatist – and he has also the Elizabethan attitude to danger. A story which I have not verified but which was currently believed in Oxford may be told in this connection. A drunken undergraduate pointed a pistol, believed to be unloaded, at Duff Cooper's head. The bullet missed him by an inch. The undergraduate collapsed with horror, but Duff Cooper did not move a muscle. "I don't mind you playing with pistols," he murmured, "as long as you're tight. But you couldn't miss me at that range if you were sober."

My brother explained that he was in no way responsible for the editorial of which they complained, and the party broke up in a mood of frustration. They did not call on me, because I was still hobbling about in a splint as the result of a mountain accident, and their code forbade them to beat up a cripple, though my brother would have been as incapable of resistance as I, for two sound legs are of no avail against twelve indignant Etonians. They complained that it was mean of me to attack them, protected as I was by crippledom from just reprisals. I was unimpressed by this plaint, for I felt that they were no more helpless against me than I should have been against them, but for my accident. We were quits, and the columns of *Isis* remained open for such reply as they chose to make.

A few days later I happened to pass the open window of a ground-floor room in Balliol in which the "Anner" were dining. I climbed in through the open window and clattered on to the floor. "I've come to return the unsolicited call which you paid on my brother. We Lunns are great sticklers for etiquette. My brother was physically incapable of ejecting you. You are morally incapable of ejecting me, for your chivalrous code will forbid you to assault a poor cripple. And your law of hospitality will, I hope, compel you to offer me a drink, for this long speech has made me thirsty." Like Queen Victoria, they were not amused. They did not fall upon me, for they were anxious not to hurt my leg. They approached me with gingerly movements and somehow managed to carry me towards the door. Three of them were told off to handle my injured leg. I emerged into the Quad in a horizontal position, and was deposited with great care on the Quad. "Next time I call on the 'Anner,'" I reflected, "I will content myself with leaving a card."

My brother Hugh, who writes under the name of Hugh Kingsmill, succeeded me as editor. A professor of literature at a Middle Western University, who took the chair for me at one of my lectures, asked me if I knew the works of Hugh Kingsmill. "It's a pity," he said, "that he incorporated his acute and penetrating criticisms of Shakespeare in a burlesque novel, *The Return of William Shakespeare*, but I learned more about Shakespeare from that book than from almost anything else that I've read. He strikes me as the most brilliant literary critic in England to-day. I hope his works are successful." I disclosed my relationship, and added that it was difficult to make a living by writing books about books. Douglas Jerrold, who is a publisher, tells me that whereas it was easy to sell five thousand copies of a scholarly book of literary criticism before the Great War, a publisher would think himself lucky if he sold five hundred copies to-day. There has been a marked degeneration of literary taste in the last fifty years.

IV

Among the books that have influenced me, few have had more effect than *Life and Habit*, by Samuel Butler, which I read at Oxford. Butler is best known for his *Erewhon* and *The Way of All Flesh*. He was something of an iconoclast, and because he detested the Calvinistic Christianity in which he was reared he is often quoted by progressives, such as Cyril Joad, as if he were a forerunner of modern Left-Wing intellectuals. In fact he was a convinced conservative. He had little use, it is true, for Anglicanism, but he had a great respect and a certain sympathy for Catholicism. He was the first to introduce me to the Darwinian controversy. A convinced evolutionist, he attacked the fallacies of the Darwinian interpretation of evolution, but because he was an amateur, a literary man, and because his inimitable style suggested a flippancy which concealed from the superficial the intense seriousness of his convictions, he was ignored by contemporary scientists, only to win recognition after his death.

Butler was a conservative because he believed that the unconscious knowledge which we inherit from our ancestors is much more reliable than the conscious knowledge which we painfully acquire during the course of our own lives. His conviction that instinct is nothing more than unconscious memory is the basic doctrine of his philosophy. His argument may be summarised as follows. A novice in the art of playing the piano picks out the individual notes, one by one, and plays them by a process of *conscious knowledge.* The practised player performs difficult pieces without effort, "often indeed while thinking and talking of something quite other than his music . . . we draw the inference that the more the familiarity or knowledge of the art, the less is there consciousness of such knowledge . . . whenever we observe a person able to do any complicated action unconsciously, we may assume both that he must have done it very often before he could acquire so great proficiency, and also that there must have been a time when he did not know how to do it . . . no man is a great hypocrite until he has left off knowing that he is a hypocrite."

This last profound observation is, I believe, the key to Hitler's psychology. Hitler, it seems, is genuinely pained when he is accused of lying or breaking faith. And if the Butler theory is true Hitler's ancestors must have been lying for thousands of years, for Butler identifies instinct and unconscious memory. Personal identity, according to Butler, is far less definite than we are inclined to believe. In a very real sense the child is identical with its ancestors. The child breathes before it talks because it has had far more practice in breathing than in talking. Its remotest ancestors could breathe, but it is only in comparatively recent times that the child, in the person of its ancestors, learned to talk. Instinct is the unconscious memory of actions which we have performed so often that we can perform them without conscious thought.

Our intellectuals, who know that they know and whose conscious knowledge finds expression in schemes of world improvement, may be compared to the child picking out the scales on the piano with its eyes firmly fixed on the score. But it is "those who do not know that they know so much, who have the firmest grip of their knowledge; the best class, for example, of our English youth, who live much in the open air, and, as Lord Beaconsfield finely said, never read. These are the people who know best those things which are best worth knowing – that is to say, they are the most truly scientific. Unfortunately the apparatus necessary for this kind of science is so costly as to be within the reach of few, involving, as it does, an experience in the use of it for some preceding generations."

Many of Butler's theories have been adopted by Spengler.

Until I read Butler I had assumed that men might be divided into those who desired and those who opposed reform, but Butler suggested the possibility that reformers might be divided into Conservatives who based their programmes on the foundation of human nature and human experience, and Radicals who ignored the immense power of inherited instincts and traditions. In a passage which I quote from memory Butler describes two methods of getting a hen to cross a road. The first is to throw small pieces of bread, not at the hen but just in front of her, and thus lure her gradually across the road.

The second method is to throw a loaf of bread *at* the hen. "And this," says Butler, "is the method of our advanced Liberals. Some of whom mistake stones for bread."

By chance I happened to read Burke while Butler's theories were still fresh in mind. Burke's essays on the French Revolution are well worth re-reading to-day, for a recurring pattern runs through the great revolutionary movements, and there is nothing which dates in Burke's attacks on the Jacobins. *Mutatis mutandis*, Burke's criticism can be applied to the Russian Bolsheviks and their disciples in Spain. Burke was no die-hard Tory. He defended with passionate sincerity the cause of the American revolutionists, and attacked no less effectively the policy of the French Jacobins. It is interesting to note that Burke's *Reflections on the Revolution in France* was inspired by a prototype of the Dean of Canterbury, a Nonconformist minister, Dr. Price, whose enthusiasm for the French regicides was as uncritical as the Dean of Canterbury's affection for the Russian Bolshevists. Rousseau, who dumped his children on a foundling school, is described by Burke as "a lover of his kind but a hater of his kindred," an epigram which applies with even greater force to modern revolutionaries. Burke awakened in me a faint distrust of professional humanitarians. "Benevolence to the whole species, and a want of feeling for every individual with whom the professors come into contact, form the character of the new philosophy."

Before reading Burke I had been artless enough to believe that the French Revolution was, in essence, a rising of the oppressed poor against a selfish aristocracy; but Burke provoked an uneasy doubt of this popular simplification of a complex problem, a doubt which was subsequently reinforced by reading De Tocqueville's classic study of the Revolution. Burke contended that the Revolution was provoked by a struggle for power between different groups, of whom the Revolutionists were perhaps the least concerned to redress the just grievances of the poor. The Jacobins were resolved to transfer the government from the landed gentry to the cities, "among tradesmen, bankers, advocates . . . and those cabals of literary men, called academies." Burke's list of English partisans reads like an intelligent anticipation of the classes who supported the Republicans in Spain and who condoned the atrocities of the Bolsheviks.

The Jacobins, said Burke, were supported by "the dissenters of the three leading denominations; to these are readily aggregated all who are dissenters in character, temper and disposition . . . Whigs and even Tories; all the Atheists, Deists, and Socinians; all those who hate the clergy, and envy the nobility; a good many among the monied people; the East Indians almost to a man, who cannot bear to find that their present importance does not bear a proportion to their wealth. . . . The monied men, merchants, principal tradesmen, and men of letters (hitherto generally thought the peaceable and even timid part of society), are the chief actors in the French Revolution." Burke did not convert me to Conservatism, for my Radicalism was too ingrained to yield to the first attack. His action was delayed, but his effect was greater than I knew at the time.

V

While at Oxford I founded two clubs, which are still flourishing: the Oxford University Mountaineering Club and the Alpine Ski Club. The former, unlike the sister club at Cambridge, did not number among its objects the organisation of roof climbing, but I kept in practice for the Alps by scrambles on Oxford pinnacles. The fact that I possessed an Alpine rope had certain incidental inconveniences, for my room came to be regarded by tardy revellers as the normal method of entering the College. But I am glad I was a roof-climber, for I shall never forget a sunrise after completing a somewhat hazardous "first ascent." Oxford had never seemed so beautiful. Her spires were silhouetted against the golden haze of a May dawn. And for the first time in my life, I felt that there were some things in England almost as lovely as the Alps. Oxford was the first English institution which I loved, and still love without qualification, and without reservation. There are indeed three experiences in travel of which I never tire: the moment when the train sweeps out of the ravines of the Jura to reveal beyond the lake and beyond the green foothills the radiant gleam of the Oberland; the moment when one escapes from the ugly terminus at Venice to discover the Adriatic washing the station steps; and the turn in the railroad which discloses the spires of Oxford.

Oxford had an erosive effect upon my Radicalism. The quiet insistence of a loveliness which has matured through the centuries must influence even the most doctrinaire of Radicals. Of all the articles which I wrote for the *Isis* there is only one which seems to me to have been written with the conviction of passion rather than with the conviction of the intellect, a panegyric of the Middle Ages. Then, as now, I was happy among hills, and could endure the plains if surrounded by the beauty of the past; but where the scenery is resolutely flat, and where the works of man are obstinately modern, I suffer from intolerable nostalgia.

As the years passed, I ceased to make my personal tastes the criterion for my views of the social order. I discovered that the politically-minded may be divided into those who accept the facts of human nature and those who plan their programmes on the naïve assumption that man is what they wish man to be. It is, perhaps, regrettable that man is a hierarchical animal, with an invincible tendency to create distinctions, but the realist starts from facts, and does not plan for the future on the assumption that a classless society is realisable in this geological period. The only result of abolishing an aristocracy of birth is to substitute an aristocracy of money, or, as in Russia, of quasi-hereditary bureaucrats.

Subversive movements have never found it difficult to attract a certain type of aristocrat, but such aristocrats never fail to remind us that their criticism of aristocracy is based on first-hand knowledge. Of all forms of snobbery, the snobbery of the Left-Wing aristocrat is the most exasperating, and it is time that a word was coined for those who insist on having it both ways, such as these aristocratic *Hibows* who claim the prestige of the intellectual without disclaiming the prestige of noble birth. I have met many Etonian Socialists, but I have not met one who regrets that he was not educated at a Board School. If one fouls one's own nest, it is always pleasant to feel that one's nest is an eagle's and not a crow's.

Mr. H. G. Wells is a typical example of the doctrinaire Radical who makes no attempt to adapt his Utopias to the nature of man. It was Mr. Wells who hailed the last war as "the war to end war," a prediction for which there was never any basis more substantial than wishful thinking. Mr. Wells cheerfully sweeps aside as irrelevant all the enduring elements in human society, religion, race, love of country and love of property. It is easy to produce blue prints for a classless society if one ignores the hierarchical nature of man; easy to draw up constitutions for a Federal Europe if one ignores the fierce tribal rivalries and racial feuds of modern Europe. Even the few weeks that I have spent in Rumania, Hungary, Jugoslavia and Bulgaria sufficed to cure me of any illusions as to the possibility of an enduring world peace, save in a slave world dominated by a single power. What was the *Pax Romana* but a peace imposed by a conquering race, a peace which endured only so long as the Roman legions were invincible?

Mr. Wells is a genius, but the feudal tradition of England, though a declining force, is strong enough to infect with class consciousness one of the greatest of contemporary writers. Who cares whether Mr. Wells was born in a draper's shop? Mr. Wells cares. He is too modest to realise that few Englishmen to-day would prefer the career of a Duke to the career of Mr. Wells. Because Mr. Wells was not educated at a public school, he has an immense dislike of the classics which are taught in public schools, and because he dislikes the classics he finds it necessary, as Mr. Belloc somewhere says, to depreciate Julius Cæsar because he spoke Latin.

My brother's anthology *Invective and Abuse* is enriched by Mr. Wells's abuse of men whom the world, in its ignorance, still considers more important than Mr. Wells. "The intensely personal tone," writes my brother, "in the following verdicts on Alexander, Cæsar, Napoleon, and Shakespeare, suggests that they are based partly on the self-evident premiss that if Alexander, Cæsar, Napoleon, and Shakespeare are great men, Mr. Wells isn't, and partly on the more debatable premiss that if Alexander, Cæsar, Napoleon, and Shakespeare are not great men, Mr. Wells is." Of Shakespeare, Mr. Wells writes: "Shakespeare's thought amounts to very little. . . . The name was never banished" (from Mr. Wells's *Outline of History*). "It was never there. Why should it be?" "Napoleon," writes Mr. Wells, ". . . this dark little archaic personage, hard, compact, capable, imitative and neatly vulgar . . . Napoleon could do no more than strut upon the crest of this vast mountain of opportunity like a cockerel on a dunghill."

It is easy to understand why Mr. Wells should wish to denigrate Cæsar, Alexander and Napoleon, for these men succeeded where Mr. Wells failed. They made history; they moulded "the shape of things to come"; but Mr. Wells's political writings are mere literature which shuffles querulously beside the march of events. The architects of history have exploited, consciously or unconsciously, the irresistible forces which Mr. Wells sweeps aside as irrelevant. Napoleon, for instance, was a sceptic, but he knew that the Church would endure to the end, and that no political system which defied religion could survive. His utterances on the theme of religion, race, aristocracy and nationalism are sane and realistic. And it is because Mr. Wells, the wishful thinker, discounts the experience of mankind and dismisses as irrelevant all forces which he personally dislikes that his predictions have been consistently wrong and his influence on politics consistently negligible.

But the instinctive motives which Mr. Wells despises are too potent even for Mr. Wells. I hope he will forgive me if I justify this remark by an incident which I observed, an incident which is all to Mr. Wells's credit. A controversy in which we engaged was ended by an invitation to lunch. Mr. Wells is magnanimous, and cherishes no personal animus against those who disagree with him. I enjoyed the lunch, and was captivated, as others have been, by Mr. Wells's charm and essential modesty. We lunched at the Garrick, of which Mr. Wells is a member. At that time the Garrick was entertaining the members of the Reform Club, which was temporarily closed for house-cleaning. The exclusiveness of London clubs is a myth, but the Garrick happens to be one of the few clubs to which an honest member of the middle classes, who had not been convicted for felony or misdemeanor, would not automatically be elected. Mr. Wells, who is a member of both the Garrick and the Reform, was most careful to remind me, more than once, that he was lunching in the Garrick, not as a guest from the Reform, but in his own right as a member of the Garrick. He walked round the smoking-room chaffing the exiles from the Reform. "You're refugees," he remarked; "I belong."

I was amazed. Though I am unimpressed by Mr. Wells the politician, I entertain a feeling of respect, bordering on reverence, for Mr. Wells the creator of Kipps and Mr. Polly. I found it difficult to believe that this great master of fiction could entertain the notion that his prestige was increased by membership of a club, however exclusive. His humility is reassuring. He will, I suppose, spend some time, when he leaves this world, in a Reform Club even less exclusive than the club in Pall Mall, but Rabelais and Boccaccio will be his sponsors for that Celestial Society which is favourably disposed to such candidates as possess the important qualification of humility.

VI

On the night of one of the post-war elections, a friend of mine took me along to a party which was celebrating the Conservative successes. I knew nobody present, with the exception of my friend, and I did not feel that I had much in common with his friends. They were rich, and as Conservative successes were reported over the radio they celebrated these victories in champagne. At that time I should have described myself as a Conservative, but I did not like my fellow-Conservatives. At least not that particular group. They were, for the most part, City people and big business magnates, very different from the country squires who still represent all that is best in the Conservative tradition, for in the country privileges are still balanced by corresponding duties. The Conservatism which is inspired solely by the effect of politics on dividends is as unsympathetic as the Radicalism inspired solely by envy. The idealistic Conservative has more in common with the idealistic Radical than either has with many of their nominal allies.

I reacted from Radicalism to Conservatism, and I passed on beyond Conservatism to a political creed the very name of which, *Distributism,* is unknown to most Englishmen. During my undergraduate days I had read the works of G. K. Chesterton and Hilaire Belloc, and their influence was one of the principal factors in my conversion; but it was not until the late twenties that I began to take an interest in their political views. Apart from these pioneers, the Distributist creed has been defended in England by many writers, notably Douglas Jerrold, Christopher Hollis, and the late A. J. Penty, and in America by that very gifted and brilliant author Herbert Agar.

Distributism is at once more radical and revolutionary than the servile creed of Socialism and more conservative than modern Conservatism. The Distributist believes in the distribution of property and the means of production. He insists that the love of property, particularly property in land, is a sane and enduring instinct which needs to be both fostered and controlled. Fostered with the object of increasing the number of people who own property; controlled to prevent the concentration of property into the hands of the few. He is opposed to the subordination of the producer to the financier, and of the countrymen to the townsmen, and he would agree with Burke and Spengler that modern democracy is too often a mask for securing the dominion of the urban proletariat over the peasant. He is convinced that the health of a nation depends very largely on the proportion of men owning their own land or their own small business, and he resents the tendency to transform the small owner into the employee of the State or of chain stores.

Switzerland is the closest approximation to a Distributist state that I know, though the word "Distributism" is unknown in Switzerland; but the success with which they have adopted, unconsciously, the principles of Distributism will be discussed in a subsequent chapter.

CHAPTER IV

Why Men Climb

MAN might be defined as an animal who invents artificial problems for the fun of solving them. The ingenious mechanism of the human body provides the athlete with a fascinating variety of intriguing puzzles. How fast can a body be propelled along a racing track? How high can a body be lifted by a pole vaulter? What is the limit of steep and smooth rock up which man can climb?

Animals are severely practical in exploiting their physical resources. An antelope may, unwittingly, break the antelope world record for a hundred metres while escaping from a lion, but he makes no effort to lower his own record until he meets the next lion. Cats climb trees to escape from dogs, but there is no Alpine Club for cats. The record-breaking appetite is peculiar to man. Men do not play football to satisfy an obscure appetite for placing a round ball between two vertical posts, for this craving could be relieved by kicking a goal on a deserted football field. The game of football consists in an attempt to solve the problem of controlling the direction of a ball in spite of the efforts of the opposing team.

Mountaineering does not consist only in climbing mountains which have been climbed before or only in the invention and solution of new problems. A virgin peak is a problem, but when a peak has been climbed new conditions have to be introduced so that the struggle, which would lose something of its appeal if the outcome were certain, may continue with redoubled zest. The ascent of peaks no longer virgin by virgin ridges or unexplored faces, guideless climbing, winter mountaineering and ski mountaineering, are the results of an evolution partly determined by the search for new problems. The mountaineer has something in common with the crossword-puzzle enthusiast, but the thrill of a solution necessarily varies with the stakes involved, and the joy of tracking down an elusive clue is inevitably more intense where the penalty for failure may have tragic consequences.

I remember leading down a great face which ended in the labyrinth of an impassable ice-fall. It was essential to hit off a miniature saddle some ten feet in breadth which interrupted the downward sweep of the rock ridge on our right. All but the immediate foreground was blotted out by driving snow, but I banked on the possibility that the shoulder would correspond to some ill-defined belt of gentler ground across the slope we were descending, and when the slope eased off – a change of gradient more perceptible to the foot than to the eye – and turned sharply to the right, suddenly the clue to our descent loomed up through the greyness. At such moments one feels not only the intellectual thrill which is the reward of a correct deduction from obscure clues, but also the more primitive joy which follows peril safely past.

Ruskin believed that he had disposed of mountaineering by his assertion that there was more beauty in mountains seen from the lowlands than in summit panoramas. But even if this were true it would prove nothing. We may agree with Ruskin that Amiens Cathedral is more beautiful than St. Peter's, but that is no reason why we should refuse, with Ruskin, to enjoy St.

Peter's. Every school of architecture has enriched æsthetic experience, and every aspect of the mountains has its peculiar appeal. Ruskin overlooked the connection between the ascetic and the æsthetic. The mountains are prodigal of loveliness, but they keep their more intimate beauty for those who tread the ascetic way. It may be true, as Ruskin asserted, that the real beauties of the Alps may be seen without danger to life or limb, but Ruskin overlooked the possibility that our appreciation of beauty is sometimes intensified by danger.

Many years ago my friends and I had spent an unlovely night in a squalid cowshed. I had curled myself up on a shelf and tried to sleep, but the cowherd supplemented his meagre earnings by taking in fleas as paying guests, and I was soon forced to escape into the open. I tried a shallow cave, and had dozed off when a goat began to nibble my boots. I woke with a splitting headache and wondered why men were such fools as to climb.

We left before dawn. I staggered sulkily up the moraine behind a lantern whose inconsequent and impish flicker failed to reveal a nasty hole between two sharp rocks into which I stumbled, barking my shin. A dishevelled sunrise uncurtained a frowsy collection of sleepy hills flecked by dirty patches of grey snow. A despondent sun lumbered above an eastern ridge and some greasy clouds trailed across the tired blue of a dispirited sky. God, how my head ached!

We meandered up an easy rock-ridge and then roped before crossing a broad, steep gully. The leader began to chip steps in the hard frozen snow. Suddenly a loud explosion from above jarred my splitting head and provoked a moment of dull resentment, transmuted all but instantaneously into gripping terror. Two thousand feet above us a rock-fall had launched itself into our gully. The leader made an instinctive movement forward and then checked. We could not hope to cross before the avalanche passed. Had any one of us been struck while we were moving we should all have been dragged down together. Burying our axe-heads in the snow, we cowered down and waited.

Separate and successive explosions re-echoed from the upper reaches of the gullies. Chronometers record the impersonal procession of objective seconds, but no chronometer can measure time as experienced by men placed as we were. I remember a pause before the vanguard of rock struck a broad ledge just above us, rebounded and screamed overhead with a comet tail of trailing dust. But we, as yet, were untouched. A friendly pinnacle deflected some big boulders down a lateral rib, but the shrapnel of smaller fragments sprayed around us, and we still lived. The main attack had spent itself, but a rolic of camp followers ricocheted off the ledges and whistled round our heads, and still our luck held. Then the sound changed: crescendo as the avalanche approached, diminuendo as the disappearing trail of rocks vanished down the gully with the disappointed rumble of innocuous thunder.

Very shakily we stood up. Nobody spoke. The leader mechanically uncoiled the rope off the axe-head, withdrew the axe and, with the deliberate movements of a man who is making a big effort to rediscipline shaken nerves, slowly began to cut steps to the edge of the gully. We scrambled on to the rocks and sat down heavily. The mountain still seemed to be quivering with a dying convulsion. The snow slopes fanned out below the gully. I looked down on to the glacier and thought of what might be lying there, quiet, motionless shapes,

> For whom all winds are quiet as the sun,
> All waters as the shore.

Then came the reaction. A hill breeze rippled over the snows and sent the blood coursing through our veins. I found myself making strange, grateful movements with my hands, as if to bathe them in the overflowing sun. Life and colour and joy had returned and the mountains had recovered their grace of outline. The morning headache had vanished, the scales were lifted from my eyes. The dullness of vision disappeared. I remember a miniature cornice, a delicate volute of iridescent colour, glinting in the sun. The wings of death had passed and in their passing (strange paradox!) had quickened our response to the beauty of the visible world whose citizenship we still retained.

"He shall dwell on high: his place of defence shall be the munitions of the rocks." The mountaineer can translate this verse from Isaiah into the memory of moments when the artillery of heaven and the munitions of the rocks bear witness to the majesty of One who dwells on high. No dawns are more terrible in their beauty than those in which the red and angry snows herald a day that breaks in splendour only to set in storm. No mountain memories are more enduring than those of moments when the black wings of the wind-tormented mist lift to disclose the embattlements of frost-riven rock. There is a tranquil loveliness in the slow drift of sun-tinted clouds across a summer sky, but their true glory and their might are hidden save from those who invade their mountain kingdom. No man knows the mountains until he has watched the approach of storm from high places. The puffs of mist down the gullies are the skirmishers which precede the grand assault. Slowly the last pools of light in the coppery glitter of a thunder sky are obscured by a blur of indefinite gloom. Wisps of filmy cloud gather the rocky towers into their greyness. The patter of hail or snow plays its staccato tune on the mountains, and finally all but the immediate foreground is blotted out by driving snow.

Many years ago I spent a New Year's Day struggling up through storm to the crest of the Eiger. A sudden lull tempted us up the final ice slope, but, just as we started, down from the summit a low mutter broke the silence and struck fear into our hearts. We knew what was coming, but were not prepared for the tornado which broke. The mountain quivered beneath the impact. Stones, whipped off the ice, screamed past like shells. A flood of loose snow poured down the ice and blotted out the steps which we had cut with such labour. I had left my climbing irons behind and was hurled out three times at full rope's length before I regained control. I remember a sudden vision of the valley below, but my companion's ten-pointed claws saved us. Slowly and with infinite care we crept down the ice, in which every step had to be recut; and when at last we felt beneath our feet the reassurance of rough and friendly rock we threw ourselves on the ground and lay huddled together for many minutes, indifferent to cold, intoxicated with the relief of safety, and far too weary to raise our voices above the storm.

But even that day had its moments of calm beauty. We had been climbing for thirteen hours and had seen nothing but the same drab foreground of ice-fretted rock and grey mist, and then suddenly towards evening we paused, for the blanket of grey mist seemed subtly changed, stirred by movements which destroyed its cohesion. The mist was beginning to disintegrate. Soon only a diaphanous veil separated us from the windy spaces of the sky. Then even this dissolved to reveal the dark blue waters of Thun and the distant ground-swell of the Jura. The western sun flooded the cold grey rocks with a golden light. The long hours of storm and darkness were a fitting prelude to this hour of mountain peace.

The most hackneyed of peaks provides the climber with a problem which he must solve afresh if he climbs it in bad weather. To lead in a storm up a ridge one has never climbed in fair weather is an even more stimulating test of mental and physical powers. There are moments when it is difficult to believe that one is contending with inanimate matter, for there is a human touch about the bluster of a storm and the peculiar malice of the wind. The wind will suddenly peter out when the mountaineer reaches good anchorage and make a great parade of having business in a neighbouring gully, only to leap upon him with an exultant scream as he leaves a secure ledge for the perils of an exposed slab. Cloudless skies and mountain valleys may inspire a mood of Wordsworthian pantheism, but the mountains of storm would incline one to pan-diabolism but for the queer sense of contending against something which is half friend and half foe:

Love thou the gods and withstand them lest thy fame should fail
at the end,
And thou be but their thrall and bondsman who wast born for
their very friend.

This rendering of the old Norse theology expresses the curious *odi et amo* attitude of the mountaineer to the mountains. Even the most sophisticated mountaineers seem unable to resist this conviction of personality in the hills. Most climbers have felt the presence of an unseen companion at times of crisis, a feeling which is the theme of a fine poem by Geoffrey Young:

I never see him, but his tread
Sounds just before my own.

When I was young I was caught by a storm ski-ing alone among the Oberland glaciers. I had been climbing for some days and I had run out of food. Most of those who have died of exposure in the Alps had exhausted themselves in the search for shelter. I did not make this mistake, and resigned myself to the inevitable while I had still reserves of strength. I divided my time between digging a hole in the snow to keep warm and taking shelter in the hole until I had once again begun to freeze. It was not until the small hours that I was in danger. But towards morning the strain began to tell. I heard siren voices in the little winds which gathered strength in the hollows of the hills. There was a caressing touch in the snow-laden breezes which moved so gently over the surface of the glacier. It would have been easy to die, if only to avoid the recurring strain of forcing myself to my feet just as my frozen limbs relaxed for sleep. While I was contending with the gathering darkness I had known the fear of night and the misery of solitude:

It darkens, I have lost the ford,
There is a change on all things made,
The hills have evil faces, Lord,
And I am awfully afraid.

But fear left me when I gave up hope of shelter and the loneliness of the snows did not oppress me. In those days I should have resisted the instinctive urge to pray as a collapse more ignoble than the surrender to sleep, but in some dim fashion I knew that I was being sustained by a Power not myself and encouraged to continue the struggle by a Companion, nagging and insistent, who forced me to my feet when I fell back half asleep, and who would never let me rest. Later I dismissed this experience as an interesting example of the recrudescence of primitive beliefs under conditions of fear and exhaustion. But perhaps I was right, for primitive man saw clearly many truths which are forgotten in the clamour of great cities, and among the mountains our intuitions of truth break through the mist of modern falsehood. It was no accident that the discovery of mountain beauty coincided with that Romantic revival which was a reaction against the dreary deism of the eighteenth century, or that systematic mountaineering began in the decade in which Darwin published *The Origin of Species*. Leslie Stephen, the agnostic, was not the only mountaineer to whom the mountains spoke in "tones at once more tender and more awe-inspiring than that of any mortal teacher":

> *φεύγωμεν δὴ φίλην ἐς πατρίδα . . .*
> *πατρὶς δὴ ἡμῖν, ὅθενπερ ἤλθομεν*
> *καὶ πατὴρ ἐκεῖ.*

These lines from Plotinus appeal to those who, like the writer, recovered in the "friendly fatherland" of the hills the belief in a friend behind phenomena. *Kai Pater ekei.* "I was found by them that sought me not; I was made manifest unto them that asked not after me." Mr. Irving might have inscribed these words on the title-page of his charming anthology *The Mountain Way*, for passage after passage bears witness to the search for some clue to the mysticism of the hills; but few are the mountaineers who follow up with the same courage the mountain clues which lead to truth and those which lead to mountain crests.

"The solemn dome resting on those marvellous buttresses,

fine and firm above all its chasms of ice, its towers and crags; a place where desires point and aspirations end; very, very high and lovely, long-suffering and wise. . . . *Experience*, slowly and wonderfully filtered; at the last a purged remainder. . . . And what is that? What more than the infinite knowledge that it is all worth while – all one strives for? . . . To struggle and to understand – never this last without the other; such is the law. . . . We've only been obeying an old law then? Ah! but it's *the* law . . . and we understand – a little more. So ancient, wise and terrible – and yet kind we see them; with steps for children's feet."

How much this passage would have gained not only in precision, but in beauty, had the writer been able to decide whether Mont Blanc was a god or the creation of God. "*La religione*," says Croce, "*è precisa. La religiosità è vaga.*" Contrast the vagueness of this Alpine religiosity with the clarity of two other writers, quoted in the same anthology, who had thought out their mountain *credo*, the first a Shintoist, the second a Catholic.

"The mountains themselves," writes Prince Chichibu, "stand as symbols of eternal life, and serve as the expression of a mighty spiritual Being."

The same conclusion emerges from the famous passage, quoted in full in a later chapter, in which Mr. Belloc describes the distant view of the Alps, which "link one in some way to one's immortality . . . from the height of the Weissenstein I saw, as it were, my religion. I mean humility, the fear of death, the terror of height and distance, the glory of God . . . and my confidence in the dual destiny."

To the Shintoist and to the Catholic the mountains speak the same language and proclaim the same truths, truths which the shy prophets of a vague religiosity dimly perceive but dare not boldly profess.

CHAPTER V

1909

I HAD spent the Easter vacation of 1909 with my friend Scott Lindsay at Hexham, before returning to Oxford, and it was at Hexham that I first met the lady who is now my wife. Mabel Northcote had never met anybody in the least like me, and she explained to her aunt that she hoped the experience would remain unique. In those days I had not begun to mellow, and whereas I have now succeeded in concealing, then I was anxious to emphasize my unpleasant eccentricities. I owe my marriage, as I owe almost everything good in my life, to the mountains, for I was asked to lecture on mountains, and in the course of the lecture I displayed my less repulsive characteristics, and I noticed to my surprise that the most interested member of the audience was a girl whose disapproval I had amused myself by provoking. Mabel shared a room with a cousin, and we carried on a long conversation about mountains through the keyhole. Towards midnight I slipped a copy of a mountaineering journal under the door. "It's getting late," I said. I looked at my watch. It was twelve o'clock on April 18th, 1909. I had just come of age.

A few days later I startled Miss Northcote with the first of a long series of proposals which broke down her resistance many years later. I returned to Oxford to discover that I had just been sent down for failing in the rudiments of Holy Scripture, an examination the main object of which was to increase the revenues of the university. This was a nuisance, for it was not easy to edit the *Isis*, the undergraduates' journal, from London, and my chances of the presidency of the Union, to which I had just been elected secretary, were not improved in spite of the fact that Balliol considerately allowed me to come up for four debates. And I did not enjoy the prospect of explaining to my future father-in-law, Prebendary Northcote, that my presence in London was connected with my lack of interest in Holy Scripture. Prebendary Northcote was the son of Sir Stafford Northcote, who was Lord Salisbury's rival for the Premiership. His statue stands in the central hall at Westminster next to Gladstone's. He was an old-fashioned statesman with no talent for political intrigue. "We don't have many politicians like old Sir Stafford," remarked an elderly registrar of births when I gave him the details about my son. As an M.P. he was entitled to have his letters franked for nothing, but he always bought and tore up a penny stamp if he posted from the House any letter dealing with his private affairs.

Prebendary Northcote had two daughters, of whom the elder, Jaqueta, has placed my children and me under a debt which cannot be repaid. He had three sons, of whom the elder two were killed in the last war. His youngest son, Harry, who succeeded his uncle as Earl of Iddesleigh, is now serving with the Welsh Guards. Few Englishmen who were born between 1880 and 1920 have escaped the ordeal of war.

I should never have been married but for a lucky accident. I am indebted for my good fortune not to my virtues, but to my most irritating, if not my most serious, shortcoming — absent-mindedness. After my fourth proposal had been rejected Miss Northcote felt that it was unfair not to give me a definite *congé*, which she did. A few weeks later the lady undergraduates' magazine published a brilliant review of my articles in the *Isis*. I was flattered and intrigued and invited the unknown reviewer to meet me. "Ten to one," I remarked to a friend, "that she's got side whiskers or a beard, but it's worth taking a chance on it." The reviewer replied that she could not come to tea with me in Oxford because she had just been sent down (another link between us), but that she would meet me in London. So we met at the Authors' Club. The reviewer had neither side whiskers nor a beard. On the contrary, she was beautiful and witty, a dangerous combination. We exchanged the scintillating epigrams which were the period pieces of the Edwardian age, and, mortified by a sudden lull in the conversation, I proposed to her, to see what she would say. She accepted me to see what I would say. She was never in the least in love with me, but she thought that it would be fun to be engaged. She had literary ambitions, and to the novelist in embryo all experiences are valuable. We exchanged letters in which sentiment and humour were felicitously blended, and during a visit to her people I came across, while searching at her behest for a book, no less than six drafts of the first ingenuous love letter that she wrote to me. I produced these six drafts with a slight air of reproach. She looked at them with interest. "I could not make up my mind," she said, "whether to send you the letter I actually sent you or this second draft. . . ."

A few days later I wrote two letters, announcing my engagement, one to a literary friend and the other to Miss Northcote. My first letter was a pen picture of my fiancée which rather pleased me. I kept a copy. It would be useful as material for a novel. I did not keep a copy of the letter to Mabel Northcote and I did not enjoy writing it. And then I put the letters into the wrong envelopes. Worse still, the first letter contained a phrase tolerant of an interpretation which I had never intended, an invidious comparison between my fiancée and Mabel. She assumed that I had chosen this oblique method of conveying to her the news of my engagement and my own estimate of my good fortune in escaping from a previous entanglement. I was horrified when I discovered what I had done, and followed it up with a letter of apology and a call. A few weeks later my fiancée told me that I had ceased to interest her; my stock of epigrams had run dry, so she broke off the engagement.

"You little know," my wife often remarks, "what a nuisance you are with your absent-mindedness."

"But if I hadn't been absent-minded," I reply, "I should not have had a chance of being a nuisance to you," an answer the controversial effectiveness of which is perhaps more apparent to me than to my wife.

II

Nineteen-nine was a decisive year in my life both for good and for ill. Fortune has few favourites, and good luck seldom lasts.

On August 28th, 1909, Scott Lindsay and I walked up Cader Idris. Scott did not feel like climbing, so I left him and began to descend the east ridge of Cyfrwy. Our British hills provide the rock climber with problems as exacting as those met with in the Alps. The climbs are shorter and once the summit is reached the cragsman can run down on grass or scree to the valley, and because he has greater reserves of time and energy he can overcome difficulties which might defeat him on a long and exhausting Alpine climb. The cliffs and gullies of Wales, Cumberland and Scotland are something more than a mere nursery for Alpine climbs. They are, in their own right, a glorious arena of adventure. Judged by modern standards the ridge I was descending is not a difficult climb, but it has a crack which, though short, has been compared with the famous "Mummery Crack" on the Grépon, and some steep pitches.

The day was perfect. The burnished silver of the sea melted into a golden haze. Light shadows cast by scudding clouds drifted across the blue and distant hills. The sun flooded down on the rocks. I slid down the crack and reached the top of the steep face of rock above "The Table." The usual route dodges the top fifteen feet of this face, and by an easy traverse reaches a lower ledge. But on that glorious afternoon I longed to spin out the joys of Cyfrwy, and I found a direct route from the top to the bottom of this wall, a steep but not very severe variation.

It was one of those days when to be alive is "very heaven." The feel of the warm, dry rocks and the easy rhythm of the descending motion gave me an almost sensuous pleasure. One toyed with the thought of danger, so complete was the confidence inspired by the firm touch of the wrinkled rocks.

I was glad to be alone. I revelled in the freedom from the restraints of the rope, and from the need to synchronise my movements with the movements of companions.

I have never enjoyed rock climbing more. I have never enjoyed rock climbing since. But, at least, the hills gave me of their best, full measure and overflowing, in those last few golden moments before I fell.

A few minutes later Lindsay, who was admiring the view from Cader, was startled by the thunder of a stone avalanche. He turned to a stray tourist, urging him to follow, and dashed off in the direction of Cyfrwy.

And this is what had happened. I had just lowered myself off the edge of "The Table." There was no suggestion of danger. Suddenly the mountain seemed to sway, and a quiver ran through the rocks. I clung for one brief moment of agony to the face of the cliff. And then suddenly a vast block, which must have been about ten feet high and several feet thick, separated itself from the face, heeled over on top of me, and carried me with it into space. I turned a somersault, struck the cliff some distance below, bounded off once again and, after crashing against the ridge two or three times, landed on a sloping ledge about seven feet broad. The thunder of the rocks falling through the hundred and fifty feet below my resting point showed how narrow had been my escape.

I had fallen a distance which Lindsay estimated at a hundred feet. It was not a sliding fall, for except when I struck and rebounded I was not in contact with the ridge. The fall was long enough for me to retain a very vivid memory of the thoughts which chased each other through my brain during those few crowded seconds. I can still feel the clammy horror of the moment when the solid mountain face trembled below me, but the fall, once I was fairly off, blunted the edge of fear. My emotions were subdued, as if I had been partially anæsthetised. I remember vividly seeing the mountains upside down after my first somersault. I remember the disappointment as I realised that I had not stopped and that I was still falling. I remember making despairing movements with my hands in a futile attempt to check my downward progress.

The chief impression was a queer feeling that the stable order of nature had been overturned. The tranquil and immobile hills had been startled into a mood of furious and malignant activity, like a dangerous dog roused from a peaceful nap by some inattentive passer-by who has trodden on him unawares. And every time I struck the cliff, only to be hurled downwards once again, I felt like a small boy who is being knocked about by a persistent bully—"Will he never stop? Surely he can't hit me again. Surely he's hurt me enough."

When at last I landed, I tried to sit up, but fell back hurriedly on seeing my leg. The lower part was bent almost at right angles. It was not merely broken, it was shattered and crushed.

I spent half an hour on that ledge before my cries were heard, and four hours before the search party arrived. Long hours. Dr. Warren, a first-class London surgeon, happened to be in the district, and thanks to his skill my leg was saved, though on two occasions preparations were made for amputation. I was in bed for four months, and two years passed before

I could climb again, and I should still be wearing a queer iron contrivance to take the weight of the knee if the contrivance in question had not gone through a window at the banquet following our first victory in the Anglo-Swiss University Ski Races. But I accepted this as an omen, and none of the gloomy things which were predicted have happened to me, and the libelled leg has carried me up many mountains and helped me to collect some cups in ski racing in the days when the standard of racing was infinitely lower than it is to-day. So 1909 still has a large balance on the credit side.

Two years after I fell I returned to the Alps, and after a training walk set out to climb the Dent Blanche, which was considered a difficult peak in the Victorian age. I left the hut an hour before another party bound for the same peak, and was overtaken before I had been climbing for two hours and met them on their homeward descent while I was still three or four hours below the top. My guide maintained an uninterrupted mutter of complaint. It was unfair, he insisted, to expect one guide to take a cripple up the Dent Blanche. I ought to have had a second guide, for I had not allowed for the fact that two inches of cork sole on my short right leg would destroy that touch which is so essential for balance or that the open wound in my shin would bump into every protruding knob. Ten hours after leaving the hut I struggled up the final slope to the summit. I remember a miniature wave of snow glinting in the sun, the ultimate symbol of a kingdom reconquered. I patted it affectionately, and then came the reaction, and I was violently sick from pain and exhaustion. Pleasure is of the body, happiness of the mind. Those moments on the Dent Blanche were among the least pleasurable and the happiest of my life. Nothing mattered, for I could still say:

> I have not lost the magic of long days,
> I live them, dream them still.
> Still am I master of the starry ways
> And freeman of the hill.

Shattered my glass ere half the sands were run,
I hold the heights, I hold the heights I won.

Those lines were written by the greatest of mountain poets, Geoffrey Young, after he lost his leg in the war, in spite of which he has since climbed the Matterhorn, Monte Rosa and Grépon. On the Dent Blanche I had felt humiliated by the criticisms of the guide, and to restore my self-respect I felt it necessary to prove that, so far from needing two guides, I could dispense with companions, so I set out alone for the Grand Combin, the highest mountain in the Alps outside the immediate neighbourhood of Mont Blanc and Monte Rosa. It was perhaps as well that I was joined in the hut by another solitary climber. We traversed the mountain together, leading alternately, and it was not until some time later that I laid the ghost of that angry guide by solitary ascents of the Wetterhorn and Mönch. On my return from the Alps I climbed the ridge off which I had fallen, only to be saddened by the contrast between the carefree happiness of the last moments before I fell and the anxious care with which I tested every hand and foothold of treacherous Cyfrwy.

III

My surgeon had lectured to me on the importance of antisepsis and had provided me with a nice little syringe for the daily cleaning of my wound. I carried out his instructions very faithfully for at least a week after I had been released from nurses, but the ritual of antisepsis is difficult for the unmethodical. I remember returning to a club hut after a long climb, and resuming the daily routine of searching for the elusive dressing, which, as usual, had wound itself round my toe. A doctor who was in the hut rushed forward to assist, under the impression that I had been struck by a stone. I lay back luxuriously, for I was tired, and it was much pleasanter to have my wound dressed by an expert than to dress it myself.

"But this is an old wound," he exclaimed.

"Don't let that deter you from dressing it," I replied anxiously, and then, of course, I was treated to the routine homily on the dangers of blood poisoning. I reminded him that Benvenuto Cellini lay on the floor of a dungeon and treated his compound fracture with cobwebs with admirable results. The doctor was unconvinced.

My distrust of experts, which I shall attempt to justify in a later chapter, owes something to my experiences with my leg. A distinguished surgeon informed me in 1924 that if I continued to walk on it without support I should be a cripple in ten years, and that a bad ski-ing fall would have very serious consequences. Acting on his advice, I had my leg fitted with a steel contraption, of great weight, and became an Honorary Lady for whose benefit young girls rose sympathetically in crowded buses and offered the poor cripple a seat. I might still be wearing this contraption, which did not make ski-ing any easier, had not the British Universities defeated the Swiss Universities in January, 1925. At the dinner which followed this happy event, as I have said, the steel contraption, somehow, went through a plate-glass window and spent the night in the snow. I had some difficulty in readjusting it when it was returned next morning by the concierge and I discarded it for ever a few days later. Having resigned from the Honorary Ladies Club I won the Scaramanga Cup for roped ski-racing, partnered by Adrian Allinson, and a few weeks later made a new ski route up the Eiger, in the course of which I was on my legs from ten at night until four on the following afternoon. None of the dreadful things prophesied by the expert have, as yet, happened.

As a result of my accident I was rejected with contumely when I applied for a commission. I spent most of the war in Switzerland in charge of arrangements for interned officers and men at Mürren and Montana hotels owned by our company.

CHAPTER VI

The Romance of a Tourist Agency

MY father was determined to make a barrister of me. He entered me for the Inner Temple, where I ate my Law Dinners and passed the first of my Bar examinations. But I never reconciled myself to his wishes, for if I had become engrossed in the Bar I should have had to sacrifice two ambitions – the first to write, and the second to shape the development of British ski-ing.

I was supremely happy for the first months of married life in Cookham, but the wander years have transformed me into a "wave man" – to quote the apt Japanese epithet for a man without roots. It is all wrong to feel, as I feel, a sense of homecoming when I enter a carriage labelled Boulogne, Delle, Biel, Bern, Brieg, Domodossola, Milan, Verona, Venezia – a litany of lovely names which mean infinitely more to me than Harrow, where I lived as a boy, or Bickley, where I spent some years as a man. The reproductions of Italian paintings which decorate the carriages that travel between Calais and Rome have the same homely atmosphere as the pictures which hang in the home which I have let.

To the townsman one bird sounds very like another, and to some people all train noises are uninteresting and indistinguishable; but no country-bred exile returning from the towns could listen with greater rapture to the farmyard sounds of his home than I to the metallic noise when wheels are tested with a hammer, the slow hiss of escaping steam, the "Pass, friend, all's well" of the station bells at the Swiss frontier, or the sonorous ding-dong which invades one's slumber as the train draws up at Delle or Biel. And just as the exile from the towns knows that he is among his own people when he meets those who grew to manhood with him, so I have friends along the great Continental highways – station-masters with whom I played as a boy in Alpine villages, porters with whom I have exchanged grumbles, not only about Hitler, but about the Kaiser. They belong, as I do, to the Estate, the Estate of Travel.

But of course this is all wrong, for a man's home should not move on wheels; a railway carriage is not a natural habitat, and a railway station, even if it be Bern or Basle, should not tug at one's heart-strings like a garden or a stream seen from the windows of one's home. A man should have fixed roots, for man was not created to live either in the inhuman environment of big cities or in railway carriages, but to play his part in the community life of a small town or village, and perhaps some day I may own a small house in the country with a garden bordered by a stream, and a black spaniel.

I introduce dogs at this stage of my narrative to conciliate the reader who is properly disedified by my nomad tastes. If I were to say crudely, "all dogs love me," I might produce a good impression on the credulous, but should irritate those who dislike such shrill blasts on the trumpet. Englishmen who never blow but merely breathe quietly down their own trumpets seldom try to commend themselves by the crude statement that dogs love them. "I don't know what it is, but dogs somehow seem to take to me" is a favourite formula. But I prefer the dog snob to the cat snob, whose faith in the superior intelligence and good taste of cats is based on the fact that he enjoys the esteem of these discerning animals. Pig snobbery, on the other hand, is attractive because it is uncommon. My friend O'Malley, with whom I founded the Alpine Ski Club at Oxford and who is now the British Minister at Budapest, has only one vanity. He is proud of the fact that pigs greet him with grunts of affectionate delight.

I am neither a cat nor a pig snob, but I can modestly claim that dogs take to me. I remember a bulldog that emerged suddenly from a side street and took to me so readily that he left with a portion of my calf between his teeth. I do not subscribe to the theory that dogs are good judges of character, for this suggests that my character is not what I believe it to be. I remember walking up a hill above Nauplia. At one point the path led between narrow walls, on each of which two dogs suddenly appeared within snapping distance of my ears. They pursued me up the path while I made semaphore movements with my stick. Of course they were Greek dogs, and may have been influenced by acute xenophobia.

I can hardly hope to have done myself much good with the reader by this doggy digression, but at least I have strengthened the case against the travel agency as a profession, for it is difficult to keep dogs if one seldom remains for more than a few months in the same place.

But though one loses much one gains something by the nomad life of a travel agent. Had Mr. Wells been a personal conductor he would have lost his illusions long before he sat down to write his recent condemnation of *Homo sapiens*. I qualified for admission to the guild of the personal conductors, a genial but cynical brotherhood, by escorting a party of pilgrims round the Holy Land. My father's eclecticism was reflected in his business, for he provided Anglicans with a Church

Travellers' Club and Dissenters with the Free Church Touring Guild, and the less expensive tours, which did not justify separate conductors for club and guild, furnished interesting data for a student of Christian reunion. In those days I described myself as an agnostic, and as such was perhaps well qualified to mediate between the Dissenters and the Anglicans who had been entrusted to my keeping. My party included a cheery Broad Churchman whom I liked, two dear old Methodists from the Five Towns who presented me with a beautiful piece of Five Towns pottery as a wedding present, an Anglo-Catholic lady who registered a formal complaint at the merging of the Church Travellers' Club and the Free Church Touring Guild, a fanatic teetotaller whose heart warmed to the Prophet in Constantinople when I reminded him that all good Muslims abstained from wine, and a timid sceptic who pretended to be a Broad Churchman until we reached Marseilles, and tried to evoke sympathy as an honest doubter during the rest of the tour.

We sailed from Marseilles on a French liner. The Italo-Turkish War was just over. The Turks had swept up a few of the more conspicuous mines in Smyrna Harbour and had fallen back on old friend Kismet for the rest. Our cautious approach into Turkish harbours delayed us, and this delay produced the first serious schism among the pilgrims. The religious associations of the firm made it necessary to avoid Sunday travelling, and we had planned for "a quiet day at Nablus" for our first Sunday in the Holy Land. Even on a weekday Nablus is not only quiet but dull, and as we had lost a day at sea we could either travel on Sunday or give up the Jericho expedition. A majority of the pilgrims preferred the turmoil of Jericho to the Sabbath peace of Nablus, but a determined Sabbatarian made it clear that there would be no quiet days, for me at least, either at Nablus or elsewhere, if I consented to desecrate the Lord's day. "It is our duty to set an example. We are Christian people travelling in a foreign land." *Ubi sum, ibi patria* is the motto of the travelling John Bull. I failed to convince her that we were, in fact, foreign people travelling in *the* Christian country.

The pilgrims had been reminded by a discreet notice that the company graciously left it to them to distribute largesse to the stewards of the line. Just as we disembarked at Beyrout an indignant steward displayed in the palm of his hand one French franc which had just been presented to him by the Sabbatarian on behalf of herself and her husband, after ten days on the boat. "I object to tipping on principle," said the Sabbatarian. I am tired of this traditional camouflage for meanness. Where tips are routine, to refrain from adequate tipping is to "defraud labourers of their wages," one of the four sins which "cry to Heaven for vengeance." I should have some respect for a person who said, "On principle I believe in tipping, but my besetting sin is meanness."

The cheap tripper has long been the butt of humorists, but the ratio of *ignorami* is no greater among those who spend ten pounds on a trip to "Lovely Lucerne" than among those who travel in the Blue Train to the Riviera. I should hesitate to lecture on the historical background of Switzerland to an audience composed exclusively of ski-ers, but I did not find it difficult to interest our summer clientèle in the associations of the country which they were visiting. In my experience there are few personally conducted parties to Italy which do not include one or two people with a genuine and instructed interest in art, whereas the decorative pilgrims who display their charms on the Lido, and who are repelled – in shorts – from the portals of St. Mark's, seldom include scholarly students of Byzantine mosaics.

No utterance of the personally conducted has pleased me more than the chance remark of a young man whom I met at Stresa. He was a client of a rival firm, and this aroused my professional interest. I asked him why he had selected this particular tour. "Well, you see, I liked this tour because it doesn't stop too long anywhere. One night in Milan, two in Venice, two nights in Florence and three in Rome. Two days is long enough for any of these high spots of culture. Of course, if you're arty it's different, but I hate picture galleries, and I run a mile when people start talking about the influence of the pre-Raphaelites on Raphael."

The staff of a travel agency is divided into those who remain at home and the foreign representatives. The London staff are convinced that the life of a foreign representative is one long holiday in romantic surroundings, a view which is not universally accepted by the personal conductors. Their sorrows have been graphically portrayed in the best of all novels inspired by the travel business, *Dogget's Tours*. The London staff, sweltering in the dog days, do their best to readjust the balance. "Our representative in Lucerne," so runs the traditional formula, "will be only too happy to fix this matter up for you." The chronic shortage of single rooms in the High Season never worries the London staff. "Of course, we can't *guarantee* you a single room, but we have asked our foreign representative at Lucerne [or Grindelwald or Zermatt, as the case may be] to do all in his power to secure one for you."

The foreign representative who received some thirty or forty strong recommendations to provide single rooms and who knew that he had only six available would look forward with dismay to the battle for *Lebensraum* which deprived arrival nights in August of monotony.

An Oxford undergraduate who was earning his keep during the Long Vacation by a temporary job at Lucerne found himself confronted by an indignant old lady of seventy. "But the kind man in your London office positively *promised* me a single room." "I'm sorry, Madam, but there are no more single rooms available." "Nonsense, young man, you must get me a single room. It's forty years since I slept with anybody." The reply of this weary and jaded young man was not in accordance with the traditions of the Free Church Touring Guild. "God forbid, Madam, that it should fall to me to break the spell."

My father lost money until he began to capitalise his own instinctive prejudices against all foreigners. Every tourist agency, of course, caters for those who believe that "Black men begin at Calais." Only the courageous venture unescorted into Darkest France. My father exploited with genius the distinction between travellers and tourists. The traveller leaves not only England but Englishmen behind when he crosses the Channel. The tourist changes his physical but does his best to preserve his social environment when he sets timid foot on the Continent.

Cælum, non animum, mutant, qui trans mare currunt.

The public Schools Alpine Sports Club, which my father founded, catered for winter sportsmen who were glad to carry with them to the Alps the social environment in which they had been born and bred. Only those who had been educated at Public Schools or Universities were eligible for election in the ordinary way. My father secured for the exclusive use of the Club a number of leading hotels in Switzerland. I have vivid memories of an indignant committee meeting summoned to protest against the action of a Swiss *hôtelier* in admitting two Germans into his own hotel. The Germans left next day.

A more difficult problem was presented by a spirited eccentric who died many years ago. Let us call him Mr. Smith, though that was not his name. Mr. Smith, a man of sixty, had led an adventurous life as a gallant soldier and an enterprising explorer. He arrived just as the Palace Hotel was opening and was irritated to discover that there were only half-a-dozen couples circulating on the ballroom floor and that even wallflowers, who were scarce, did not seem anxious to dance with him. He accordingly took the floor alone, and waltzed slowly round holding an imaginary lady in his right arm and a cigar in his left hand. Mild protests only elicited vigorous abuse, so a committee meeting was hastily summoned and Mr. Smith was invited to appear. He was extremely angry, but no normal Englishman can face with equanimity the prospect of being asked to resign from a club, so he accepted our invitation.

"I'm a barrister," he began, "of thirty years' standing, and I'll sue you all for libel."

As an obscure member of the Inner Temple I felt entitled to draw his attention to the distinction between libel, which must be written, and slander, which is spoken. But Mr. Smith was not easily silenced. "My action was a protest," he shouted, "because no women were provided." Somebody remarked that he had come to the wrong address. The chairman, an Air Force officer, said, "Excuse me, sir, but I object to your talking about these ladies as 'women.' " "I belong to Brooks's and White's," replied the undaunted Smith, "and in Brooks's and White's we call them women." We managed to persuade our friend that we bore him no ill-will, but hoped that he would discontinue solo dancing with a cigar.

When the members of the committee came down to breakfast next morning, the concierge, with a broad grin, handed each of them Mr. Smith's visiting card, on which was inscribed, "To challenge to a duel with pistols." Mr. Smith was a curler, so I saved my honour by replying that, as the recipient of the challenge, I had the choice of weapons, and that I chose battle-axes on ski. A retiring member of the committee who had not received a challenge was so distressed by the thought of losing this interesting memento that he lured Mr. Smith into the bar to insult him.

The Club exercised a great influence on the development of winter sports. Ski-ing was introduced into the Alps by Norwegians and their pupils, but the development of downhill racing was due to British initiative, and the Roberts of Kandahar Challenge Cup, named after the first Vice-President of the Public Schools Alpine Sports Club and first held in 1911, is the world's senior challenge cup for downhill ski racing. The

Club also inaugurated the Oxford and Cambridge Ice Hockey Match and the Oxford and Cambridge Ski Races. The former event developed out of a scratch game between Oxford and Cambridge players at Beatenberg. Had I not broken my leg it is possible that I might have played in the first Oxford ice-hockey team, a claim which will sound presumptuous only to those who did not witness the first of these annual matches. The Oxford goal-keeper had never been on skates before and had to be assisted between the goal-posts at half-time. His attitude to such shots as did not actually strike his person would have qualified him for a seat on a non-intervention committee, and the shots which struck him only failed to score when he fell forwards instead of backwards.

Mürren, in its first winter season, occupied more space in the society papers than St. Moritz. My father was proud of beating St. Moritz at its own game, but as a convinced Liberal he felt it necessary to justify to himself his success in exploiting class distinctions in the interests of his business. "I have tried," he often remarked, "to make people travel together and failed. I've lost a lot of money trying to mix people on their holidays. I now realise that it is no more snobbish for a public-school man to prefer meeting his own type at Mürren than for a Free Churchman to patronise the Free Church Touring Guild when he goes to Lucerne."

Like most of those who have risen in the world, my father was interested in what may be termed the Who's Who scale of values. I remember a concierge who had been sent in search of this invaluable reference work informing me that "Sir 'Enry wants ze book OO IZ OO," but my father's interest in these things was merely a variation of the Bradshaw * mind. Specialisation in one small field of knowledge is one of the ways in which the mind takes refuge from the intolerable burden of ascertaining facts. Two brothers, both masters at Eton, were reputed to be infallible on Bradshaw. One of them, in reply to

* Bradshaw – the British Railway Guide.

the question, "Does your brother know his Bradshaw as well as you do?" said, "Not quite. He's a bit weak on the Sunday locals." But nobody would have accused either of these brothers of a snobbish reverence for railway directors. "Rank," said Jowett, "is not a dispensation of Providence, but it is a fact." There is nothing snobbish in recognising or in believing that man is instinctively hierarchical and that a hierarchical society therefore corresponds more accurately to his nature than an egalitarian society. The distinction between the snob and the feudalist corresponds to the distinction between the Man and his Office. A saint who had been presented to one of the Borgia Popes fell at his feet in an ecstasy because he was the Vicar of Christ, and then rose to her feet and denounced him for his crimes. She drew the correct feudal distinction between the Man and his Office. A feudalist might be defined as a man who respects the Office in spite of the Man, and a snob as a man who respects the Man because of his Office. The feudalist may believe in the value of a peerage; the snob would prefer to dine with a bore who was a peer rather than with an interesting man who was a commoner.

My father was a feudalist *malgré lui.* In theory he was opposed to the House of Lords. In fact he believed in the aristocratic principle, but he never attempted to cultivate eminent people, though he was glad to have them on his committees. His idea of bliss was to preside over an ecclesiastical meeting or to take the chair at a lecture on one of the Hellenic Travellers' Club cruises. He had an immense faith in the value of a classical education and was infinitely more impressed by academic than by social distinctions. He was happiest in the company of parsons and scholars, and of all the clubs which he founded there was only one for which he cherished an enduring affection – the Hellenic Travellers' Club.

Had my father been a snob he would not have died, as he did, a poor man, for he would have adjusted his standards to suit his clientèle. He nearly ruined the firm by his pro-Boer campaign, and when the news of his defeat as a Liberal candidate for Parliament reached Switzerland his clients burst into applause. For in pre-war days advanced political views were not as yet a social asset.

His own principles were unaffected by such success as he enjoyed. In the early days of the Public Schools Alpine Sports Club my father tried to enforce the rule which was usual in pre-war London clubs, forbidding the playing of cards on Sundays in public rooms. Indeed, he contrived to force a by-law to this effect through a committee meeting at Lenzerheide. The local chairman, whom we will call Sir William, gave his services in return for tickets and accommodation, but his services did not include endorsing ridiculous rules about card-playing. "Sir Henry," said the baronet of ancient lineage, "you're using me as a decoy duck."

"Yes," said my father, "and I'm very much obliged to you, Sir William."

My father was always very much obliged to his decoy ducks, but he never allowed them to influence his policy. He was essentially a theocrat and was sanguine enough to believe that theocracy could be imposed upon his winter clients if only he could contrive to force resolutions through amenable committees. He was a teetotaller, not from principle but for the sake of his health. He always offered his guests wine, but he was convinced that hotel bars encouraged the young to drink to excess, and he imposed upon the committee a rule ordering all hotel bars to be closed at 11 P.M. He knew nothing about dancing, but he suspected that modern dances which described themselves as "Bunny-hugs" were very wicked. People who take dancing seriously and who master every new step as it appears are usually too interested in the intricate technique of modern dancing to exploit this subtle art for purposes which can be achieved more directly by other means. But my father had made up his mind, and committee resolutions which he had drafted, vetoing the Bunny-hug, were duly circularised to the Club, and formed the theme of a poem in *Punch*. Our rivals were delighted, and Mürren, which was fashionable from 1911 until 1914, acquired the reputation of a place where grown-ups were treated like school children.

Theocracy was not an outstanding success even in Calvin's Geneva. It was an outstanding failure in Sir Henry Lunn's Mürren.

CHAPTER VII

Portrait of a Liberal

FEW words are more ambiguous than "Liberalism." Liberals of the Manchester school invoked Liberalism in their efforts to liberate economic activity from State control, whereas modern Liberals are even more anxious than Socialists to extend the sphere of the State's activities. When Lord Shaftesbury, the Conservative, introduced the Factory Acts to liberate small children from the tyranny of the machines, John Bright and Cobden protested in the name of Liberalism against any attempt to fetter the economic activities of the factory owners. In the early twentieth century Mr. Lloyd George, in the name of Liberalism, introduced compulsory insurance.

My father's Liberalism was derived not from Manchester but from Nazareth. He was one of the last survivors of those Victorians who were Christian Liberals as opposed to Secular Liberals. The Liberalism of the convinced Christian must always be qualified by the conclusions which he draws from the great premiss that man is made in the image of God, and therefore has rights which no dictator and no democratic majority can override. Secular Liberalism, on the other hand, with its deification of the "General Will," inevitably leads to the servile state. If man is nothing more than first cousin to the chimpanzee there is no reason why a dictator or a dictatorial majority should not put him behind bars. It is only man's supernatural estate which guarantees his personal dignity and his inalienable rights.

The Renaissance, like Liberalism, had two aspects, Christian and secular, for the Church which saved the classic learning during the Dark Ages was the patron of the great revival of classic learning. Secular Liberalism had its roots not in the Christian but in the pagan Renaissance, which denied, if only by implication, the supernatural values, and accepted as its only criterion the truncated and impoverished humanism which ignores all values save those of this world. Pagan humanism promised emancipation from divine authority, but condemned its dupes to inevitable tyranny, for man is free only within the framework of an authority which guarantees his rights because it respects his nature. The Byzantine Church of Tsarist Russia had its origin in the Greek schism which revolted against the authority of Rome. German Lutheranism represented a yet further stage in the deification of private judgment. The flight from authority has led neither Russia nor Germany to the land of liberty. No tyranny of the Dark Ages was more ruthless and more satanic than those which are to-day crushing out the last remnants of liberty from the countries in which Hitler and Stalin rule. The pact between these dictators should have surprised nobody, for there is an identity of aim in the Russian and Prussian forms of that anti-Christian Socialism which is the final end of secular Liberalism.

Freedom survives in England because we are still a Christian country with an instinctive, rather than a conscious, conviction that authority is derived from above, and that man has rights of which no democratic majority may deprive him. The fact that the Church of England is established and that England is legally a Christian country is a protection against the tyranny of secularism.

Secular Liberalism was born on the shores of Lake Geneva in the salons of Madame Necker and Madame de Staël. Its basic doctrine was defined in the proposition: "It is contrary to the natural, innate and inalienable right and liberty and dignity of man to subject himself to an authority the root, rule and measure and sanction of which is not in himself."

The word "liberalism" has been the greatest asset to the Liberal Party, for the word implies that a love of liberty is the distinguishing characteristic of Liberals. If this were so we should all be Liberals, for we all love our own liberty. Milton was a Liberal of this school. He did not write against marriage until his own marriage was a failure, or protest against the licensing of books until his own tracts had been condemned as immoral. And he did not refuse the post of censor when it was offered him, for that post carried a handsome salary. The French Liberals, who sowed the seeds of the French Revolution, wished to be liberated from the authority of the Church and the King and hoped to transfer the privileges of the nobility to themselves, but they had no intention of liberating the proletariat from the authority of the intellectuals and the bourgeoisie. Bright and Cobden wished to liberate their party from the authority of the House of Lords, but they opposed the liberation of small children from the tyranny of the factories. Whig aristocrats sympathised with every revolution abroad and successfully prevented revolution at home.

Liberalism, however, would never have captured the allegiance of good men had it been nothing more than selfishness disguised by a thin veneer of hypocrisy. English Liberals have always included among their leaders men who believed not only in liberating themselves but also in liberating those with whose religious or political views they disagreed. Thus Sydney Smith justified his support of Catholic emancipation by arguments which would have been endorsed by most of those who agreed with that measure.

"I am as disgusted," he wrote, "with the nonsense of the

Roman Catholic religion as you can be: and no man who talks such nonsense shall ever tithe the product of the earth, nor meddle with the ecclesiastical establishment in any shape; but what have I to do with the speculative nonsense of his theology, when the object is to elect the mayor of a country town, or to appoint the colonel of a marching regiment? Will a man discharge the solemn impertinences of the one office with less zeal, or shrink from the bloody boldness of the other with greater timidity, because the blockhead believes in all the Catholic nonsense of the real presence?"

British Liberalism, at its best, reflected the characteristic English virtues – tolerance, a sense of fair play and the conviction that differences should be settled by free discussion rather than by force. Liberalism prevented the secession of Canada and might have prevented the virtual secession of Eire, had Home Rule been granted when Gladstone proposed it. The noblest flower of Liberalism was the Christian peace which brought the disastrous South African War to its end.

Liberalism, like charity, should begin at home, and my father made a real, if only a partially successful, effort not to interfere too much with his unruly family. But by temperament he was an authoritarian. Nothing could have been less democratic than my father's attitude towards the directors of companies of which he was the chairman. He could never distinguish between a public company and a family concern, or realise that directors were elected, at least in theory, to represent the views of shareholders rather than to support the chairman against their better judgement. If directors opposed him, as they sometimes did, he was genuinely grieved and perplexed, but never vindictive. He was a benevolent dictator and retained the affectionate loyalty even of those who, like my Uncle Holdsworth or the oldest member of the firm, Mr. Elkington, must often have found him exasperating.

Like all Liberals, he was a great believer in international co-operation and friendship. He organised municipal parties to Germany and parties of German Burgomeisters to England. He was knighted for his services to Anglo-German friendship, though it is, of course, only too patent that the German desire for British friendship in 1913 was inspired by the same motives as in 1939, a desire for our neutrality until all other enemies had been disposed of. The ineffectiveness of Liberal internationalism is due, among other things, to the fact that English Liberals instinctively think of foreigners as members of inferior races who are fortunate to merit the sympathetic interest of English Liberals, and who would be wise to accept their leadership in the campaign for a united Europe.

Few men have travelled more than my father, and few men could have been less interested in the countries through which they travelled. America was an exception, but then the Americans spoke English and were thereby promoted into a class of honorary Englishmen. My father was delighted by the signal honour, conferred on few Englishmen, of election as an honorary member of the Mother Chapter of the Phi Beta Kappa fraternity. He had a vague feeling of affinity with the Germans and an ingrained distrust of the French. He liked the Swiss, but he seldom returned from abroad without murmuring, "There's no country like England and no people like the English." He had a gift for languages, and mastered enough Greek in a few weeks to pass his university examinations in that language, and he read the Greek Testament as easily as the Authorised Version; but he was so little interested in the foreigners whose political and ecclesiastical co-operation he desired that he never bothered to master enough French or German to ask his way to the station. I have only heard him use one French phrase which contained four French words. Sugar disagreed with him, and I have often heard him ask for "*cacao, pas de chocolat*," but he always got chocolate. My son Peter tells me that once when the train was drawing out of Vicenza past the usual advertisement my father remarked thoughtfully, "I wonder why so many of these Italian stations are called *Olio Sasso*."

Friendship between nations cannot be manufactured by societies or by men who believe in internationalism as an ideal, but who remain obstinately national in their own personal outlook. It is difficult to feel any genuine affection for foreigners unless you live among them, learn their language and take the trouble to understand their cultural background:

L'amore di qualunque cosa è figliuola d'essa cognitione.
L'amore è tanto più fervente quando la cognitione è più certa.

International friendship cannot be mass produced by ideologists of the Left "who are so occupied with the rights of man that they have completely forgotten his nature." Burke's famous comment on the English sympathisers with the French Jacobins explains, among other things, the failure of the League of Nations.

My father's Liberalism was, in the main, ideological, but his Christianity had its roots in experience. His internationalism was "progressive," but his views on wealth, and its dangers, were reactionary, for they were derived through John Wesley from the mediæval scholastics. Most Christians abandon as insoluble the problem of applying the Christian teaching on wealth. Wesley's difficulty was not to discover the solution to this problem, but to believe that a problem existed. "Where is the difficulty?" he said. "Provide yourself and your dependents with simple food and plain raiment and give away the rest." As a young man he discovered that he could live on £28 a year. When his income rose to £400 (thanks to the sale of his books) he still lived on £28 and gave away the rest. "He who has enough to satisfy his wants," wrote a mediæval theologian, "and nevetheless labours to acquire riches, either in order to obtain a higher social position, or that subsequently he may have enough to live without labour, or that his sons may become men of wealth and importance – all such are puffed up by a damnable avarice, sensuality and pride."

Liberalism arose, as that distinguished Socialist, Professor

Laski, insists, as the result of a widespread desire to liberate the rich from the restrictions which the mediæval Church imposed upon money-making. "Whereas in the Middle Ages the idea of acquiring wealth was limited by a body of moral rules imposed under the sanction of religious authority, after 1,500 years those rules, and the institutions, habits and ideas to which they had given birth, were no longer deemed adequate. They were felt as a constraint. They were evaded, criticised, abandoned, because it was felt that they interfered with the exploitation of the means of production. New conceptions were needed to legitimise the new potentialities of wealth that men had discovered little by little in preceding ages. The Liberal doctrine is the philosophic justification of the new practices." *

Professor R. H. Tawney, in his brilliant book *Religion and the Rise of Capitalism*, describes the gradual transformation of the mediæval doctrine that the acquisition of wealth was a drudgery or temptation into the dogma that the acquisition of wealth was a moral duty.

My father had a genius for making money which was only equalled by his talent for losing it and for giving it away. In his rare moments of prosperity he was always ill at ease, but was at his best in the more congenial climate of financial stringency. As a young man he had founded a successful business and abandoned it for the mission field. He involved himself in an unfortunate controversy with Methodism because he maintained that Methodist missionaries would be more effective if their standard of living were more in accordance with that of those among whom they worked. He founded the Free Church Touring Guild and the Church Travellers' Club, and limited their profits by restrictions which he himself insisted on imposing. The bulk of the profits had to be given away to charities

* I have quoted this passage from the *Rise of European Liberalism* in my book *Communism and Socialism* (p. 36), in the introduction to which I have tried to summarise the mediæval attitude to money-making. For a fuller treatment of John Wesley's attitude I may refer the reader to my Life of John Wesley, pp. 340 *et seq.*

nominated by him. Had he been commercially-minded he could have obtained the necessary ecclesiastical backing for about twenty per cent of the sums which he disbursed in charity. Hundreds of poor parsons received free holidays, and many good causes in which he was interested benefited by this arrangement. As he retained complete control over the distribution of charities, he could have reinvested these in the business and distributed the income on the capital thus invested. I urged this course; for though I was in sympathy with his policy, I believed that it would be better to provide rather fewer parsons with free holidays than to imperil a business which was a source of income to so many good works, but it was impossible to control my father when there was money to give away. "Money never stays with me," wrote John Wesley; "it would burn if it did. I throw it out of my hands as soon as possible lest it should find its way to my heart." Those words might have been inscribed on my father's tomb. He and my mother occupied four rooms in the Albany Hotel, Hastings, which the company owned. He never wished for a car or a big house or any of the outward and visible signs of success. "If only people," he often said, "would realise how much fun they can get by giving money away they wouldn't buy cars." My mother shared his bizarre views. Had she taken the vow of poverty which is binding on members of religious orders, her life would have been no different. She worked in an East End parish, and as an old lady of seventy she would take buses from her work to the station before facing the long journey down to the south coast, to save the taxi fare for her charities.

During the post-war boom the business began to make money, and my father, an incurable optimist, promptly began to dispose of a non-existent fortune. He limited his own income by deed to £500 a year, over and above his expenses at the Albany Hotel, and, after allotting shares which he believed would provide reasonable incomes for his children, set aside the income from his shares to be administered for charity. A pessimist has been defined as a man who has lived with an optimist; hence my lack of interest either in the "Trust" or in my own hypothetical share in this legacy, for I never believed that these shares would pay a dividend – nor did they. "Fairy Gold" was the family term for the incomes which we were to draw from a non-existent fund. I wish that my father could have foreseen the embarrassing consequences of his action, for he was represented in both the British and the American press as a philanthropist who had distributed millions in charity, with the unhappy result that he was bombarded by appeals from all over the world. This legend was revived at the time of his death, and most people assumed that a man who had given away millions must have left some thousands to his family, whereas beyond a small annuity to his widow he left nothing, for the shares in the family business had passed, long before his death, to the new owners. I have no regrets, but though I have no ambitions to be wealthy, I cannot afford the expensive luxury of being considered rich.

On one occasion when my father was addressing a group of young Methodists he quoted Wesley's famous will: "I leave no money to anyone because I have none."

"I wonder what *you'll* leave," interjected a sardonic sceptic.

"Wait and see," replied my father cheerfully. But God took him literally, and his will might have been modelled on John Wesley's.

My father, though he remained a Methodist lay preacher, had been confirmed in the Church of England, and had a great sympathy with the Anglo-Catholics. He claimed to be a member of the Catholic Church. He was one of the few Protestants who championed the Nationalists, and though he was an old man of seventy-seven when the war started there was no sign of flagging energy in the vigour with which he conducted his campaign. He even succeeded in carrying an amendment to a vote of sympathy for the persecuted Protestants in Germany at the Annual Methodist Conference, with the result that a somewhat embarrassed conference expressed their sympathy with the persecuted Christians in Russia, Germany and Spain.

He was a member of the Shadow Cabinet of the Liberal Party and a vice-president of the Liberal League, but his relations with the Liberal Party were strained by their attitude to the Spanish War, and severed by their attack on the Munich Agreement.

My father was never happier than when he was one of a minority. He enjoyed a fight and he never refused an appeal for help. Of many tributes to him, the one I liked the best was paid to him on the occasion of his knighthood by that great Victorian journalist W. T. Stead:

"I shall fail signally in the duty which I owe to an old friend and to the world at large if I do not pay my tribute to the services to humanity which have given him a well-merited place in the roll of knighthood. He is one of those men for whom a knighthood is the most appropriate of all honours, for he is a knightly soul, constantly riding out on some perilous quest, from which he emerges time after time, bruised and battered and wounded sore, but never daunted or disheartened."

CHAPTER VIII

Germany in Defeat: a Memory

"I CANNOT understand," a friend of mine impatiently exclaimed, "why any decent German supported Hitler with enthusiasm."

The Nazi movement did not surprise those who visited Germany between the Armistice and the Treaty of Versailles.

Thanks to a chance encounter with Mr. (now Sir George) Young, I travelled through Germany at the end of January, 1919. George Young is the elder brother of my great friend Geoffrey Young, the mountaineer. He was in the Diplomatic Service for some years and was the author of a textbook on Turkish Law which won high praise in Turkish legal circles. George Young has a touch of genius, but I do not suppose that he makes a very comfortable subordinate. The Foreign Office must have sniffed out the latent heretic in George Young, for during the war, instead of making use of his great knowledge of the Near East and his brilliant qualities, they sent him to Portugal in a minor capacity. This was more than he could bear, so he resigned the Diplomatic Service, enlisted in the Artillery and got a commission after a few months, and contrived to get himself demobilised within two or three weeks of the Armistice. Politically his sympathies were with the Left, a fact which had no doubt injured his career in the Diplomatic Service, and when I met him he was on his way to Germany as the correspondent of the Radical *Daily News*.

On January 29th, 1919, I boarded the steamer at Romanshorn and said good-bye to Switzerland. A Swiss on board introduced himself to us as a *Times* correspondent. "*The Times*," he said, "thinks that a neutral can get information which no Englishman could get. If an Englishman turns up, the Germans will give him a tremendous welcome and then do their best to hoodwink him. They haven't changed. They are as militaristic as ever and are already beginning to plan the next war." Young sniffed contemptuously, but I am inclined to think that our Swiss friend was not far wrong.

We landed at Lindau. The senior officer in command there was a sergeant, all officers of higher rank having been ejected by the Revolutionaries.

It was at Lindau that a deplorable lapse on my part defined, at the outset of our journey, the relationship between Young and myself, for it was in consequence of this lapse that he assumed the rôle of the helper and assigned me the rôle of the helpee. George Young is the most superb helper that I have ever met. He has done all the sort of things that helpers do, and if only I had accepted from the first the rôle of helpee all might have been well. But my vanity incited me to vain and futile competition. Anybody who has climbed without guides has at least acquired the art of travelling among mountains without being killed and does not readily resign himself to the rôle of the personally conducted passenger, which I should have done from the first. But my reaction to his super-efficiency was as ungenerous as Monsignor Knox's to my pseudo-efficiency, and though I was not shamed into helpfulness, such little talent as I have was ruined, and I disgraced myself by leaving at Lindau a precious trunk which Young had entrusted to my care. This trunk contained food, which Young, with superb adroitness, in defiance of all war-time regulations on the subject of importing and exporting food, had smuggled through three frontiers. And it was I who left the trunk at Lindau.

Young said nothing. He looked serenely contemptuous and went in search of a Red Guard.* In a quiet undertone which was infinitely effective, he murmured that we were Englishmen of enormous consequence and that any tampering with our possessions would lead to very serious results. A banknote changed hands. The trunk arrived a few hours later at Munich, unopened and undisturbed.

My self-respect might have recovered from the loss of this trunk had not George Young combined ruthless efficiency with strong silence. He talked very little, which was sad, for I have seldom met anybody who was better worth listening to when he did talk. He would have been an easier companion if he had sometimes said things which were not worth listening to. I am naturally garrulous, and as such I am always at a disadvantage with the silent.

The train from Lindau to Munich was comfortable and well-sprung – one of the few good trains left in Germany. It was kept running between Lindau and Munich as propaganda. The old railway officials still functioned, but the Red Guards were in command and the railway staff treated them with profound respect. At one station, twenty or thirty stray soldiers tried to board the train, but they were vigorously repulsed by the Red Guards, profoundly abused and reminded that their passes did not admit them to fast trains.

"Things are getting better," remarked an Austrian in my carriage. "I was in Austria just after the Armistice, travelling near Vienna. The soldiers boarded the train and kicked the civilians into the corridors. An officer came up and remon-

* This was during the short-lived Communist revolution of 1919 in Bavaria.

strated, and was promptly killed. Another officer expostulated. He reminded the men that the officer they had just murdered had been through the whole campaign, and had always been noted for his great consideration for the troops under his command. They killed him, too. . . . It was a terrible time – terrible. Some of the troops just commandeered any motor lorry that was handy, and rode through the villages shooting off their spare ammunition."

We slept at Munich. Breakfast next morning inspired me with profound respect for the tenacity of the German race, but perhaps those who in Germany decided the issues of war and peace did not begin the day with black bread flavoured with aniseed, acorn coffee and turnip jam. Everything in Germany was *ersatz* (substitute). We drank *ersatz* coffee, we ate *ersatz* bread and *ersatz* jam, and washed ourselves with *ersatz* soap. At least, we should have done had not the soap brought from Switzerland lasted out our visit.

After breakfast I wandered disconsolately through Munich, trying to evoke the old pre-war Munich which I loved, but I could establish no link between pre-war Munich and this sorrowful city, or between the cheerful Bavarian crowds of the days that were dead and the long processions of despairing men in dirty, war-stained field-grey uniforms. Perhaps *ersatz* beer had helped to produce this *ersatz* München.

Munich was under the control of the Soldiers and Workmen's Council (*Arbeiter und Soldatenrat*). Soldiers arriving there were informed by posters at the station that they should apply to this council for food and lodging; but the Red Guards were pink rather than red, and had little use for the genuine Spartacists * who were still making trouble in Berlin. The Spartacists who came to Munich from Berlin on propaganda bent were usually thrust into prison and sent back to Berlin a few days later.

* The German Communists took the name of Spartacists, from Spartacus, who led a slave revolt in ancient Rome.

We left in the evening for Berlin. The train was terribly overcrowded; Young inquired whether there was a carriage reserved for diplomatists on an official mission, and, on receiving an affirmative reply, induced a Red Guard to unlock a carriage reserved for three members of the American Legation in Berlin. When the Americans put in an appearance, Young remarked imperturbably that he hoped they would extend the courtesy of their reserved carriage to an English diplomat and his companion. Young travelled with a complete set of alibis. He was equally impressive as the traditional diplomat and as a Left Wing intellectual with advanced views. He had provided himself with introductions to representatives of every shade of opinion from the extreme Right to the extreme Left.

We fed well, Young having filled a thermos with boiling water from the railway engine and produced his camp cooker, which laid a sound foundation for breakfast. As we ate, hungry Germans peered through the carriage window. We collected some food and distributed it. A depressed-looking soldier with a husky voice who had just left hospital nearly cried when I handed him a sandwich.

The train took nearly double the pre-war time for the journey to Berlin, for in the Armistice terms Foch had secured all the railway engines worth having, and those that the Germans still possessed were always getting overheated owing to the absence of copper.

We had registered our precious food trunk to Berlin and had some difficulty in collecting it. A Red Guard, wearing the red brassard of the Government *Sicherheit* troops, challenged us. Trunks filled with food, he said, were liable to confiscation. In moments of great emergency Young always gives the impression of muttering under his breath, and drops his voice to a full-blooded whisper. He had, he remarked, been treated with profound deference from the moment that he entered Germany. He hoped, for the sake of the Red Guard, that Berlin would not prove an exception to the general rule. The Red Guard would probably have confiscated the trunk had Young shouted, but he was overawed by the self-possession (and therefore the importance) of an Englishman who did not bluster or shout even when threatened with the confiscation of food.

The fish takes the water for granted and only begins to gasp when removed from its natural environment. Well-to-do folk who have led sheltered lives and who have never come into contact with war or with revolution accept as inevitable and preordained a framework of civilised life. The routine appearance of eggs and bacon and crisp rolls at breakfast surprises them as little as the punctuality of the sun. It must be almost impossible for such people to realise, emotionally no less than intellectually, what it feels like to begin the day with coffee made from acorns and with black bread made largely from potatoes. The black bread was so unwholesome that few Germans escaped violent indigestion during the later years of the war; indigestion which left its obvious mark on their complexions.

George Young, of course, had a trunk of food, but as I was only staying a week I made no inroad on that store, and I lived during that time as a rich German might have lived. "Rich" because, owing to the shortness of my stay, I could afford to pay ten shillings for one reasonable meal, consisting of soup, a plate of indifferent meat and a few potatoes. The restaurant in which we lunched thus luxuriously was officially closed, and the meat was smuggled meat. We crawled down dark passages before being admitted by a password to a private room where Americans, press correspondents and other *cognoscenti* escaped from the horrors of hotel food.

The hero in *Das Schopfer*, which I saw one evening in Berlin, made a great hit. His airy suggestion, "What about having a snack of food, shall we say something light, a sausage or a spring chicken?" brought down the house. The theatre reverberated with ironic laughter and with reminiscent sighs for prewar food. There was a shortage of all forms of grease, and soap was difficult to obtain. I always kept a few bars of chocolate and soap in my pocket, for these were talismans which opened most gates. An important official in the coal department whom I met in the train to Hanover wrapped up a piece of chocolate which I gave him and said, "I can't thank you enough. I shall take this home to my children." He was wearing an immense fur coat, pre-war, and it was with some diffidence that I offered him a cake of soap, for in normal times I should hesitate to approach the great with so ambiguous an offering. His gratitude was touching. "Oh, but I am robbing you. *Ich beraube Sie*. You are too kind. Can you really spare it?" I assured him that I could spare it, and I saw myself as the hero of a new version of the Sir Philip Sidney story in which soap took the place of water: His dirt was greater than mine.

The effectiveness of our blockade and the poor quality of *ersatz* clothing were all too evident in the dingy clothes and the drab uniforms. The prevailing effect was one of unrelieved squalor. One does not often see a radiantly happy face even in peace-time cities, but a London tube or a Fifth Avenue bus usually reveals a cross-section of human emotions ranging from self-confidence to anxiety or even despair. The corresponding cross-section in Berlin had begun with anxiety, and ended with despair. It would be difficult to convey by photograph, and it is impossible to suggest in words, the impression produced upon an observer from outside by this atmosphere of unrelieved gloom. Whenever I think of Berlin in 1919, I see again that dreary straggle of depressed humanity. I see the sallow, liverish complexions and the unending procession of dirty field-grey uniforms and the rising tide of despair reflected in every face. The Germany of Sedan had crumbled into dust. The new Germany, which was bred by revolution out of defeat, was preparing to drink the dregs of bitter humiliation. "America is our only hope, Wilson our only friend." How often did I hear some such bitter, despairing comment! But even in January most Germans guessed that Wilson would prove a broken reed.

Only one thing in Berlin was not *ersatz*—the drama. Shakespeare and Ibsen, Sudermann and Schnitzler were played nightly to full houses. There was nothing worth seeing when I returned to London. *Chu Chin Chow* was attracting audiences as enthusiastic and almost as numerous as those in Berlin which continued to applaud Shakespeare and Ibsen.

An election was in progress when I arrived in Berlin. The town was full of posters. A bewigged Prussian cavalry officer in eighteenth-century uniform urged the electors to remember the old Prussian *Geist*, which, however, was one of the things which most Germans were very anxious to forget. None the less it was the Prussian *Geist* which saved Germany from collapsing into Communism. Hard things have been said, and with justice, of the Junkers. They lacked culture and were deficient in "sweetness and light," but they did not lack the basic virtue—courage. The Junker had not the charm and the breeding of the Austrian aristocrat, and he lacked the mature self-assurance of our English nobility. His arrogance was apt to be raw and blustery, but he stood—none better—the iron test of war. For over four and a half years the Junkers were in the forefront of the battle. When the home front collapsed they still held on grimly. Some died at their machine-gun outposts, some in rearguard infantry action, and one and all continued to the last to hold their men together, and to resist, until the High Command demanded an Armistice. When the Reds seized control those who still loved the old Germany called for volunteers to save her from Communism. The Junker, though he had had his bellyful of fighting, still rolled up in his thousands to volunteer.

We began our war with an appeal for volunteers and we ended it with conscription. This order of events was reversed in Germany. I have often wondered if the methodical Germans filed away photographs of our recruiting posters, which could have been obtained from newspapers, on the off chance that they might be useful one day. The posters which I saw in Berlin in 1919 were strangely reminiscent of our own. I noted with amusement variations of the familiar "There is a place in this row for you," and again of the Spartan mother urging the reluctant son, "Go, lad; your country needs you, and I must not keep you."

Due credit, however, for originality should be given for an amusing poster which represented a German and a Russian in conversation. "*Sag' mal, Ruski, was ist denn das Bolshevismus?*" (Tell me, Rusky, what is this Bolshevism?), to which the Russian replied: "Bolshevism is perfect equality. Nobody has anything to eat."

There were moments when it seemed that Germany might go the way of Russia. Even conservative Munich endured a period of Red Dictatorship. The middle classes, however, are much stronger in Germany than in Russia, and the German people as a whole have a sense of discipline which is in itself an insurance against the Communistic impulse to rebel against authority from above. The Russian counter-revolutionary movement failed because it assumed the character of a foreign invasion. The White Army invaded Red Russia from without. But the German Whites fought the revolution from within. Some of them sent their wives and children to Switzerland or to Holland, but they themselves remained in the storm centres and organised the resistance to the Reds.

The German Spartacists were inspired with sullen resentment against the class which they held responsible for the miseries of the war. They did not know what they were fighting for, but the Rheinhardt battalion knew that they were fighting to save what was left of the Germany which they loved from utter destruction. Men die more readily to save what they love than to damage what they hate.

The casualties in the Berlin street fighting were not very heavy. Those who had survived the war felt that it would be a ridiculous anticlimax to get killed in a street brawl, but the Spartacists should be given full credit for enriching military science with one important tactical discovery. Where cover was scarce, and barricades had not been erected, the Spartacist was taught to lie flat on the ground and to transfer his hat from his head to the seat of his trousers, thereby deflecting the enemy fire to a less vulnerable portion of his anatomy.

Characteristic of the Junkers who saved Germany before ever Hitler had been heard of was an elderly Prussian whom I met on his way to volunteer.

"When the war broke out," he said, "I was on my way back to Germany from Africa. I enlisted at once, and somehow managed to get to the front in a few days. For three weeks I was in the battle line, and I have been in it, off and on, ever since. I was twice wounded. I was fighting when the Armistice came. My men fought wonderfully to the end; the discipline was good and they fought with great courage. Our allies were dropping off like ripe fruit; the home front was cracking. We were fighting a rearguard action without that hope of reserves which kept you going at Mons. We were outgunned and outnumbered, but the Army held firm. In parts of the line there may have been demoralisation, but my battalion stuck it to the end. It was the sailors who wrecked the situation. Curse those damned sailors! They've been *faul* for two years. If the infernal *Asrats* (*Arbeiter und Soldatenrats*) hadn't broken loose two days before the Armistice, we might have got much better terms. We were beaten not so much by the enemy as by the *Etappen-Schwein* (Base-hogs). The present situation is terrible. The Entente are merciless. . . . They've destroyed our Prussian military system of which we were so proud . . . they might be content with that."

I asked him what he thought of the Kaiser. He considered that the Kaiser committed a fatal mistake when he decamped so suddenly. That precipitated the Revolution. He ought to have stayed on.

Ludendorff? "Well, Ludendorff mixed much less in politics than those damned Socialists make out. He was a good soldier, and Hindenburg is a fine man too. He has placed his services at the disposal of the Socialists. He's not a politician. He is primarily a soldier, and he will serve a Socialist Government as faithfully as he ever served the Kaiser. If he had resigned the whole thing would have gone to ruin. Say what you will of those old Junkers, there is something fine about them. Their officers have a conception of duty which is really wonderful. No matter what happens, their first thought is the State. Perhaps they may be ruined, but they still carry on. Country first – nothing else matters."

CHAPTER IX

From "Pale Ebenezer" to "Roaring Bill"

THE memory of that long straggle of broken men, meandering through the City of Despair, haunted me after I returned to England. I wrote some articles for the *Nation*, and other papers, with no hope of influencing the movement of events. In search of sanity I called on Mr. Massingham, Editor of the *Nation*, for Massingham had still kept alive the flame of all that was best in Victorian Liberalism. A Swiss statesman who read the *Nation* regularly throughout the war described it as the most convincing of all arguments for England. "England," he said to me, "may lose the war, but it has not lost its balance and its broad humanity. That Massingham should be allowed to write what he pleases in the fourth year of a disastrous war is a wonderful tribute to the Liberalism of your country."

I found Massingham in a mood of deep dejection. "The worst thing about war," he said, "is the spate of emotional stupidity that it unlooses. The English are not really vindictive. All this 'hang the Kaiser' business is alien to their real character. They'll be the first to make friends with the Germans, but meanwhile we'll be saddled with a peace which will produce war in twenty years."

In the early days of the war those who believed that open diplomacy would ensure a sane peace and prevent the recurrence of war founded "The League of Democratic Control." I joined this League, only to discover that the one chance of a reasonable Peace Treaty depended on Mr. Lloyd George's power to resist "democratic control." Mr. Sisley Huddleston, in a book which is, perhaps, the most illuminating of all studies of the post-war years (*In My Time*), reproduces his interview with "a high authority" in which the Premier stated the case for a generous Peace. The Premier's name was not mentioned in the interview, but it was clear who was the "high authority" quoted, with the unhappy result that "democratic control" came into play. Three hundred and seventy Members of Parliament signed a telegram of protest to the Premier, and the Premier yielded to their demagogic clamour. The "Hang the Kaiser election" was the first-fruit of King Demos's intrusion into the discussion of Peace terms.

Feudalism, like every other system of government, had its characteristic defects and its characteristic virtues. Chivalry was one of its finer products, for chivalry is aristocratic in origin. It is the consequence of a way of life based on self-discipline and on pride of caste. The cultured cosmopolitanism of mediæval Europe was confined to the class which could exchange thoughts in Latin, the language of all educated men, and which had its roots in the culture of Christendom. It is easy to regard every foreigner as the devil, if you never move out of your own village; but the aristocrats who met at Vienna belonged to an international society whose standards and whose outlook differed only in accidentals. The British mob demanded that Napoleon should be hanged, just as their successors demanded that the Kaiser should be hanged; but Metternich and the Iron Duke exchanged contemptuous glances, and it was men of their tradition that were responsible for a wise and humane peace. Britain and France have not fought against each other since Waterloo, but the Treaty influenced by "democratic control" gave Europe only twenty years of uneasy armistice.

I draw attention to the virtues of the aristocratic outlook, not because I have any illusions about aristocracy, but because I have even fewer about pure democracy. Social reformers may be divided into two groups: those who wish to make the poor richer and whose ideal is to level up and transform Demos into an aristocrat, and those who wish to make the rich poorer and who are anxious to level down the aristocracy to the level of Demos. I have every sympathy with the former and none with the latter. I believe that any system of government will work if the rulers are sincerely determined to translate Christianity into action, and that no system can work if it is corrupted either by the selfishness of the rich or by the envy of the poor. I find it difficult to understand how any man of adult intelligence can accept with uncritical enthusiasm any of the existing varieties of either authoritarian or democratic government, or regard any system as more than a makeshift, for our effective choice is not between the good and the bad, but between the bad and the worse. It is, I think, the duty of the political critic to draw attention to the defects of the existing order and the virtues of the order which it has replaced, for it is only by comparing the good in what has gone with the evil in what has come that we are saved from self-complacency. Representative government, which, at least, allows us the pleasure of getting rid of those who misrepresent us, is certainly better than any other rival system, but that is no particular reason why we should be uncritical in our adulation of King Demos, or assume that modern democracy is the best form of Representative Government.

In the first months of 1919 we still anchored our hopes to

the Messiah from beyond the seas who was to bring redemption to a troubled Europe; but it was only a jerry-built Messiah who crossed the Atlantic. Wilson was a man of good intentions ruined by egoism. He was ambitious to be remembered as the architect of the League, and to secure his League he was ready to sell his principles. He could have rallied liberal opinion in Great Britain against demagogic control. He could have insured Europe against war for fifty years. But he turned sorrowfully away, for he made great concessions. Europe asked for the bread of peace and he gave them a stone, the marble façade of the League of Nations. He was not outwitted, as many Americans insist, by the slick diplomatists of Europe. He was offered advice by Americans on the spot, Americans who knew Europe. If he was deceived, he was deceived, not by Clemenceau, but by his own wishful thinking.

It was something of a blow to me after the Armistice to find that chivalry began with the soldiers. I was educated in a tradition of anti-militarism. The evils of war were emphasised and re-emphasised by my father. And though my father liked soldiers when he met them, and had a bias in favour of engaging retired officers because, as he rather artlessly remarked, they knew how to obey, I instinctively contrasted the character whom we now call "Colonel Blimp" with the humane ideologists of the Left. And even as late as 1919 I was both shocked and surprised to discover that the demand to feed the starving should have come, not from the churches, or the politicians, but from the soldiers.

A few days after the Treaty of Versailles had been ratified by the British Parliament, Sir Donald Maclean, leader of the Liberal Party in the House of Commons, was staying with my father at Hastings. I asked him why he had allowed the party to vote for the Treaty. He replied that it would have been difficult and unfriendly to spoil the general effect of harmony and of rejoicing that the war had officially come to an end. Yes, it would have been difficult, but had the Liberals voted against the Treaty of Versailles, Liberalism might be in power to-day.

The British are intensely militaristic in time of war, and intensely pacifist in time of peace, a dangerous combination which encourages potential enemies to believe in British decadence. Once Peace had been signed, we adopted "Never again" as a national motto, and did everything in our power to ensure that "Soon again" should be our fate. There are two schools of pacifists – those who believe that it is wrong to kill and those who believe that it is unpleasant to be killed. It was the ignobler pacifists who dominated our policy in the post-war years. I have some respect for the pacifist who maintains that we should surrender the possessions which we took by the sword, and that disarmament should coincide with a general share-out of the British Empire. He is at least consistent. I do not agree with him, for I think Lord Rosebery was right when he maintained that the British Empire was the greatest secular force for good in the world (the operative word is, of course, "secular"), and I should be sorry to see any of the natives under our rule transferred to Germany, even if Germany were governed by rulers very different from the Nazis. But at least such pacifists are consistent. There is, however, nothing to be said for the pacifists who were naïve enough to believe that we could hold by the pen what our ancestors took by the sword.

Big Business was reluctant to pay for military security, and the Left were anxious to deflect money from the fighting to the social services. It was therefore easy to persuade the public that our fellow-members in the League were ready to defend our empire and the frontiers of France. A fantastic chimera. War is the result of original sin and will disappear in a world of angels. Collective security is as unrealisable an ideal as collective chastity. A league to abolish adultery could not fail more disastrously than the League to abolish war. I shall be reminded that the duel has disappeared. It has only disappeared from the Anglo-Saxon world as the result of the disintegration of the feudal emphasis on personal honour. It has not disappeared from the Latin countries. The disappearance of the duel, which was always condemned by the Church, is one of the few good things which we owe to the "progress" which partially replaced the ideals of the soldier by the ideals of the merchant. But the duel is preferable to "liquidation" as practised in Soviet Russia, the Utopia from which all traces of feudalism have disappeared. Mr. Belloc's epigram on "The Pacifist" crystallises our post-war search for universal peace:

> Pale Ebenezer thought it wrong to fight,
> But Roaring Bill, who killed him, thought it right.

Our British Ebenezers have made things delightfully easy for the Roaring Bills.

Pale Ebenezer enriched his propaganda with dramatic and moving descriptions of men dying in agony in No Man's Land, an argument which is valid against waging war for any but the most irreproachable of causes, but which is essentially un-Christian if exploited to justify passive resistance to lawless aggression. There are ideals for which men must be prepared to emulate the Christian martyrs who endured not only death but the extreme of bodily torture in defence of those ideals.

Those of us who do not believe that perpetual peace can be achieved by any form of league are often accused of cynicism by the self-styled idealists. But there is nothing idealistic in refusing to face uncomfortable facts or in surrender to the sloppy, pain-dreading temper of a false humanism. I remember a conversation towards the end of 1931. A well-known Bishop had just preached a sermon at Geneva, to the effect that the war had been a terrible blunder and that the Germans were very nice people indeed. My friend, a devout High Anglican, cordially agreed. "What good did the war do?" he sighed. "What is the point of war? It brings nothing but evil in its train." "Perhaps," I replied, "and so does a plague; but the effective choice in this wicked world is often between a greater and a lesser evil, and not between evil and good. We do not ask ourselves, 'What good do plagues do?' We do not repeat in a melancholy refrain, 'Plagues bring nothing but evil in their train.' We mobilise doctors and nurses and antiseptic ammunition to repel the hostile microbes. And if we don't, the casualties are multiplied indefinitely. Of course the war left Europe worse than it found it, but what sort of a Europe would it be if Germany had won and if Prussianism was triumphant? If a mad dog comes down my street I do not sadly sigh, 'What good are mad dogs?' I shoot the dog or the dog bites me."

He sighed indulgently. "I'm an idealist, and we shall never understand each other."

This piqued me, for I too have my ideals, and I resent the attempt of those who disagree with me to represent themselves as the only idealists. The question at issue was not whether any ideals were better than no ideals, but whether his ideals were better than mine. I asked him whether he had ever preached a sermon in favour of raising the blockade or of reasonable peace terms. He looked thoughtful, and said nothing, for he had been a militarist when England was at war, and became anti-militarist when England was at peace. He had been anti-German when Demos was anti-German, and he became pro-German when Demos became pro-German. And I knew that he would be anti-German again before long, for I was following with anxiety and interest the rise to power of a house-painter whose programme for a new Europe had escaped the attentions of my friend. More recently, he has moved votes of sympathy with Niemöller, the brave Lutheran imprisoned by the Nazis; but he was too discreet to remind his fellow-Christians that Catholics were not being imprisoned, like Niemöller, but tortured and murdered by the thousand in Republican Spain. He has recently received high ecclesiastical preferment.

He is not a conscious time-server. The mental fashion of the day is his natural habitat. He is as unconscious of his environment as a fish of water, and – like the fish – he would gasp helplessly if removed from that habitat. And yet I am convinced that he would face a firing party without flinching if the tragedy of Spain were to be repeated in England.

"The English," a shrewd friend of mine remarked, "just beg people to deceive them, and are more grateful to those who oblige than any other people." I am not sure that I agree. I think that the Germans would compete in any championship for wishful thinkers, perhaps because they originated the doctrine of "justification by faith."

Those who believed in Hitler as a bulwark against Communism had more justification than those who persisted in regarding Stalin as the keystone of resistance to Nazi aggression; for Hitler was once a sincere opponent of Bolshevism, and has, perhaps, not yet abandoned his designs on the Ukraine. Stalin, on the other hand, has never had the least intention of helping the democracies to defeat Germany. Lenin destroyed the only democratic government Russia has ever had. Why should Stalin fight for British democracy? Stalin's consistent objective has been a world war. Whenever I mentioned on the platform the twelve wars of aggression which Soviet Russia has waged,* I have asked any person present in the audience who can name three of these wars to hold up his hand. This challenge has never met with a response. The contrast between the enthusiasm with which Fascist aggression has been advertised and the conspiracy to ignore Soviet aggression is not necessarily sinister, for we were right to regard Germany as Public Enemy Number One; but our determination to believe in Soviet Russia as an ally of peace-loving Powers was merely a symptom of that mischievous wishful thinking which is the principal cause of our present distress. I remember a well-intentioned Catholic of Left-Wing sympathies who defended the popular thesis that Russia was essentially unaggressive. Why do intellectuals so

* I gave a list of these wars in Chapter XI of my book *Communism and Socialism*, which also contains a summary of the wars waged by previous revolutionary governments.

seldom read history? Every socialistic revolution begins by proclaiming its passionate love of peace, but is inevitably driven to seek escape from internal difficulties in foreign adventure. Neither the French Revolution of the eighteenth century nor that of 1848, nor the Russian Revolution, nor the National Socialist Revolution of Germany, escaped the consequences of revolutionary dynamics. Nothing could be more artless than to accuse Stalin of "treachery." Treachery to whom? Since when has that ruthless dictator shown any sympathy with democracy? Stalin is one of the most brilliant politicians that Europe has ever known. He has obtained the world war for which he had worked so patiently, the war which, so he hopes, will bring Bolshevism to the Rhine, and which has already given him control over the Baltic provinces. He encouraged the Poles to believe that he would assist them with arms, and he therefore ensured that they would not accept a compromise with Germany, and at the very last moment he signed the pact with Berlin which encouraged the Germans to invade Poland.

Christian civilisation is to-day in greater peril than when the Turks advanced to the walls of Vienna. In those days there was one, and only one, enemy to be met and conquered. To-day the explicit atheism of Stalin is allied with the implicit atheism of Hitler; but we possess not only the material, but, if we mobilise them, the spiritual resources to meet this grim challenge.

"Our Europe," writes Mr. Belloc, "cannot perish. Her religion – which is also mine – has in it those victorious energies of defence which neither merchants nor philosophers can understand, and which are yet the prime conditions of establishment. Europe, though she must always repel attacks from within and from without, is always secure; the soul of her is a certain spirit, at once reasonable and chivalric. And the gates of hell shall not prevail against her. Her component peoples have merged and remerged. Her particular famous cities have fallen down. Her soldiers have believed the world to have lost all because a battle turned against them. . . . Her best have at times grown poor and her worst rich. . . . She will certainly remain."

Postscriptum (June 10, 1940)

I bring this chapter, begun during the first weeks of the war, to an end in the darkest hour, as yet, of this tragic struggle. Italy has declared war and only a miracle can save Paris.

I spent a day in Paris on my way home from Italy, and lunched with my friend Alec Dru, one of the assistant military attachés, on the day after the German tank attack had forced a deadly breach in the French defences south of Sedan. Alec Dru quoted a century-old prediction of the greatest of Danish philosophers, Kierkegaard, to the effect that Christianity would, one day, be taken away from Europe to teach Europe its value. It may be so, but I am still confident of ultimate victory.

The disasters of to-day vindicate the prescience of Spengler, who diagnosed with uncanny insight the malady which has given Hitler his splendid chance. "For world peace," writes Spengler, "which has often existed in fact, involves the private renunciation of war on the part of the immense majority, but along with this it involves an unavowed readiness to submit to being the booty of others who do *not* renounce it. It begins with the state-destroying wish for universal peace and it ends with nobody moving a finger so long as misfortune only touches his neighbour. . . . Life if it would be great is hard; it lets us choose *only* between victory and ruin, not between war and peace, and to victory belong the sacrifices of victory."

Denmark was often cited by pacifists as an example of a small country which was prosperous in spite of, or even because of, the fact that it had no colonies and no effective means of resistance to military aggression. The Danish Premier is said to have remarked that Denmark preferred butter to guns. The Germans have got the Danish butter, and the Danes have the German guns.

CHAPTER X

A Poor Trumpet, but My Own

WHEN I wrote *Roman Converts*, an indignant Catholic exclaimed, "By what right does this authority on ski-ing and auction piquet criticise these eminent converts?" (Auction piquet is a card game for two, which I invented.) When I inaugurated a campaign for the recognition of downhill racing and the slalom, the Norwegians replied – "Who is this Englishman who presumes to reform ski-ing? We Norwegians are born with ski on our feet." When I found myself involved in a controversy with Dr. Coulton, who signed two appendices in a book which he published "G. G. Coulton, D.Litt., Litt.D., F.B.A., Fellow of St. John's College, Cambridge," I was reminded by the great expert that I had been sent down from Oxford for twice failing in the rudiments of Holy Scripture. And when I argue with scientists about science and religion, they reply that I am not a scientist.

It is clear that I can only establish, to the reader's satisfaction, my right to criticise the obscurantism of certain scientists by a vigorous blast on my own trumpet. A scientist who reviewed my book *Alpine Ski-ing* remarked that, though I was not a scientist, I had the makings of a scientist. The book in question was the result of scientific research, in the correct, but not in the fashionable, sense of those words.

Systematic mountaineering dates from the fifties of the last century, but the exploration of the High Alps on ski only began with Paulcke's traverse of the Oberland in 1897. Twelve years later Professor Roget and the present writer traversed the Oberland from end to end, in January, 1909. This was, I believe, the first ski mountaineering expedition of any importance by an Englishman. In the years that followed I spent many months studying and photographing snow surfaces in winter and in spring, and my book *Alpine Ski-ing*, in the opinion of modern experts, laid the foundation of modern snow and avalanche craft. Gerald Seligman has written the classic book on the subject. He is a real scientist, and has spent months investigating snow with all the paraphernalia of scientific instruments. I was relieved to discover how well my empirical theories had stood the test of scientific investigation. So far as the purely practical aspect of snowcraft was concerned, I do not seem to have left a very great deal for my successors to discover.

Marcel Kurz, incomparably the most experienced ski mountaineer, began to write a book shortly after my own book was published. He paid my book the compliment of translating several chapters of it, and remarked, rather wistfully, that it was odd that, though the English were the last to explore the Alps on ski, they were the first to produce a satisfactory study of snowcraft from the ski-ing angle. An abbreviated form of *Alpine Ski-ing* was translated into German, and the book itself into French. In recognition of my work on snowcraft I was elected an honorary member of the crack climbing club of France (the Groupe de Haute Montagne) and of the Appalachian Club of America.

Apart from the satisfaction of having helped to make ski mountaineering safer and pleasanter, I am glad that I wrote this book for many reasons.

In the first place, I soon discovered the distinction between fact collecting and fact co-ordinating. One of the most popular of modern illusions is that state-organised scientific researchers must necessarily produce scientific discoveries. Those, however, who collect facts are not necessarily skilled in co-ordinating them, and those who co-ordinate facts are not always the same people as those who have collected them. Watt, who invented the steam engine, was not a scientist in the accepted sense of the term. He was an artisan. A veterinary surgeon discovered pneumatic tyres. Browning, who invented automatic weapons, made his first gun at the age of thirteen out of the scrap iron in his father's shop. De Saussure, the father of modern geology, must often have seen erratic boulders and moraines many miles from the limits of existing glaciers. Agassiz and Forbes observed glacier-polished rocks many thousand feet above the present glacier levels. But neither De Saussure nor Agassiz co-ordinated the facts which they had seen. The fact that glaciers must at one time have covered the plains of Switzerland was discovered by a simple chamois hunter, Perrandier, who noticed a block of granite lying on the limestone near Neuchâtel, and who correctly deduced that the granite had not grown like a toadstool, and must therefore have been transported to its present site by some agency, and that the only possible agency was a glacier. Perrandier therefore concluded that glaciers must, at one time, have covered the plains of Switzerland. De Saussure, Tyndall, Agassiz and Forbes were great scientists, and many were the facts about glaciers which they collected. But it was left to a chamois hunter to co-ordinate the limited number of facts at his disposal and to demonstrate the existence of prehistoric glaciers.

And here is an example from my own experience. Everybody knows that snow is transformed into ice by pressure and by gravity. Hence the origin of ice slopes in movement – that is, of glaciers. But stationary ice slopes are common in the High Alps, particularly in the late summer. The accepted explanation of the transformation of a slope from snow in May to ice in August (*e.g.*, the summit slope of the Wetterhorn) was that the *surface* of the slope was melted by the sun or by rain and transformed into ice by a succession of night frosts. Now ice slopes are common in the High Alps, but are unknown on grass mountains, though the snow which covers grass mountains in the winter and spring is subject to the same processes of alternate melting and freezing that transform snow into ice at high altitudes. None of the scientists who specialised in glaciers had apparently noticed this anomaly, which continued to puzzle me until I happened to notice the stratified snow resting on a roof constructed of some kind of metal sheeting. The lower stratum, immediately above this impermeable sheeting, was ice. Why? Because the moisture which drained downwards from the summit layer, exposed to the sun, could not penetrate into the roof itself, and consequently formed a substratum of sodden snow which was transformed into ice by the night frosts. When snow rests on grass, the moisture from the thawing upper stratum escapes into the grass, and no ice forms. When snow rests on rock, the moisture forms a substratum of ice on the rock. The summit slope of the Wetterhorn is not transformed into ice superficially. It is not the summit layers which are changed into ice as the summer advances. What happens is that the top layer melts away, revealing the permanent substratum of ice.

Neither scientific training nor scientific apparatus would have helped me to co-ordinate the facts which that stratified snow on the roof provided.*

Few experts realise the distinction between the appeal to experience where the thesis advanced is admittedly based on experience, and the appeal to experience where the theory advanced is based on deductions from admitted facts.

* Ice is now beginning to appear on grass mountains served by funiculars. The effect of thousands of ski-ers using the same course gradually produces a brick-like crust which can be almost as impermeable as rock.

If I were leading a party in the High Alps, I should expect a novice to defer to my view that a particular slope was, or was not, likely to avalanche, and in this case the appeal to experience and expert knowledge would be valid. But if a novice and I were arguing in the valley, and if the novice based his case not on his own experience, but on facts which I admitted, or on facts which I myself had collected, and if he tried to prove that those facts did not justify my conclusions, it would be invalid and irrelevant to appeal to my status as an expert.

It was never more important than it is to-day to defend the right of the amateur to draw his own conclusions from the facts which the specialist has collected. Samuel Butler's brilliant criticism of Darwinism, which has been endorsed by many modern scientists, was ignored because he was a literary man. He admitted that he had made no original experiments, and remarked that an architect does not quarry his own stone. "If the facts are sound," he wrote, "how can it matter whether A or B collected them? What are the fact collectors worth, if the fact co-ordinators may not rely on them?"

Finally, my own position as an international expert in the organisation of downhill racing and in the theory of snow-craft has weakened my faith in the infallibility of experts.

Many years ago, when I was still a comparative novice in ski mountaineering, I engaged one of the most famous guides to accompany me on a difficult expedition. He began to lead across a slope which I was convinced would avalanche, and I refused to follow. A few seconds later, the slope avalanched, and the guide escaped death only by a miracle. A few years later Geoffrey Samuelson, who knows a lot about snow but who has fewer chances than I to study snowcraft, warned me that Telemark slope on the Palace run was dangerous. I disagreed. The slope itself did not avalanche, but an avalanche fell from the slope above. Samuelson was right, and I was wrong.

In a later chapter of this book I describe the disastrous race for the World Championship at Innsbruck. I was one of the committee which permitted a race to start under conditions which resulted in serious injuries to one competitor in three.

And now, little trumpet, you have earned a rest. Your strident blasts have achieved their objective. The walls of the expert Jericho have crumbled, and the timid defenders can no longer shelter behind their reputations. They must meet argument by argument, for the issue will be decided, not by rival trumpet blasts, but by the keen, decisive sword of dialectic.

CHAPTER XI

Adventures in Psychical Research

LET me conciliate the reader, outraged by my claim to scientific status, by the offer of an honourable compromise. Let him concede me scientific curiosity, and I will abandon all claims to a Fellowship of the Royal Society.

Felix qui potuit rerum cognoscere causas. Strange how few people are anxious to experience the felicity of those who know the "causes of things." The Greeks had a word for this type of curiosity. *Zetesis* means more than "curiosity," the nearest English equivalent. The word defines an attitude to life, an eager spirit of inquiry, concerned not only with the "how" but with the "why" of phenomena.

The Greek and the mediæval thinkers were interested in origins rather than in processes. Why was man created? What is the power behind phenomena? Our age is mainly interested in processes, in the way the machine works, including the human machine, rather than in the source of the machine's power.

My own variety of *zetesis* is practical rather than metaphysical. I studied snow because I did not wish to be killed in an avalanche. I spent a great deal of time investigating psychical research because I wanted to discover what would happen to me if I was killed. "Just what I expected," exclaims the Freudian. "Fear of death and wishful thinking explain your conversion to Catholicism." Puritanism, which may be defined as disapproval of innocent pleasure, takes many forms. The Puritan Manichees thought it sinful to eat meat or drink wine; the Puritan Catharists condemned the pleasures of sex, even between married couples. The Calvinists destroyed the glories of mediæval art and architecture because they disapproved of pleasure inspired by the beauty of art. The Freudian puritan condemns the pleasures of truth, and is firmly convinced that a belief is necessarily false because it happens to be consoling.

I once spent a night out among the glaciers in a storm. I was convinced that I would survive, a consoling thought, and I did survive. The reasoned case for surviving was stronger, but not much stronger, than the reasoned case for survival in the next world. Juries do not refuse to award a verdict because both barristers are influenced by wishful thinking in their belief that they can convince the jury. A jury listens to the arguments, and is uninterested in the motives which induce barristers to accept a particular brief.

Wishful thinking has never been one of my accomplishments. I am not sanguine by disposition. I have never believed that I would realise my earliest ambition, to achieve fame as an author. I believed in immortality long before I became a Catholic. If I were a wishful thinker I should be a convinced reincarnationist, for the only form of survival which appeals to me is the possibility of returning to the beloved Mountains of Youth. I accept the Beatific Vision on trust, but do not pretend to understand the happiness of a timeless world of absolute truth. Moreover, Catholic eschatology is not particularly cheerful. There is always the possibility of ending up in Hell, and the certainty that if one squeezes into Purgatory one will spend a very long time in a state of extreme discomfort.

My interest in psychical research was provoked not by wishful thinking, but by scientific *zetesis*. The phenomena reported, if genuine, involve a complete revolution in our scientific ideas.

I have sat with Mrs. Leonard, the best-known English subjective medium, and with Evan Powell, a well-known "physical medium." Mrs. Leonard in trance conditions often revealed knowledge of facts which she had no means of ascertaining by normal processes, but she never produced physical phenomena such as levitation, movement of objects without contact, materialisation, and so on.

The medium, whether subjective or "physical," goes into a trance until the "control" in the spirit world puts in an appearance. The "control" acts as a medium for the spirits. The spirits communicate through the control, and the sitters in the séance communicate through the medium. Red Indians and small children are popular as controls. "Great Hawk" is Evan Powell's control; "Feda," Mrs. Leonard's. Feda should be sent to a school for defective children, and Great Hawk to a reservation for backward Indians. Their range of ideas is as limited as their vocabulary.

By way of preface to what follows, let me state my own conclusions. I believe that 95 per cent of these phenomena are due to fraud or malobservation. I believe that there remains a residue of genuine supernormal phenomena, some of which are due to the agency of low-grade intelligences. I do not believe that the dead communicate through mediums, but I am prepared to credit the intelligences responsible for these phenomena with a telepathic power of picking our brains, and weaving scraps of information into a connected story. I suspect that they enjoy these opportunities of meeting pleasant, if slightly credulous, people and do their best to prolong these periods of social intercourse by playing up to any lead provided by the sitter.

The soundness of an hypothesis varies with the number of

facts which it explains. The materialistic hypothesis offers no explanation of the fact that certain mediums undoubtedly possess supernormal powers of acquiring information about their sitters which they could not have acquired by normal means. The spiritualistic hypothesis leaves unexplained the mental deterioration of the dead, and the large element of downright silliness in the alleged communications. "Phinuit," the spirit control of the famous American medium, Mrs. Piper, claimed to be the spirit of a French doctor. He startled sitters by the accuracy of his knowledge of their past histories. One day a sitter made a few remarks in French, but there was no reply from Dr. Phinuit, formerly of Metz. He explained that he had had so many English patients that he had entirely forgotten his native language. The tentative hypothesis, advanced above, explains not only Phinuit's clairvoyant faculties but also his ignorance of the French language.

It is only fair to quote the spiritualist reply to the sceptic who is unimpressed by spirit communications. I was once asked to debate spiritualism before an audience of spiritualists presided over by the Duchess of Hamilton. In reply to my criticism of the conversational powers of such spirits as I had met, the Duchess put me quietly and effectively in my place: "We cannot all expect to get into touch with the highest spirits" – and the audience was left to deduce that Arnold Lunn was the sort of person who did not mix with the best spirits, either in this world or in the next. *Noscitur a sociis.*

Sir Arthur Conan Doyle arranged my first sitting with Powell. We had tea before the meeting in Sir Arthur's house, and I was introduced to an earnest spiritualist who told me that his son was very interested in the quantum theory. He specialised in higher mathematics. I asked if he was studying at Oxford or Cambridge. "Oh no, he's a graduate of the spirit universities. He passed over last year." This sort of thing is embarrassing. (Incidentally, I cannot understand why spiritualists should be so prejudiced against the monosyllables "death," "died," and the like. Even those who believe most firmly in immortality refer to death as death.) During tea, somebody referred to a book of mine, and Sir Gilbert Parker, the novelist, remarked that his only psychical experience occurred during a recent illness, when the room seemed full of lights. The medium heard both these remarks, and wove them very skilfully into the subsequent performance.

After tea we adjourned to a small room in another house. The medium was roped into his chair, and I counted the knots, and verified them after the séance. Behind the medium was a small alcove containing a table on which there were some flowers. The medium went into a trance, and Sir Arthur led us in a hymn. Mutterings from Evan Powell, who in private life is a Welsh coal merchant, and then suddenly Great Hawk began to address the company in pidgin English, or rather in pidgin Welsh. The sitters were introduced: "Glad to meet you, Great Chief." "Glad to meet you, Great Hawk," replied Sir Arthur. Miss Stead, who was present, was addressed as "Squaw Stead," and I was greeted as "Chief Push-Pen." I protested that I never used a pen, but my request to be addressed as "Chief Strike-Typewriter" was ignored.

I was beginning to be bored, when suddenly little flames, which recalled the Pentecostal flames, fell in great profusion through the darkness. Suddenly that curious white substance known as ectoplasm began to filter out of the medium's body, a grey cloud which slowly organized itself into the shape of a delicate hand, like a woman's, extended over a ball of flame. The light of the flame showed through the edges of the ectoplasmic fingers, much as an electric globe shows through the edges of fingers which enclose it. The hand moved slowly round the circle. We had promised not to release hands, but my feet were free, and I moved them about in front of me as the hand approached, hoping to expose an accomplice, if any. But though the hand paused within two inches of my body, my foot touched nobody. At that time I wore, in consequence of a mountain accident, a large iron splint, the joint of which I could never remember to keep adequately oiled. It squeaked abominably. "Listen to the psychic vibrations," remarked Sir Arthur. Another "spirit" took a hand in the game and carried round the flowers, which I had seen on the little table before the séance began. The flowers were thrust into my face, and once again my errant foot moved through the empty air. "Are those flowers a hallucination, Chief Push-Pen?" asked Great Hawk. Great Hawk was the most unconvincing of spirits. He had no difficulty in producing long sentences and long words such as "hallucination," but he would affect to stumble over simple words – "Me no spik English welly well."

The direct voice, on the other hand, is an impressive phenomenon. Great Hawk's voice was merely a variant of Evan Powell's, but suddenly the room was filled with voices, an attractive woman's voice among others. "Do you remember, my dear, those psychic lights?" said the voice to Sir Gilbert, who had lost his wife a few months previously. I asked him, after the séance, whether the voice was recognisably his wife's. His reply was a hesitating negative. Once again the "spirits" had worked in a scrap of information, gathered before the meeting, in the effort to build up a character.

The direct voice is one of the few psychic phenomena which, if fraudulent, are more difficult in the dark, for a ventriloquist can produce no effect in the dark, a fact which the reader can test for himself by firmly shutting his eyes next time he is present during a performance by a ventriloquist.

Shortly before the end of the séance, I heard a whisper in front of me. "It's horrible, it's horrible." "Don't be afraid," said the spiritualist whose son is studying higher mathematics, "You've nothing to be afraid of. We are all trying to help you." "You haven't heard him properly," said Sir Arthur, "the word is 'Horace,' not 'horrible.' I knew a Horace once." And the spirit, anxious to oblige, moved over slowly to Sir Arthur and "horrible" became "Horace."

I do not base my belief in the reality of supernormal phenomena on my experiences at this or any other séance, but on experiments carried through under the strictest and most exacting scientific control, and, in particular, the experiment with the ectoplasmic gloves which is described in the next chapter.

CHAPTER XII

The Conflict between Science and Atheism

MANY people would devote themselves to that branch of scientific research which investigates the evidence for events alleged to be caused by supernatural agents, but for their unquestioning acceptance of the basic dogmas of a Victorian sect, a sect which owes its influence to the fact that it has never been identified by a label.

The Bishop who confirmed me at Harrow sent me to the Rationalists in search of a reasoned basis for relief, and the Rationalists in their turn encouraged me, in my reaction against the blind faith with which they accepted their dogmas, to search elsewhere for rational grounds for belief.

In this chapter I can only summarise in outline the positions which I defended against the spirited criticisms of Professor Haldane and Professor Joad. Those who are bored by religious controversy have probably abandoned the book at this point. If they are sanguine enough to continue, they might skip this chapter and the next and resume their plucky search for something of interest at Chapter XIV.

Materialists have exploited with success the defects of the scientific terminology. There is, as yet, no word which describes a sect, which claims to speak for science, and which asserts that science establishes the dogmas of materialism. Christians have fallen into the foolish habit of writing as if scientists, as such, were biased against the supernatural, and as if the alleged conflict between science and religion existed only in the imagination of people who know little of science and less of religion.

I remember listening to a long rambling broadcast lecture on the history of science. The speaker was indebted to a Catholic scientist, Marconi, for the opportunity to broadcast a talk, of which the central theme was the inevitable conflict between science and religion, and the historical opposition of the Church to science.

The Church, in the nineteen centuries of her existence, has never opposed scientific research, has been generous in her patronage to scientists, and has numbered among her children many of the greatest of European scientists. The one blot on a glorious record is the notorious Galileo case. In 1543 two Cardinals financed the publication of a work in which Canon Copernicus advanced the view that the earth revolves round the sun. The reigning Pope accepted the dedication of this book, and none of the nine Popes that followed took exception to the Copernican doctrine. In 1596 Kepler was hounded out of Germany by the Lutherans for teaching the Copernican theory, and took refuge with the Jesuits, among whom he continued to teach the blasphemy of the moving earth until he died.

Galileo would not have been molested had he not trespassed on the preserves of the theologians. Not content with teaching the Copernican theory, he insisted that theologians must have blundered in their interpretation of the famous passage in which

Joshua commands the sun to stand still. Now of all experts, few are more touchy about their status than theologians or more resentful of amateur criticism. But though Galileo got into trouble, he was treated with a consideration which would certainly not have been shown to any other amateur theologian, a consideration which was prompted by the respect which his scientific attainments inspired. "In the generation which saw the Thirty Years War," writes Professor Whitehead, F.R.S., a non-Catholic, "and remembered Alva in the Netherlands, the worst that happened to men of science was that Galileo suffered an honourable detention and a mild reproof before dying peaceably in his bed."

The French Jacobins sent Lavoisier to the guillotine because, as Robespierre remarked, "The Republic has no need of chemists." Thousands of scientists have been imprisoned and shot in Russia. If science refutes Catholicism, and establishes atheism, it is odd that scientists should have been persecuted by atheists in power and consistently encouraged and assisted by the Church.

I propose to describe the Victorian sect whose basic dogma is the irreconcilability of science and religion as Huxleyites, for Thomas Huxley may be regarded as their founder or at least as one of their principal prophets. Huxley had much in common with religious revivalists. He developed a marked pulpit manner and entitled a volume of his essays *Lay Sermons*, a tradition which his grandson Julian Huxley has maintained in his book *Religion without Revelation.* Scientific religiosity certainly had no more popular preacher than Thomas Huxley.

Thomas Huxley invented the word "agnostic," and was, perhaps, the first to enunciate the principles of what is now known as Behaviourism. But though he wrote a great deal of nonsense, he also wrote a great deal of sense. In an enlightened moment he even destroyed the whole basis of Huxleyism by admitting that "the philosophical difficulties of theism are neither greater nor less than they have been ever since theism was invented." It would, perhaps, be possible, by a judicious selection of his sounder remarks, to do for Huxley what Mr. Alfred Noyes has done for Voltaire. Huxley was still living on the Christian tradition. He was a better man than most Huxleyites, just as Darwin was a better man than most Darwinists. So long as he confined himself to natural science he was loyal to the ideals and to the method of science, but he ceased to be a scientist and became a neo-Lutheran when he approached the subject of the supernatural. Justification by faith, a negative faith, was his guiding principle in his attitude to phenomena which could not be fitted into the framework of natural law.

He lacked *zetesis*. The Dialectical Society, having appointed a committee to investigate the phenomena alleged to have been produced by the greatest of physical mediums, David Home, were startled and shocked when the committee failed to discover fraud and insisted that they had witnessed levitation in broad daylight. Huxley was invited to join the committee and to continue the investigations. He replied with a criticism of the intellectual calibre of spirit conversation. But the point at issue was not whether the alleged spirits were intelligent, but whether certain physical phenomena had occurred. If it were true, as the investigators claimed, that heavy bodies, in some instances men, had been seen "to rise slowly in the air and remain there for some time without visible or tangible support," an *a priori* case had been established for the investigation of phenomena which, if true, would have revolutionised the attitude of Victorian scientists. The true scientist should be above the snobbery which refuses to investigate phenomena merely because they are accompanied by undignified trimmings, such as silly spirit chatter, floating tambourines, and such. To the true scientist no fact is common or unclean.

Scientists have never been persecuted by the Church, for pioneers only suffer from the jealousy and obscurantism of their own colleagues. The pioneers of psychical research, amongst them many distinguished Fellows of the Royal Society, suffered in reputation by defying the fashion of the moment. Sir Oliver Lodge, for instance, lost the Presidency of the Royal Society because his heterodoxy shocked the high priests of orthodox science. A distinguished Fellow of the Royal Society made a remark which was highly significant. "I'm glad you're taking up this question of evolution. Of course the evidence for it is very weak, but I can't say so, because I've a wife and family to support. This is a job for an amateur with nothing to lose."

The Huxleyite accepts with uncritical faith two basic dogmas. First that all phenomena are explicable in terms of natural law, and secondly that "spirits" do not exist. There is no justification whatever for either of these *a priori* assumptions. As that great French scientist, Professor Richet, who never formally renounced materialism, remarks, "Why should there not be intelligent and puissant beings distinct from those perceptible to our senses? By what right should we dare to affirm on the basis of our limited senses, our defective intellect, and our scientific past, as yet hardly three centuries old, that in the vast cosmos man is the sole intelligent being, and that all mental reality always depends upon new cells irrigated by oxygenated blood?" The Huxleyite always assumes that he can draw blank cheques on the future to explain any phenomena inexplicable in terms of natural law. Had a Huxleyite met St. Denis, who is alleged to have carried his head in his hands after decapitation, the Huxleyite would have exclaimed, "Very puzzling, but science will one day explain the fact that certain exceptional, and no doubt pathological, persons can survive decapitation." Clearly it is useless to investigate the alleged existence of unknown agents, if all evidence for their reality is to be swept aside as irrelevant. Surely a scientist who suspects the existence of an unknown agent should proceed by the technique of exhaustion, and should admit, at least as a working hypothesis, the existence of a new agency, when he has failed to explain the phenomena in terms of existing agencies. It was this technique which led to the discovery of Neptune. The courses of planets are predictable by astronomers, for they are determined by known forces – the attraction of the sun and the attraction of the other planets. Before Neptune was discovered astronomers observed certain perturbations in the movements of the known planets which were inexplicable in terms of existing agencies – that is, of the sun and of the planets known to exist at that time. Leverrier correctly assumed that these perturbations must be due to an unknown planet, and as the result of intricate calculations he succeeded in directing his telescope to that part of the heavens where Neptune was visible, and in selecting a moment when Neptune was sufficiently near to the earth for its existence to be revealed by the telescope. But had Leverrier employed the Huxleyite method, he would have dismissed the perturbations as irrelevant. "For the moment," he would have exclaimed, "I cannot explain these deviations in terms of the planets known to me. But I know by faith that there are no other planets, and I am confident that astronomical science will one day explain these unaccountable deviations of planetary courses without invoking any planets other than those which we already know."

The Huxleyite recognises no objective criterion of evidence, to be applied impartially both to phenomena which do and to phenomena which do not support his preconceived theories. Let me briefly summarise the examples I selected to illustrate this point in the course of my correspondence with Professor J. B. S. Haldane, F.R.S.*

First let us consider the evidence for evolution. The animal kingdom is divided into groups known as phyla, classes, orders, families, genera and species. Of these the phyla, to which all mammalia belong, is the largest group, and species the smallest. The zebra and quagga are different species of the same genus. The horse and zebra belong to different genera of the Equidæ family.

* This correspondence was published under the title *Science and the Supernatural* (Eyre and Spottiswoode; in the U.S.A. by Sheed and Ward).

The geological record does not suggest the theory of evolution by descent, for though the record proves, what nobody denies, that there have been considerable changes *within the limits* of species and genus, the record as a whole bears witness to the fixity of types. The new types appear suddenly. The first shells are perfect shells. The record reveals no experiments in shell-making or feather-making, and as Berg, a Russian scientist working under an atheistic government, admits, there are no transitional forms between vertebrates and invertebrates or between reptiles and birds. "No one knows," writes Sir Arthur Thomson, "how feathers are evolved . . . there is no hint of transition between feathers and scales." There is no satisfactory series of lineage fossils linking even the small divisions of the genera, and no such series linking one family to another family. The geological record suggests what I have called *minor evolution,* – that is, small changes within the framework of the same genus, – but negates the theory of major evolution – that is, changes transcending the limits of the family.

To this the evolutionist replies by an appeal to the evidence which is not there. The geological record is admittedly imperfect, and by an unhappy coincidence it has retained the evidence which suggests fixity of type, and mislaid the missing links necessary to establish evolution. Faith, as I remarked to Haldane, is the substance of fossils hoped for, the evidence of links unseen.

Mr. D. Dewar, a well-known zoologist, has proved that every genus of European land mammal existing to-day has left a record on the rocks. The odds against any individual member of a genus leaving a fossil record are, of course, very large, but Mr. Dewar's statistics suggest that the odds are strongly in favour of one individual, at least, among the millions that compose a genus surviving in fossil form. Now if evolution be true, millions of genera, of which no fossils exist, must be presumed to have existed to link the different families together. It is certainly surprising that *every* genus of existing European land mammal is represented in the record, but that all the genera necessary to prove the evolutionary theory have disappeared. Mr. Dewar is a Fellow of the Zoological Society, but his revolutionary discoveries were refused publication in the *Proceedings* of the Society, on the advice of a palæontologist who refused his *imprimatur*, on the ground that the evidence, which was not refuted, "led to no valuable conclusions." Valuable to whom? I refer the reader to Mr. Dewar's book, *Difficulties of the Evolution Theory*.

Catholics are, of course, free to accept the evolution of man's *body* from the body of lower animals, a belief which raises no difficulties for the theist, and one need not be a Catholic to protest against the attempt to impose as a dogma a theory which is beset with difficulties. Yves Delage, a famous scientist, admitted that evolution was accepted "not so much for reasons deduced from natural history, as for motives of personal philosophic opinions." Justification by faith, in fact. And he added, "If one takes one's stand upon the exclusive grounds of facts, it must be acknowledged that the formation of one species from another species has not been demonstrated at all."

The evolution controversy is confused by the inability of many evolutionists to realise the point at issue. The simplest of fundamentalists does not believe that fishes and men were created simultaneously, and it is therefore irrelevant to trot out evidence which proves succession, as if succession were identical with evolution by descent. Sir Arthur Keith, for instance, makes a great point of comparing the evolution of watches with the evolution of man. The modern watch is very different from a sixteenth-century watch. He forgets that every watch owes its existence to an act of special creation. His analogy would be sound only if he could prove that a stop watch and a grandfather clock were blood relations, descended from a common ancestor.

Again, evidence which suggests evolution within the framework of species or genus, which nobody denies, is frequently produced as evidence of major evolution, which is the point at issue; and the fact that a few transitional forms are known which possess characteristics of two different genera or families is produced as coercive evidence in favour of a common ancestor. But just as the human creator will use the same ground plan for different varieties of motor-cars, so there is no *a priori* reason to suppose that the Creator would not necessarily start *de novo* every time He wished to create a new type.

A glaring case of faulty logic occurs in an essay of Professor Haldane's entitled "Darwinism To-day." Though Sir Arthur Keith habitually uses "Darwinism" as the equivalent of "evolution," it is important to recognise that Darwinism is the least plausible of all attempts to explain evolution, a theory that was first promulgated by Buffon in the eighteenth century. Darwinism is the theory that all living species have evolved under the influence of natural selection, blindly selecting those fortuitous variations which make for survival. A mindless environment blindly selecting chance variations produced in the course of ages from the rocks, sea and air of the primeval planet the brain of a Shakespeare and the emotions with which we listen to Beethoven's Fifth Symphony. Darwinism is philosophically absurd since you cannot get plus out of minus, and scientifically false for many reasons, of which the most convincing, perhaps, is the fact that if the survival of the fittest was what Nature aimed at it is difficult to understand why the evolutionary process should have begun with rocks, which are still existing, and ended with a baby, which is lucky if it survives to three score years and ten.

Darwinists frequently confuse natural selection as a fact with natural selection as an agent of evolutionary changes. Every epidemic is a case of natural selection. The fittest to survive survive. Darwin was not concerned to establish this truism, but to prove that natural selection explains such changes as, for instance, the evolution of a wingless reptile into archæopteryx, the parent bird.

"The assertion is sometimes made," writes Professor Haldane, "that no one has ever seen natural selection at work." What moron made this suggestion? Every epidemic is a case of natural selection at work. "It is therefore worth while," continues Professor Haldane, "giving in some detail a case recently described by Harrison." Professor Haldane then describes a wood containing dark pines and light birch. In one division of the wood the birches were almost entirely ousted by pines; in another part the pines were replaced by birches. Where light birches were replaced by dark pines, the white moths, which show up against the dark pines, are gradually disappearing, whereas the dark moths are increasing in number. No doubt; but the white moths are still white, and the dark moths still dark, and all that this illustration proves is that a badly camouflaged moth is more likely to be spotted by the enemy, owls or bats as the case may be, than a well-camouflaged moth. But no amount of "natural selection" will transform a wingless reptile into a bird, or a gun into an aeroplane.

Mr. H. G. Wells, who collaborated with Professor Julian Huxley in the production of that readable and informative work *The Science of Life*, pours ridicule on silly people who allege that Darwin maintained that "natural selection, in Heaven knows what inconceivable way, *produced* variations." Mr. Wells then commits the very blunder of which he has accused the hypothetical anti-Darwinist. Mr. Wells had a good look at the passage from Professor Haldane which I have just quoted, and decided that it would not do, as it stood, but might, if dressed up a little, be made to suggest that new characters emerged under the influence of natural selection. Professor Haldane wrote: "The assertion is sometimes made that nobody has ever seen natural selection at work." Mr. Wells interpolated a few words of his own, accidentally omitted the quotation marks and the quotation read – "The assertion is sometimes made that natural selection has never been seen at work in the production of new characters." I reviewed the book, and asked what new characters had appeared, whereupon Professor Haldane demanded an apology on the ground that I had attributed to him "an obviously silly remark." I thus found myself in the happy position of apologising to one Darwinist for attributing to him an "obviously silly remark" made by another Darwinist. Mr. Wells's interpolation was, in effect, implied in the original text, and I do not myself see that there is much to choose between Professor Haldane's pointless illustration and the "fortuitous variation" introduced by Mr. Wells. All this trouble would have been avoided had Professor Haldane and Mr. Wells received that training in exact thought which clarified the mental processes of the mediæval scholastics.

Let us now compare the evidence for three different types of phenomena, the first and second of which are rejected on *a priori* grounds by the Huxleyites, and the third of which is accepted with uncritical faith.

I. *Ectoplasm.* Ectoplasm, as already explained, is a white substance which emerges from the body of a medium, and, in the case of complete materialisations, organises itself into the shape of a human body. Professor Richet and Dr. Geley, two well-known scientists, performed the following experiment at the Institut Metapsychique, which has been recognised by the French Government as "of public utility." They introduced into the séance room a bowl of paraffin wax. The medium, Kluski, was rigidly controlled, and in due course a spirit form materialised out of the ectoplasm which had emerged from the medium's body. The alleged spirit, hereinafter referred to, for the sake of brevity, as the spirit, was requested to immerse its hand in the liquid paraffin wax, and to withdraw it. A human being who repeated this experiment would find his hand covered by a thin, fragile shell of paraffin, about one sixteenth of an inch in thickness. As a human hand could not pass through the narrow opening where the paraffin had solidified round the wrists, it would be impossible for a human being to withdraw his hand without breaking the paraffin shell. The spirit had no such difficulty. It dematerialised; and the spirit hand vanished into thin air, and the paraffin shell remained. Shells of clenched fists and even of clasped hands have been produced in great numbers. I should add that Richet coloured the paraffin which he employed for this experiment with chlorestin, in order to refute in advance the objection that the medium might have introduced the paraffin gloves himself. But this objection is of no help to the sceptic, for professional moulders working in daylight have been unable to duplicate these ectoplasmic shells. The paraffin gloves which they produced were made in different sections and show signs of the join. Houdini, perhaps the greatest conjuror that has ever lived, worked for months at Notre Dame University in the attempt to duplicate these shells. I have seen the results, shapeless lumpy wax fingers, pressed together and extended, so as to permit Houdini, with infinite care, to wriggle out of the wrist. But Houdini never produced a paraffin shell of clasped hands, or of a single hand with clenched fingers.

The medium worked in the dark; Houdini in daylight. The medium used paraffin which Richet had introduced, Houdini used his own materials. The medium was rigidly controlled, at a considerable distance from the paraffin. Houdini worked alone in a laboratory. I leave the sceptic to explain how the medium produced, at the first attempt, paraffin shells which the greatest of conjurors failed to duplicate after weeks of patient effort.

II. Peter de Rudder was a Belgian labourer whose leg was broken in 1867. Seven years passed and the bones were not united. He visited the shrine of Oostacker at which our Lady of Lourdes is venerated. His bones suddenly united. The detailed evidence, including the doctor's report, is summarised in my correspondence with Professor Haldane, who wrote: "I think the odds are that the bones were united, and the septic wounds healed, in a few hours." Professor Haldane, of course, refused to accept the hypothesis of a miraculous cure.

III. No cure is reported as a miracle at Lourdes until it has been examined by a committee of doctors. Any doctor, Catholic or non-Catholic, is entitled to serve on this committee. In my correspondence with Haldane I cited some of the more remarkable cases – sudden cures of blindness, ulcers, club feet, tuberculosis, and so forth.

Let us compare the evidence for the ectoplasmic gloves and the Lourdes miracles with the evidence for the evolution of a wingless reptile into a bird. "There is no hint of transition," writes Professor Sir Arthur Thomson, "between feathers and scales." In the case of the supernormal phenomena cited above, we are dealing with phenomena which took place, not millions of years ago, but in the contemporary world, phenomena which were observed and recorded by men with expert scientific or medical knowledge. In the case of the archæopteryx we have no basis for our belief that this bird, which appears suddenly in the geological record, is descended from a wingless reptile save a rash inference from certain reptilian characteristics, an inference which is only plausible if we assume that the Creator could not use similar ideas in the creation of very different types.

In conclusion, let me repeat that I am not in the least concerned to deny the possibility that the body of man may have evolved from that of lower animals, though I should require more evidence than I have as yet discovered to believe that the process was a purely natural one.

All I am concerned to establish is that those who believe in evolution and who reject all supernormal phenomena clearly choose their beliefs on the same principle that a woman chooses a hat, to suit the fashion of the moment. Huxleyism is merely a modern form of justification by faith.

CHAPTER XIII

The Return to Reason

MY deepening distrust of Huxleyism, and of much that paraded itself as modern thought, was reinforced by reading, during 1929, *Science and the Modern World*, by Professor A. N. Whitehead, a distinguished non-Catholic philosopher and mathematician, and a Fellow of the Royal Society. "The Reformation and the scientific movement were two aspects of the historical revolt which was the dominating intellectual movement of the later Renaissance. . . . It is a great mistake to conceive this historical revolt as an appeal to reason. On the contrary it was through and through an anti-intellectualist movement . . . based on a recoil from the inflexible rationality of mediæval thought. The Middle Ages formed one long training of the intellect of Western Europe in the sense of order . . . the habit of definite exact thought was implanted in the European mind by the long dominance of scholastic logic and scholastic divinity. The habit remained long after the philosophy had been repudiated, the priceless habit of looking for an exact point, and sticking to it when found. . . . I do not think that I have even yet brought out the greatest contribution of mediævalism to the formation of the scientific movement. I mean the inexpugnable belief that every detailed occurrence can be correlated to its antecedents in a perfectly definite manner, exemplifying general principles. Without this belief the incredible labour of scientists would be without hope . . . to this day science has remained an anti-intellectualist movement based on a naïve faith."

Under the influence of this impressive tribute to mediæval thought, I began to read the mediæval scholastics, and, in particular, the greatest of them, St. Thomas Aquinas. He appealed to me for many reasons.

Temperamentally I am a sceptic, and am uninterested in creeds which cannot justify themselves at the bar of reason. At Harrow not only did I never hear a reasoned case for Christianity, I was not even allowed to suspect that such a case existed. Personal experience was the basis of my father's faith, and personal experience, though convincing for the "experient," has no validity as an argument for those who do not share this experience. My father insisted on the power of faith to conquer temptations against chastity. I was by no means convinced that there was much to be said for refusing to accept such romantic adventures as came my way. To-day it is the difficulty of the Christian code, rather than the difficulty of the Christian creed, which keeps most people out of the Church, and the only reasonable defence for the code is to prove that it follows logically from a creed whose truth can be established by reason.

The Catholic Church, I discovered, does not appeal to faith or expect the potential convert to accept her claims until he has satisfied himself that they are rational. She approaches the Bible in the same spirit in which she approaches any other historical book, and applying the method of history proves that Jesus Christ established His claim to be God by rising from the dead. It is not until she has proved the credentials of the Church by reason that she asks us to accept on the authority of the Church doctrines which we have no independent means of verifying. In other words our attitude to the Church may be compared with our attitude to a specialist called in to diagnose an obscure disease. Having satisfied ourselves by reason that his credentials are reliable, we accept his diagnoses, which we have no means of independently verifying. Incidentally I think it was Professor Powicke who remarked that there was never an age in which more men took more beliefs on authority than our own.

I was impressed by the fairness with which St. Thomas summarised the principal arguments which tell against his thesis. Professor Thomson, F.R.S., somewhere comments on the contrast between the objectivity with which St. Thomas states and meets the arguments against the Faith and the evasive conspiracy of silence with which the arguments against evolution are ignored. The contrast between the confident rationalism of St. Thomas and the timid emotionalism of our modern prophets was the theme of my book *The Flight from Reason*, a theme which was treated as an entertaining paradox by most reviewers, for in 1931 the anti-rational tendencies of modern thought were implicit rather than explicit. Luther's "justification by faith" had not yet degenerated into Hitler's "We think with our blood." But the suicidal tendencies of modern thought were apparent to competent observers. The principal characteristic of modern philosophy is an implicit premiss which, in effect, denies the validity of all philosophy. If Marx and Freud are to be believed, neither Freud nor Marx should be believed. Marx maintained that the religion, philosophy and art of a given period are the by-products of its economic processes. Scholastic theology is nothing more than the mirror of the feudal system of land tenure. But, if this be true, Marxist Communism is nothing more than the mirror of the *laissez-faire* liberalism and industrialism of Victorian England. It has no objective validity. Freud maintained that the reasons with which a man justifies his beliefs are nothing more than rationalisations invented, *post hoc*, to justify beliefs imposed upon him by his environment and sexual complexes. We can safely ignore the reasoned arguments with which a man defends his belief, for we shall discover all that is worth knowing about those beliefs by psychoanalysing the man in question. If this be true, we shall learn all that is worth knowing about Freudianism by psychoanalysing the Freudian. These modern thinkers are busily engaged in sawing away the branch on which they are sitting.

The Church is the last refuge of Rationalism, and those rationalists who still remain outside the Church are only able to record a wistful protest against tendencies which we predicted but which they do not understand. My friend Cyril Joad, for instance, is a rationalist, and to the third edition of *Is Christianity True?* which consists of letters which we exchanged, we contributed a joint preface. In spite of our basic disagreement on Christianity, we reaffirmed our faith in reason and our joint rejection of the last and vilest of modern superstitions, the theory that reason is nothing more than a cork bobbing about in the sea of emotion and sex.

Joad is uninfected by the vanity of the moderns who regard ultra-scepticism as the hallmark of a superior mind. In an early stage of my correspondence with Professor Haldane, he remarked that he was prepared to admit that he was "nothing but a biologically and socially convenient fiction." A man who doubts his own existence is not easily convinced of the existence of God. In my reply I quoted Mr. Chesterton's remarkable prediction. The old sceptics, said Chesterton, doubted the existence of God; the modern sceptics doubt their own existence. "We are on the road to produce a race of men too mentally modest to believe in the multiplication table . . . the creeds and the crusades, the hierarchies and the horrible persecutions, were not organised, as is ignorantly said, for the suppression of reason. They were organised for the difficult defence of reason. Man by a blind instinct knew that, if once things were blindly questioned, reason would be questioned first."

Haldane has justified Mr. Chesterton's prediction, for, in our correspondence, he professed himself "willing to consider the possibility of exceptions to" the statement that $2 \times 3 = 6$. The half-educated may be impressed by this silly pose, the only point of which can be to reinforce the contrast between the alleged humility of the man of science and the alleged dogmatism of the Christian. But the most cursory examination of Professor Haldane's writings reveals the fact that his humility is highly selective and barely extends beyond the multiplication table. The inconsequence of modern thought finds few more striking illustrations than this Haldane blend of dogmatism about things which are doubtful, such as evolution, and sceptical humility about things which are certain, such as the multiplication table.

We find the seeds of the new scepticism in Darwin. "With me," wrote Darwin, "the horrid doubt always arises whether the convictions of a man's mind are of any value or at all trustworthy. Would anyone trust the conviction of a monkey's mind?" The mind can be trusted when it draws the conclusion that it has developed from the monkey's mind, and that therefore all the conclusions which it draws are untrustworthy. We have travelled a long distance from the logic of Aristotle to the logic of Bedlam, from faith in reason to doubts of the multiplication table.

The mediæval scholastics, I concede, overrated the power of pure reason to solve all problems in this world and in the next. "To them," writes Henry Adams, "words had fixed values like numbers, and syllogisms were hewn stones that needed only to be set in place in order to reach any height or support any weight." One need not abandon one's faith in reason to agree with Spengler that intellectual concepts are far less potent in the moulding of history than the unconscious forces, race, blood, and tradition. It is irrational to plan a Utopia on the assumption that men will be more influenced by the intellectualism of the doctrinaires than by their own deep-rooted and subconscious beliefs.

II

In spite of their faith in reason, the scholastics were saved from the folly of modern intellectualism by their recognition of the fact that human reason, though adequate to demonstrate the credentials of a supernatural revelation, cannot independently verify doctrines received on the authority of that revelation, whereas the modern intellectual acknowledges no such salutary check to conceit. His roots are in himself, and he recognizes no power higher than himself.

St. Thomas Aquinas, on his deathbed, dismissed his own monumental contributions to philosophy as "mere straw." He did not mean to depreciate the importance of philosophy, for he knew that the Catholic philosopher must, like our Lord, hold his own against the doctors in the Temple and talk to them in the language which they understand. But he knew that the intellectual approach is inferior to that mystical approach which is open to the simple and the uneducated.

Contrast the humility of St. Thomas's "mere straw" with the bumptiousness and oblique self-praise of the following passage from Mr. H. G. Wells's recent book *In Search of Hot Water:* "Nevertheless, the authentic writer and artist and scientific worker are the aristocrats of the human community. There is nothing above them under heaven. They are masters. *Cher maître* is no idle compliment to them. They work on honour and under no man's direction. They are subject to an inner necessity to do the utmost that is in them."

Perhaps the operative word is "authentic," for most artists and writers work for pay under the direction of fashion. On the greatest issue of recent years, Russian Communism, the majority of intellectuals have blinded themselves to the truth and prophesied smooth things. Even those, the majority, who had not the courage of their convictions, and who remained outside the Communist Party, joined the conspiracy of silence which concealed the horrors of that evil tyranny. The world which refused the unpalatable medicine of Christianity was only too anxious to be deceived, only too ready to believe that the Russians had found the secret of Utopia on earth. The "inner necessity" to which Mr. Wells's *chers maîtres* yielded was the dictation of Maître Demos. They have proved themselves servile lackeys of Plato's "Great Beast," the uninstructed opinion of the mob. "They have studied the humours and the wishes of the great and powerful beast, and the sounds which make it tame or fierce . . . and after mastering this knowledge, they call it wisdom, and construct on this basis a system . . . calling the things which please the beast good, and the things which irritate it evil."

Admittedly life has always been difficult for the independent writer. A stockbroker can hold what views he wishes, for a stockbroker sells stocks, but a writer sells ideas, and if his ideas are unfashionable he starves.

It is easy to understand why cowards should depreciate heroism, and why those who have no stomach for war should poke fun at Colonel Blimp, but art and letters decline, as Mr. St. John Ervine insists, when this inversion of values becomes fashionable.

"Let a man be either a hero or a saint," writes Spengler. "In between lies not wisdom but banality." Art flourished when men admired the hero and reverenced the saint. Art began to decline when men reverenced the artists and neglected the saints. Modern Europe can produce no art to set beside the supreme achievements of feudal Europe or feudal Japan, the Europe in which, not the intellectual prototype of H. G. Wells, but the warrior was in supreme control. An age of unbridled individualism always coincides with a decline of art, for the artist works best within an authoritarian tradition. The greatest masterpieces have been produced in times when art was a trade, and when artists were regarded as honest tradesmen. "Edward II's court painter," writes Dr. Coulton in his interesting book *Art and the Reformation*, "had no more tincture of ecclesiastical dignity than his cook." A contemporary of Chaucer's, Da Imola, a professor at Bologna, tells us that many people were astonished that Dante should have immortalised "unknown men of mean occupation," such as Giotto and Cimabue, but that Dante thereby proved his genius, for he realised that "even petty artisans" are anxious to earn honour, in proof of which the good professor mentions the curious fact that painters actually append their names to their works.*

"All evil," said St. Thomas, "is the result of mistaking means for ends." Art and letters are not ends but means. It is only in ages of artistic sterility that men proclaim as their ideal "art for art's sake." What is art, as Samuel Butler somewhere says, that it should have a sake? Art is not an end, but a means to an end, a window opening on to a world of eternal values. The final end of man is not artistic self-expression but eternal beatitude, and all that contributes to this end is good and all that does not contribute is indifferent, if it be not actually evil. The Church which enriched Europe with the greatest masterpieces of art and song is, as Mr. Belloc says, "careless of these things, for she has her roots in something other, that something which our moderns hate. Yet out of that something other came all the art and the songs of the Middle Ages, and what art and what songs have you?"

Many years ago I visited the Frari at Venice with a don, who was something of an authority on Catholic art. He admired Titian's masterpiece over the high altar, and discoursed very brilliantly on its peculiar excellences. Then we turned a corner to discover a working woman saying her prayers before a very different representation of the Madonna, a wax doll of exuberant and defiant gaudiness. My friend winced. "Why, oh why," he asked, "must these Romanists ruin their most ador-

* See *Art and the Reformation*, p. 82.

able churches by these too, too utterly frightful monstrosities?" Even then I did not agree. Though I was not a Catholic, the doll in some queer way seemed to have more right in that church than my sensitive friend. Its very gaudiness helped to establish the distinction between a church, which is the natural home for lowbrows and highbrows, and a museum in which my friend would feel at home and the Venetian woman ill at ease. There was something in the Frari for all tastes. The Church can meet the doctors in the Temple on their ground, and the artist on his, but she remains "careless of these things, for she has her roots in something other."

I do not feel at home in modern churches, every effect of which conforms to doctrinaire standards. The aseptic atmosphere of such churches is slightly chilling. There is a wealth of meaning in Heine's phrase "great-hearted dirt." I remember being shown round a great modern cathedral, much admired by those who know. Everything was in perfect taste, but how I longed for the friendly evidence of living, popular and vulgar art. I would gladly have exchanged the "Stations of the Cross" by a renowned modern sculptor for the Frari doll. But, of course, it would be useless to introduce the Frari doll into a modern church. The doll is at home in the Frari, because the donor thought it wonderful and because many of the faithful far preferred it to Titian's Madonna. The mixture of masterpieces and gaudy horrors is attractive, because, and only because, it bears witness, not to the conscious striving after contrast, but to a long process of organic growth in the course of which the Church has adapted itself naturally to the changing tastes of different generations and of different individuals.

"Because we have no dogmatic theology of our own," Professor Gilbert Norwood once remarked, "we have no cathedral architecture of our own." Noble architecture and great art are necessarily the flower of religious faith, for art achieves greatness only when it reflects values which are unaffected by the accidents of time and space.

The Gothic impulse reappeared in our own age in the character of Mickey Mouse, who has (or rather had) much in common with Gothic gargoyles. Mickey's appeal is universal, and transcends the limits of race. Like the Gothic gargoyle, he belongs to another world than this, and holds out hope of an escape from the limitations of natural law. All genuine art offers us a release, if only imaginary, from the tyranny of fact. I have watched the rapt expressions on the faces of audiences while Mickey was on the screen. Slaves of circumstances, they were entranced by the vision of a world in which man (and Mickey) is liberated from the compulsion of terrestrial law. Mickey, escaping from the Devil, in the form of a monstrous cat, shooting into the sky in defiance of gravity when the cat is ready to pounce, or leaping across vast chasms, is the symbol of a self which is only imprisoned for the moment in the limitations of time and space. His appeal is (or was) faintly religious, but Mickey has passed all too rapidly through the Spenglerian cycle. I loved him best in the Gothic phase before inspiration had been subordinated to technique. Baroque Mickey was bearable, but Royal Academy Mickey has already arrived. Nothing but a return to the Faith can save Mickey or modern art from inevitable decline.

III

I had approached my study of the mediæval Scholastics unhandicapped by the usual prejudices against Catholicism, for I had spent three years (1921–1924) in the attempt to solve a problem which puzzles many people, but which most people are content to leave unsolved. Here is a Church committed, so I believed, to fantastic and irrational doctrines and which yet continues to make converts among men distinguished not only for intellectual gifts but also for intellectual integrity. I am glad that in my book *Roman Converts* I had the honesty to confess that I had discovered no solution to this problem. I discovered, of course, that most of the beliefs with which Catholics were credited were not, in fact, held by Catholics.

I am perplexed by the curious lack of *zetesis* which moderns display in this matter of an institution which gave Europe her religion, her law, her noblest art and sweetest song. Surely it should be regarded as an integral part of a liberal education to know something, if only in outline, of the philosophy of a Church which still enjoys a world-wide influence? Why is it that so few people pause, as I paused, after asking themselves how Catholics can hold such and such a belief? Why is it that so few people are interested to discover whether in point of fact Catholics do hold the belief in question? I can offer only a tentative answer to this question.

It is a fact that the Church's prestige has notably increased in recent years. The failure of secular Liberalism to produce the new earth which was offered in exchange for the old heaven is responsible for a reawakening of interest in the traditional remedies for our distracted civilisation. The Mid-Victorian Liberals were convinced that the Church would scarcely outlive the century, but it is secular Liberalism which is on its deathbed and the Church which is enjoying a new lease of life. In my youth I thought of the scholastics as pedants who argued about the number of angels who could dance on a pin; I lived to see the Protestant president of a great American university, the University of Chicago, insist that a return to scholastic philosophy is the only hope for American education. Professor Adler, a Jew and, as yet, not a Catholic, lectures on scholasticism in the heart of the Middle West to enthusiastic audiences, very few of whom are Catholics.

It would be easy to collect from the writings of men normally hostile to the Church, men such as Dr. Inge, Mr. Bernard Shaw and Mr. H. G. Wells, astounding tributes to Catholicism. Mr. Wells, for instance, entered Rome with all the usual prejudices, but was temporarily thrown off his balance by the Eternal City. "The Scarlet Woman," he writes, "of my youthful prejudices was not in evidence. Protestantism, I perceived, had not done justice to Renascence Rome. Here, quite plainly, was a great mental system engaged in a vital effort to comprehend its expanding universe and sustain a co-ordinating conception of human activities. That easy word 'superstition' did not cover a tithe of it. . . . In spite of my anti-Christian bias I found something congenial in the far-flung cosmopolitanism of the Catholic proposition. Notwithstanding its synthesis of decaying ancient theologies and its strong taint of other-worldliness, the Catholic Church continues to be, in its own half-hearted fashion, an Open Conspiracy to reorganise the whole life of man. If the papal system had achieved the ambitions of its most vigorous period, it would have been much more in the nature of that competent receiver for human affairs, the research for which has occupied my mind so largely throughout my life, than that planless Providentialism which has characterised almost all the political and social thought of the nineteenth century. Catholicism is something greater in scope and spirit than any nationalist protestantism. . . . I have lived for years in open controversy with Catholicism and though, naturally enough, I have sometimes been insulted by indignant zealots, I have found the ordinary Catholic controversialist a fair fighter and a civilised man, worthy of that great cultural system within which such minds as Leonardo and Michael Angelo could develop and find expression. . . . It is a question too fine for me to discuss whether I am an outright atheist or an extreme heretic on the furthest verge of Christianity — beyond the Arians, beyond the Manichæans. But certainly I branch from the Catholic stem." *

It would be easy to parallel this passage from the writings of other men during those moments when they remember that they "branch from the Catholic stem," but a momentary

* *Experiment in Autobiography*, by H. G. Wells, p. 574. (Gollancz.)

approach to the Church is usually followed by a recoil. Mr. Aldous Huxley, for instance, never wrote anything better than that Catholic tract, *Brave New World*, in which he satirised the basic doctrines of the Huxleyism in which he was educated. But his next book was on a much lower level. Mr. Shaw followed up "St. Joan," his greatest play, with "A Black Girl in Search of God." And Mr. Wells in his recent *The Fate of Homo Sapiens* indulges in futile shrewish attempts to saw through the stem from which he branched.

Mr. Wells illustrates the lack of *zetesis* in the modern attitude to the Church. In the passage from which I have quoted above he wrote "beyond the Aryans," a mistake which I have allowed myself to correct; and in his most recent work he betrays the usual ignorance of the doctrine of the Immaculate Conception, and sniffs at theologians for excogitating a "sinless" begetting for the Madonna. There is something to be said for getting one's facts right even if one is writing about something as unimportant as Catholic doctrine. It is curious that the one subject on which men of academic status do not lose caste by writing nonsense should be the Church which founded most of the universities in Europe.

A popular variant of what may be called the compensation complex, which in this case is the anxiety to believe the worst of an institution of which one suspects the best, is the refusal to admit that a convert may have joined the Church because his reason was convinced that the Church's claims were true. Any motive must be preferred to this. Conversion is often attributed to love of ritual. I do not think that this motive was a factor in my own conversion. I first attended Mass in August, 1907. I was climbing with a Catholic, and my father made the Catholic promise to take me to church at Sion. "I know there is no Anglican service, so Arnold had better go to Mass"—an interesting example of my father's tolerance. I was not impressed by Mass. It seemed to me inferior, so far as ritual went, to a military funeral. I do not think I went to Mass more than half a dozen times in the quarter of a century that elapsed between attending Mass at Sion and entering the Catholic Church.

I cannot myself detect much difference between the mental processes which led me to certain conclusions about avalanches and those which led me to the conclusion that the Catholic Church had established her claims. In both cases I spent many years in the examination of the available evidence. I entered the Church along the road of controversy and by the gate of reason. I clarified my mind by three controversial books, in the first of which (*Difficulties*, with Father Ronald Knox) I attacked, and in the second and third of which I defended, the Catholic position against Cyril Joad and Professor Haldane. And I did not become a Catholic till I had satisfied myself that I had found a satisfactory answer to the worst that could be said against the Church.

I ceased to be an Anglican at Harrow, and I became a Catholic shortly after I satisfied myself that Christ rose from the dead. I spent some years on this, the greatest of historical problems, in search of a rational explanation for the disappearance of Christ's body from the tomb. The disciples, who had fled in cowardly dismay after the Crucifixion, returned to Jerusalem to preach with unshaken confidence the resurrection of our Lord. Why did not the Pharisees produce the body of our Lord to refute them? It is a sound canon of historical criticism to give weight to theories advanced by contemporaries to discredit an alleged occurrence in which they refused to believe. The Pharisees, who had every interest in disproving the Resurrection, could produce no better alternative theory than the allegation that the disciples had stolen the body. If they had stolen the body, they would have known that Christ had not risen from the dead, and men do not break with their own Church and their own nation and their own friends and face martyrdom to proclaim what they themselves know to be a monstrous and superfluous lie. If one case had been established of a resurrection from the dead, no historian would deny the resurrection of Christ. This miracle is denied, in face of the evidence and in deference to the *a priori* doctrine that miracles do not occur. My own investigations of psychical research had convinced me that supernormal events, probably due to spirits, have been demonstrated beyond reasonable doubt, and I had therefore no great antecedent difficulty in accepting the greatest of all supernormal events.

In spite of the affection and deep respect which I still feel for the Church of my baptism, I could not return to the Anglican Church, for I found it impossible to believe that a Church which leaves its clergy free either to accept all that Christ taught or to deny much that He taught could be part of the Church which Christ founded. The infallibility of Christ, not the infallibility of the Pope, is the real issue which divides Christians.

I said something to this effect in reply to a diplomatist who asked me why I had become a Catholic. "You seem to have accepted," he answered, "the infallibility of the Pope as a logical but disagreeable consequence of your belief in the infallibility of Christ. If I ever became a Catholic, which is unlikely, I should accept the infallibility of Christ because I do not find it difficult to believe in the infallibility of the Pope. I was accredited for some years to our Legation at the Vatican, and I was tremendously impressed by the immense sagacity of the Papacy. I began to suspect that the Papacy was in touch with sources of information denied to ordinary mortals. By contrast our European statesmen seemed like children, blundering amateurs. The silly futility of their ephemeral solutions stood out against the serene confidence with which the Papacy continued to proclaim the old remedy, which – for all I know – might work if it was seriously tried out. And I felt that whereas politicians are mere opportunists living from hand to mouth, the Papacy remembers the centuries and applies to the apparent novelties of modern foolishness the yardstick of immense experience. Didn't the late Pope quietly dismiss Nazism as a mere revival of the

Julian heresy? To us Hitler represents a new problem, a modern peril, but the Church has seen many Hitlers come and go, and will outlive them all."

It is, of course, easier to reach the conclusion that Catholicism is true than to implement this conclusion. I was not attracted by the Catholic way of life. Like most sophisticated moderns I felt a fool on my knees, and only resumed with immense difficulty the habit of prayer. It is still an effort, for my turn of mind is scientific rather than devotional. I did not welcome the fact that friends, who thought me mildly clever, would wonder whether I was suffering from a sudden softening of the brain. Two ski-ers motored down to see me the day after I was received. They gave a reassuring report. "It's all right," one of the young racing toughs was reported to have said; "it's only old Arni pulling a quick one on us."

Above all, it is difficult for those who have once subscribed to the creed of humanism, the belief that man is the measure of all things, to overcome their prejudice against the alleged intolerance of a Church which refuses to compromise on the doctrines which she proclaims as true. The modern world confuses two very different things – intolerance of error and intolerance of men in error. The former is usually right, the latter usually wrong.

I am, for instance, an uncompromising bigot on the question of the multiplication table, whereas Professor Haldane is willing to admit the possibility of exceptions to the statement that $2 \times 3 = 6$. I am intolerant of his heretical distrust of certain truth, but, even if I were a dictator, I should not intern Professor Haldane, or deny him the freedom to proclaim his views. Moreover, I do not assume that those who are orthodox on the multiplication table are necessarily, in other respects, more intelligent, or better citizens than those who trifle with mathematical heresies. "Love men, slay errors," said St. Augustine, and where ecclesiastics have followed this golden rule they have remained true to the spirit of Christ, who was uncompromising in His condemnation of fashionable sins, and infinitely tolerant of unfashionable sinners.

A man is not necessarily a bigot because he believes in the Resurrection, or comes to the conclusion that Christ founded a visible Church, and that the Church in question is the Roman Catholic Church. Many bigots have rejected as inconclusive the evidence on which the Church bases her claims, and many men of wide tolerance have accepted those claims. The real criterion of bigotry is less the nature of our beliefs than our attitude to those who do not share our beliefs. There are bigots in every Church. Bigots, I am told by travellers, are not unknown in the Protestant districts of Ulster.

The ever-growing peril of militant atheism is achieving at least one good result. It is forcing Christians to realise that the beliefs which unite them are more important than those which divide them. There are, I suppose, Catholics who believe that all Protestants go to Hell, but I have never met them. Nor have I met a Catholic who would dissent from the following pronouncement by Dr. Karl Adam, Catholic priest and professor of theology: "Not merely a Christian life, but a complete and lofty Christian life, a life according to the 'full age of Christ,' a saintly life, is possible – so Catholics believe – even in definitely non-Catholic communions."

During the Spanish War my father appealed in the columns of *The Times* for a united Christian Front. Cardinal Hinsley in the course of his reply wrote as follows: "Pius XI explicitly appeals in his letter *Divini Redemptoris* to all who believe in God. Between those who believe in Christ as true God and true man and worship Him there should be charity – an effort to draw nearer to Him and so nearer to one another. This means not only friendly relationship but mutual help in defending the civilisation which is founded on the truths enunciated in the Nicæan Creed. Sir Henry rightly insists on this bond between us. Let us be frank. There have been in the past misunderstandings and faults of manner on both sides, and of temper or a lack of charity in controversy. These, our failings and differences, the enemies of religion have exploited. But the realisation of a common peril is drawing Christians together in practical sympathy." The response to this joint appeal was rather disappointing, but much has happened since 1937, and the alliance between two dictators for the destruction of Christian civilisation has already led to a revival of religion in Great Britain, and to friendlier relations between Christians of the different communions.

CHAPTER XIV

King Albert of the Belgians

Contemne mortem, nihil triste est, cum hujus metum effugimus.
— SENECA

"A STRANGE moral transformation," wrote that great American philosopher William James, "has within the last century swept over our Western world. We no longer think that we are called upon to face physical pain with equanimity. The way in which our ancestors looked upon pain as an eternal ingredient of the world's order, and both caused and suffered it as a matter of course, fills us with amazement. We wonder that human beings could have been so callous."

These lines were written before the Great War proved that modern man was as capable of heroic endurance as his ancestors, but in the reaction following the war the pain-dreading temper which William James condemned found expression in the more extreme forms of pacifism.

Twenty-five years have passed since King Albert decided that a nation can pay too high a price for peace. Before the war the word "Flanders" evoked memories of a glorious past, but it was the refrain of a lost romance which sang to us in the carillon of Bruges. To-day the Flanders battlefields are more impressive than the mediæval glamour of Ghent, and there is a new triumphant note in the bells of Bruges since they rang out their welcome to the King – riding home in triumph through the country which he had saved.*

Our pacifists sometimes forget that self-respect, national or individual, is not the least of the imponderables for which men are prepared to pay a heavy price.

Throughout the war the King and Queen were more often in than out of the front-line trenches, and were never out of range of enemy guns.

"I will not be deprived of my rights as a citizen because I happen to be a King," was a favourite saying of his. As a king his life was so precious to his country that his advisers made every effort to keep him out of the trenches in war and away from the mountains in peace. But the King refused to be deprived of the right to which, as a citizen of Belgium, he was entitled, the right to imperil his life as and when he pleased.

To the King mountaineering was not mountain travel, but a duel between man and mountain. It is, of course, the determination to preserve the reality of that contest which is responsible for all new developments in mountaineering. The King sought out the climbs which tested him to the limit of his capacity, knowing well that this involved definite risks, since no man can measure himself fully against the mountains without peril.

He climbed a great deal alone among the small but difficult rock peaks which are within easy motoring distance of his villa on Lake Lucerne. He was not at his best on snow and ice, but he was a magnificent rock climber, and it was as an active partner, and not as a passenger, that he achieved a series of brilliant guideless climbs. Two members of the Kandahar Club, Walter

* This chapter was written before the outbreak of the present war.

Amstutz and Gotlieb Michel, were his companions on expeditions of exceptional difficulty. Amstutz has given a list in *Die Alpen* of the King's climbs in the Dolomites and the Engelhorner and elsewhere. It is a list of which even a modern cragsman might be very proud.

On one occasion, as the King was creeping along an extremely exposed and treacherous traverse, one of his companions showed signs of perturbation. The King looked over his shoulder down into the depths below, and said, "Death is the fate of all true Alpinists," a remark which did little to reassure his companion.

It would be false to suggest that his real life began and ended among the mountains. He took an active interest in everything which concerned, directly or indirectly, his country's welfare. He was a man of wide reading and knowledge. He often startled experts by the soundness of the views which he expressed on their own particular jobs. He was engrossed in his work, but bored by the incidental ceremonial, and moved with resignation among cheering crowds, journalists and press photographers. He accepted all this as part of the job, but woe betide the luckless man who attempted to photograph him on his holiday.

A vivid scene comes back to me as I write. A little man cowering beneath the sudden impact of six feet three of royal wrath. . . . "I tell you it is insupportable. I have not lost my rights as a citizen because I happen to be a king. . . . You have invaded my private liberty in the most monstrous fashion."

He loved the mountains for many reasons, of which not the least was the fact that they provided him with an escape from the king business.

"I shall go back to Belgium," he said, looking out on to the mountains, "and for the next few weeks I shall have to deliver and to listen to an interminable series of speeches in connection with the centenary of our independence. Though I shall keep awake during the other speeches, I shall find it difficult not to go to sleep during my own. . . . Talk . . . talk . . . talk," he sighed gently; "but in the summer I shall be back in the mountains."

The King was the most modest man I have ever met. He continued quite simply to ignore the universal conspiracy to treat him as one of the heroic figures of the age. Out of office the one thing which he was anxious to forget was that he was a king. This, perhaps, explains his fondness for a very uncomfortable form of travel. The King and the Queen often went for long tours in the Alps on a motor bicycle, the Queen riding pillion. They travelled incognito and put up at the smallest of inns. Once when the King turned up with his bicycle in front of a smart hotel, the concierge waved him on. "You will find the kind of hotel you want further down the road."

His conversation was salted by his sense of irony. Of a friend of mine, a great mountain painter and a convinced spiritualist, he remarked: "I enjoy your friend's conversation on art, for he is a fine artist, and I am glad to hear his views about Europe and its difficulties; but though I can listen to him I cannot discuss, for one cannot discuss European problems with a man who replies, 'Excuse me, but that is not correct, for the spirits have told me so-and-so.' "

To no man has the freemasonry of the mountains meant more. He loved, when the day's work was done, to collect a few Alpine friends and to forget what Burke calls "the solemn plausibilities of the world." My wife and I had been honoured with an invitation to stay with the King and Queen at the Château de Laaken. The King had just returned from a day's scrambling on the pinnacles of the Meuse. "We're lucky," he said, "to be able to train our muscles for the Alps on these crags. They're short but difficult." It was on one of these short but difficult crags that he was to die. After dinner the King produced albums full of Alpine photographs. I remember him pausing over a photograph of one of the Oberland peaks. "This ridge . . . has it been climbed? I think it would go . . ." And then followed an animated discussion with Count Xavier de

Grunne, a gallant Belgian mountaineer. And the two heads bent together over the album. "Just like two schoolboys plotting some new devilry," as somebody disrespectfully remarked. My last memory of that event is of Xavier de Grunne canvassing the possibility of reaching the first floor of the Palace via the chimneypiece in the main hall.

The manner of his death was, as the *Alpine Journal* truly remarked, consistent with the principles by which as man and king he lived. He knew full well the dangerous character of the vegetated pinnacles of the Meuse, but believing wholeheartedly, as he did, in the national value of climbing as a discipline of character, he threw himself into the exploration of these cliffs, which he hoped would become a home climbing-ground for his people.

That death is of no great importance, and that the discipline of danger is an integral part of any life which is worth living, was the philosophy by which the King lived, and for which he died. And it may be that the years of life which would have remained to him would have proved of less value to his country than the inspiration which Belgians yet unborn will draw from the lonely pinnacle beside the Meuse, consecrated for ever to the memory of the mountain King.

The Queen was the daughter of the Duke of Bavaria. Her father would have been a scientist had Fate permitted. He studied medicine, passed his examinations as an oculist and was at the disposal of the tenants on his estate when their eyes gave trouble. The Queen's sister, Countess Toerring, inherited her father's scientific tastes. I remember a long discussion about the difference between the Darwinian and Lamarckian theories of evolution. The Queen asked us to explain the distinction. "The essence of Darwinism," I began, "is natural selection, which selects the variations fitted to survive. Creatures which are ill adapted to their environment become extinct."

"Did you hear that, Albert?" said the Queen. "Creatures that are ill adapted to their environment gradually become extinct. That is sad news for kings and queens."

But if all kings and queens were like King Albert and Queen Elizabeth there would be no republics.

The King, with his queer sardonic attitude, was the last to suspect the depths of devotion which he, and the Queen, inspired. "I don't give twopence," said Admiral Sir Roger Keyes, who rode behind them on their triumphant return through Belgium, "for this king business, but I just love those two dear people." Certainly it was not the king business, it was not even the gratitude to a king who had deserved supremely well of his people, which tugged at the heart-strings of the vast concourse which watched the King pass to his rest.

Much of the affection which citizens feel for their sovereign is merely an extended form of egoism. Old ladies who snuffle into their handkerchiefs as a king or queen is borne by to the grave are really crying over their own dead youth, for in some dim way they link together their own lives with the lives of their rulers. And when the ruler passes they feel that something of them passes too. But the immense sorrow of the silent people between whose serried ranks the King passed by belonged to a very different order of emotion. *D'antico amore senti la gran potenza.* And against that *gran potenza* death itself will not prevail.

CHAPTER XV

Greek Olympics

"THERE are some people – and I am one of them," wrote Mr. Chesterton, "who think that the most practical and important thing about a man is still his view of the universe. We think that for a landlady considering a lodger it is important to know his income, but still more important to know his philosophy. We think that for a general about to fight an enemy it is important to know the enemy's numbers, but still more important to know the enemy's philosophy. We think that the question is not whether the theory of the cosmos affects matters, but whether in the long run anything else affects them."

Mr. Chesterton's thesis might be illustrated from the realm of sport. I have watched the rapid degeneration of international ski-ing from the day that Hitler assumed power. I have seen young German racers evolve from pleasant and chivalrous sportsmen into semi-militarised athletes who raced to demonstrate the superiority of the Nazi philosophy to other creeds.

I was present during the Nazi Winter Olympics of 1936, I refereed one of their races, and had every opportunity to contrast the spirit of the old Germany, still represented on the committee of which I was a member, with the spirit of the new Germany which was the dominant influence in the games.

It is impossible to understand the Greek Olympics, the mediæval tourneys, or the Nazi Olympics except in relation to the prevailing philosophies, Greek, Christian and Nazi, which determined their spirit and tradition.

The degradation of modern international sport, a degradation for which the dictators largely are responsible, emerges very clearly from a comparison between Greek and Nazi Olympics.

The first known date in the history of the Olympic Games is 868 B.C., when the Games were reorganized by Iphitus, King of Elis. The athletic records of Olympia date from 776 B.C., and the Games were held at four-year intervals until they were finally abolished in A.D. 398. Our information about them would be more complete if the Greeks had been interested in records. The rivalry between the different states was reflected in the keenness of the Olympic competition, but it was the competition between man and man which interested them, and not between man and a formula. It was his opponent that the Greek athlete wanted to beat and not the record for the course. In sport, as in art, the Greek concentrated on "the bodily present moment." We can rely on the Olympic records for the names of the victors and for the nature of the events, but they are not uniformly reliable, as may be gathered from the fact that Phayllus is credited with having jumped 55 feet, about double the existing jumping record.

What of the spirit in which the Games were played? It will shock those who believe that sportsmanship was invented by the English on the playing fields of Eton to discover that the sporting code of the Olympic Greeks was as high as, perhaps higher than, our own, though less high than that code of chivalry which was born not in England but in France. In the modern Olympic oath *in ritterlichem Geiste* is translated *esprit chevaleresque* and "true spirit of sportsmanship." It was a pity that the word "chivalry" was not used in the English rendering, for the ideal of "sportsmanship" is an impoverished form of the old ideal of chivalry. But perhaps the word "sporting" is as native to an age of tanks as "chivalry" to an age of cavalry.

The word *ritterlich* originally meant something very different from "chivalrous." The *Ritter*, in the days before feudalism had been transformed by chivalry, was a plague to the countryside, and his memory still survives in the German proverb, *Er will Ritter an mir werden* ("He wants to play the bully over me").

"The duties," writes Professor F. J. C. Hearnshaw,* "imposed by the chivalry vows were numerous: to fear God and maintain the Christian religion; to serve the king faithfully and valiantly; to protect the weak and defenceless; to refrain from the wanton giving of offence; to live for honour and glory; to despise pecuniary reward; to fight for the general welfare of all; to obey those placed in authority; to guard the honour of the knightly order; to shun unfairness, meanness and deceit; to keep faith and speak the truth; to persevere to the end in all enterprises begun; to respect the honour of women; to refuse no challenge from an equal and never to turn the back upon a foe."

The mediæval code of chivalry was the result of an attempt, never wholly successful, to impose Christian virtues on the feudal knighthood. The ceremony of initiation was religious, and was preceded by a twenty-four-hour fast and an all-night vigil in the chapel. During the ceremony the knight's sword was solemnly blessed, a ritual which will deeply shock our pacifists. Great importance was attached, at least in theory, to the Christian virtue of humility. "*Servez Dieu*," said the great knight Bayard, "*et il vous aidera; soyez doux et courtois à tout gentilhomme en ôtant de tout votre orgeuil.*" The national bragging which is ruining international sport is removed from the true ideals of chivalry. Of the ideal knight Chaucer writes:

* *Chivalry*, p. 24, Kegan Paul.

And though he was worthy he was wise,
And of his port as meek as is a maid.

In the code of chivalry, as in other codes, there was a considerable discrepancy between high ideals and actual practice, but there is no historian who does not recognise the immense influence of chivalry in imposing a code of courtesy, consideration and good manners on the lawless feudal knights.

The ideals summed up in the Greek word *aidos* are rather nearer to the ideals of chivalry than to the modern sporting code. *Aidos* at least found a place for religion. "*Aidos*," writes Mr. Norman Gardner,* "is the direct opposite of *hubris*. It is the feeling of respect for what is due to the gods, to one's fellow-men, to oneself, a feeling that begets a like feeling towards oneself in others. It is the spirit of reverence, of modesty, of courtesy. Above all, it is a sense of honour, and as such inspires the athlete and the soldier, and distinguishes them from the bully and the oppressor.

"In sport *aidos* is that scrupulous sense of honour and fairness which is supposed to be the essence of sportsmanship. It is *aidos* which makes a man 'a straight fighter,' εὐθυμαχος, the epithet with which Pindar describes the boxer Diagoras."

We can trace in the old Olympic Games that inevitable cycle from which no sport is exempt, the cycle which ends in joyless over-specialisation. It is as idle to inveigh against specialisation as to complain that our arteries gradually harden in old age. Man is by instinct competitive. It is competition which forces up the standard in sport, and it is the rising standard which in turn renders specialisation inevitable for those who still desire to compete.

There is nothing new in the folly which seeks to measure national achievements by the barometer of sport. In Greece, as in the modern world, there were men who firmly believed

* I refer the reader who desires a technical description of the various events to the classic work on Olympia from which many of the facts in this chapter are taken, *Greek Athletic Sports and Festivals*, by Norman Gardner (Macmillan).

that few things were more important to a state than victory in athletic events. When Alcibiades was attacked by Nikias in the assembly he replied much as a modern athlete might reply, that he had entered seven chariots and taken the first three places at Olympia and brought great glory to Athens thereby. Who cares to-day whether Athens beat Sparta at Olympia or at any other athletic meeting? Who cares to-day how far the discus was thrown by the young man who caught Myron's fancy? That young athlete lives because art endures. Few things are more ephemeral than athletic fame, and only one thing more lasting than art.

"It is a foolish custom," wrote Xenophanes, "to honour strength more than excellent wisdom. Not though there were among the people a man good at boxing or in the Pentathlon or in wrestling – not for his presence would the city be better governed, and small joy would there be for a city should one in contest win a victory. These things do not make fat the dark corners of the city."

Specialisation produced in Greece the same evils which it is producing in modern sport. The successful athlete was idolised during his active career, and too often left stranded when his racing days were over.

"Of all the countless evils throughout Hellas," said Euripides, "there is none worse than the race of athletes. In youth they strut about in splendour, the pride of their city, but when bitter old age comes upon them they are cast aside like threadbare garments."

It is not professionalism but specialisation, of which professionalism is the inevitable product, which transforms sport from a pleasure into a business. The true amateur, for whom games are a relaxation and not the main business of life, cannot hope to compete either against the genuine professional or against those so-called amateurs who consecrate their lives to athletic success. Gradually the true amateur dropped out of the Olympic Games. The smart young men of Athens refused to compete against the professionals, and only entered for the chariot races which remained the monopoly of the rich. Greece during the Persian Wars was a nation of athletes. The Athenians of the Peloponnesian War had ceased to be athletes and had become onlookers.

The Olympic Games were associated with religion and with culture; the modern Games have no such associations. The Olympic competitors invoked Zeus Herkeios; the modern Olympic Oath is not an oath but an affirmation. In our law courts the conscientious atheist "affirms" but does not take the oath, for an oath by definition implies supernatural sanction. It is as impossible to imagine the old Olympic Games without the religious processions and the great sacrifice to Zeus on the morning after the full moon as it is to conceive of a modern bishop opening the modern Olympic Games.

Even more significant is the cultural contrast. The old Games gave us the Odes of Pindar and Greek sculpture. The modern Games enriched neither Art nor Literature. Greek art was the product of Greek religion, and the religion of Greece was humanism. The gods were reflections of man, of his vices and his ambitions no less than of his virtues. The Greek had little sense of sin, perhaps because there was no sin for which he could not plead a precedent in the behaviour of Olympian deities. He believed vaguely in survival, in a dim, phantom after-life, which filled him with dismay. "The man *himself*," says Homer, "lies on the battlefield." Death was the end of "the man himself." His soul, a pale ectoplasmic phantom, joined the witless ghosts of the shadow land.

Man is the hero of Greek, God of Hebraic literature. "There are many wonderful things," says Sophocles, "and the most wonderful is man." "Lord, what is man that thou art mindful of him," said the Psalmist, "or the son of man that thou regardest him?" "Whereas God is a conclusion to the Greek," writes Sir Richard Livingstone, "for the Hebrew he is the main premise." Homer judged nature solely with reference to human needs. He looked at the mountains and saw them in relation to man. He did not like them. "The mountains are covered with mists," he said, "which is bad for shepherds and better than night for thieves." To the Hebrew the mountains were a sign of the majesty of One who was before the mountains were brought forth. "God shall come down from Lebanon, and the holy one from the shady and thickly covered mountain. His majesty has covered the heavens, and the earth is full of his presence."

To the Hebrew the soul was the supreme reality; to the Greek the body. Even Plato quotes with approval a Greek proverb which ranges in order of merit the best things of life, health, personal beauty, wealth and youth. "No man," says Aristotle, "can be happy who is ugly," a depressing verdict from which I most heartily dissent.

Humanism is a religion for the young and the successful. It has no message for the underdog or the old. It is not a uniformly cheerful religion even for the young. A stream of melancholy runs through Greek literature. "It is better to be a servant in the house of the living than a king among the dead" (Homer). "Not to have been born is better for mortals than not to look upon the light of the sun" (Bacchylides). "In a brief life there is trouble upon trouble" (Simonides). It is easy to multiply these random quotations taken from three characteristic Greek authors.

Greek humanism determined the character of Greek art. It is curious that Sir Richard Livingstone, who is perhaps the wisest, and certainly the most readable, of modern Hellenists, and who has analysed with felicity and insight the contrast between the theism of the Jew and the humanism of the Greek, should be less sensitive to the no less striking contrast between the culture inspired by theism and the culture inspired by humanism. He is not the first whose judgement has been clouded by the glamour of Greece.

"The Greeks," writes Sir Richard, "are the authors of the

most beautiful poems, the most beautiful statues and the most beautiful buildings in the world." So much for Shakespeare, Michael Angelo and Chartres. I am sure that Sir Richard, had he pursued his comparison between the Jew and the Greek, would have admitted that there is no poetry to compare with the finest passages in Job, in Isaiah or the Song of Solomon, and no stories to match the great stories of the Old Testament. Nothing in Homer rivals the humanity and insight, realism and dramatic power with which the life story of David is unfolded, and it is to David's lament over Jonathan which those who admire the idealistic forms of Greek friendship turn for the supreme expression of this friendship in literature. The superiority of the Bible, judged solely as literature, is a superiority of spiritual insight. The vision of the Hebrew was more penetrating than the vision of the Greek.

The art which we owe to the Olympic Games, and with which we are therefore directly concerned, was due to the demand for statues of the Olympic victors. The Greek sculptor was assisted by the habit of nudity in these Games which originated when Orsippus dropped his loin-cloth in a race and was supposed to have gained an advantage thereby. Whereupon loin-cloths were discarded with the same rapidity as skirts by women athletes of to-day. Thanks to the Olympic Games, the Greek sculptor was able to study the naked human body in every phase of strenuous and graceful movement, and, as a result, he enriched the world with statues unrivalled in their representation of the bodily surfaces of man. But the soul is missing, for a Greek statue is impersonal. Pheidias and Praxiteles reproduced with faultless accuracy every external detail of the body; Donatello and Michael Angelo achieved a biography in stone. Compare the Ægina pediments at Munich with the statues on the Porte Royale at Chartres. The Ægina statues tell us all that the sculptor knew, or rather all that the sculptor wished to know, and nothing more. The mysterious stone shapes on the Porte Royale at Chartres provoke the "obstinate questionings" which the Greek mind evaded. These sublime masterpieces of Gothic statuary move us as the Greek never moves us, for they awaken desires which the body cannot satisfy, and which even art itself is powerless to appease. The Greek sculptor was content to aim at finite ends. Those who aim at the infinite must fail, but their failure is more glorious than a limited success. The sublimest art awakens discontent with art itself, that divine discontent which finds expression in the sonnet composed by Michael Angelo in the shadow of death,

Nè pinger nè scolpir fia o piu che chieti
L'anima volta a quell'amor divino
*Ch'aperse a prender noi in croce le braccia.**

Michael Angelo and Shakespeare are concerned not only with the three dimensions of the body, but also with the fourth dimension of the soul. If you doubt this, read the *Agamemnon* and *Macbeth* side by side. Man is the subject of the Greek sculptor, and not any particular man. "Man is the hero of Greek tragedy," writes Lowes Dickinson, "Tom, Dick or Harry of the modern novel." Greek drama is the drama of situation and not of personality. The personality of Hamlet matures inwardly towards the catastrophe, whereas Œdipus, as Spengler says, stumbles on a situation. It is the situation in which Œdipus finds himself, and not his personal character, which makes the play. Œdipus is a type of humanity, and any other individual, so the dramatist implies, would have reacted as Œdipus reacts.

The Greek admitted that he hated the *apeiron*, that which has no limits. In thought and in art he concentrated on what Spengler calls "the bodily present moment." Spengler has traced the influence of this Greek instinct through a variety of art forms, and though I do not accept his explanation of the contrast between the Greek concentration on the finite and

* "Neither painting nor sculpture can give rest to the soul that turns to the divine love whose arms opened on the Cross to embrace us." LVI.

the Gothic on the infinite, I acknowledge a profound debt to the genius with which he has analysed Greek, Gothic, Byzantine and Renaissance culture in his book *The Decline of the West.*

The Greeks would have understood the fascination of ski racing, but would have been baffled by the mountaineer. If there were mountain lovers in classical Greece they kept their emotions to themselves. There is no trace of this feeling in Greek literature.

There are many who not only love mountains, but who are also interested in the historical background of romantic mountain worship. It is for them that I write, and they will, I hope, forgive a digression on Greek art. It is not irrelevant to the discussion either of the Olympic Games or of the Greek attitude to nature. The contrast between the Parthenon and Chartres is the clue to the even greater contrast between the Greek and the modern feeling for nature.

The Greek, as we have seen, disliked the idea of infinite space, and he avoided the horizon line in his landscape reliefs. Inevitably he must have disliked the far horizons visible from a mountain summit. The lines of the Parthenon are subtly curved so as to direct the eye inwards; the entablature of the Greek temple binds the building to earth and prevents the eye from escaping upwards along the line of the columns. To the Greek an aiguille soaring into the infinite sky would have been as repulsive as a Gothic spire.

The humanism which finds expression in Greek art explains the Greek attitude to nature. This attitude remains virtually unchanged from Homer to Plato. Nature to the Greek is only beautiful in so far as she is subservient to human needs. "Every Homeric landscape intended to be beautiful," writes Ruskin, "is composed of a mountain, a meadow and a shadowy grove." Homer likes trees because trees provide man with shade in summer and with firewood in winter. He is particularly fond of rain, a fact which will not surprise those who know the parched Greek landscape in summer. Odysseus' Ithaca is rocky and rough and therefore disagreeable, but at least there is "always rain."

The Greek feeling for nature, like Greek art, is concerned with the external surface. The Greek sculptor was uninterested in the personality of his sitter, and to Homer a mountain was nothing more than an impersonal lump of rock. The "pathetic fallacy," as Ruskin describes the modern habit of attributing personality to nature, is almost unknown in Greek literature. Ruskin quotes Keats's description of a wave breaking out at sea:

> Down whose green back the short-lived foam all hoar
> Bursts gradual with a wayward insolence.

"Homer," continues Ruskin, "could not by any possibility have lost sight of the great fact that the wave, from the beginning to the end of it, do what it might, was still nothing else than salt water; and that salt water could not be either wayward or insolent. He will call the wave 'over-roofed,' 'full charged,' 'monstrous,' 'compact,' 'black,' 'dark-clear,' 'violet-coloured,' 'wine-coloured,' and so on. But every one of these epithets is descriptive of pure physical nature . . . they are as actual and intense in truth as words can be, but they never show the slightest feeling of anything animated in the ocean. Black or clear, monstrous or violet-coloured, cold salt water it is, and always will be."

I know that the neo-Hellenists will challenge this verdict on Greek feeling for nature, but when the neo-Hellenist has scraped together an uninspiring collection of impersonal references to "shadowy mountains," "meadows by the grey sea," and the like, he is uneasily conscious of the contrast between these bleak phrases and the authentic note of nature love. He accordingly plays the trump card of Greek restraint. He forgets that the Greeks were neither restrained nor reticent about the things which provoked their admiration, such as physical bravery and masculine beauty. The coldness with which they referred to the beauty of nature should be compared with the enthusiasm of their references to the beauty of the human body.

The title of Mr. Smythe's book, *The Spirit of the Hills*, would have been frankly incomprehensible to the Greek. The spirits *in* the hills, yes, hostile spirits perhaps, whom it might be advisable to propitiate. "If one imagines," as Mr. Ridley remarks, "a being dwelling in a fountain, it is just because one does not think of a fountain as a being in itself." Mr. Chesterton makes the same point when he remarks that the Greek could not see the wood for the dryads.

Nothing could be less Hellenic than the Wordsworthian sense

> Of something far more deeply interfused,
> Whose dwelling is the light of setting suns.

The modern habit of reading our own sentiments into nature and of attributing to nature a quasi-human personality is infinitely remote from the Greek attitude. Ruskin's phrase "the pathetic fallacy" is most unfortunate, for it is humanism that is pathetic and fallacious, whereas the attribution of personality to nature is an approximation towards the truth which banishes the sadness of pure humanism. It is not true that the wave is "nothing but salt water"; its beauty is the expression of eternal beauty. Poetry which confines itself to a statement of objective physical facts is of a lower order than the poetry which attempts to interpret the spiritual implications of physical beauty.

Latin poetry is a far more hopeful quarry than Greek literature for the nature worshipper. The mountain lover will search in vain in Greek poetry for anything which suggests, however faintly, his own joy on escaping from the town, which the Greek loved, to the hills which the Greek hated, but he will find this note of rapture in the poem with which Catullus celebrated his return to the mountain-girdled lake of Garda:

Salve, o venusta Sirmio atque ero gaude
Gaudete vosque o Lydiæ lacus undæ
*Ridete, quicquid est domi cachinnorum.**

The "pathetic fallacy" again, for waves do not rejoice or laugh.

The Greek was a humanist with the courage of his opinions, which is more than can be said for the sentimental humanists of our own age. He was unashamed in his worship of physical beauty and physical health. There is no literature in the world more free from sentimentalism, humbug and false heroics. To take one instance, the Greek usually fought bravely, but never pretended to enjoy fighting. The Greek soldier in one of Plato's dialogues remarks that brave men and cowards are equally depressed at the approach of the enemy and equally elated at his departure.

Death is the supreme touchstone of sincerity, and on this theme Greek directness is most effective, particularly in contrast with Roman literature. Seneca proses on interminably in the hope of allaying his own fears, and only once does he face up to the reality with that sudden outburst of sincerity with which he reacts from his own special pleadings. *Et adversus mortem tu tam minute jacularis.* Lucretius, noblest of all the poets of scepticism, spoils the austere beauty of the concluding lines of his third book by a false analogy intended to be consoling. Horace takes refuge in wistful sentiment. But Aristotle goes to the point with Greek directness. "For death it is a dreadful thing. It is the end." "The life to which I belong uses me," writes Mr. H. G. Wells, "and will pass on beyond me and I am content." Mr. Wells escapes from reality into the mists of sentimental metaphor, but the Greek faces facts like a man.

Nowhere would a revival of Greek directness be more valuable than in international sport, that great stronghold of senti-

* "Hail, beautiful Sirmio, and rejoice with your master, and you waves of the Lydian lake rejoice, and laugh out all the laughter that is in my home."

mental humbug. Those who speak at prize-givings or banquets should read and re-read the funeral speech which Pericles delivered over the bodies of the Athenian soldiers who had fallen in the Peloponnesian War. No contrast could be greater than the contrast between the platitudinous compliments which are common form at athletic banquets and the opening passages of the Periclean speech, disconcerting in their candour and frank acceptance of the limitations of human nature.

"Praise of other men is only tolerable," Pericles begins, "in so far as each man in the audience thinks that he too could perform the exploits which are being praised. Anything which goes beyond these limits incites his envy and his scepticism."

And how does he set about consoling the parents of the soldiers who have died? He holds out no hope of an immortality in which he did not believe, but he faces with dignity and resignation the inescapable fact of death.

"Console yourselves," he says, "that for the greater part of your life you have been happy, and remember that what remains will be short. Comfort yourself with the thought that in your useless old age you will enjoy the respect of your neighbours."

Cold comfort this, but is there anything else to be said to those who "sorrow without hope"?

Greek art, architecture and drama may, perhaps, have been overpraised, but it would be impossible to overpraise Thucydides or Aristotle, to overvalue our debt to Greece, or to exaggerate the freshness and modernity of the Greek solution to the problems which recur in every age.

TAILPIECE

Olympic Literature, Old and New

Pindar on great athletes:

That man is happy and song-worthy by the skilled, who, victorious by might of hand or vigour of foot, achieves the greatest prizes with daring and with strength, and who, in his lifetime, sees his son, while yet a boy, crowned happily with Pythian wreaths. The brazen heaven, it is true, is inaccessible to him; but whatsoever joys we race of mortals touch, he reaches to the farthest voyage.

From the "Tages-Programm" (English Edition) of the Fourth Winter Olympic Games:

ARE YOU A SPORTSMAN?

As a player:

1. Do you play the game for the game's sake?
2. Do you play for your team and not for yourself?
3. Do you carry out your captain's orders without question and criticism?
4. Do you accept the umpire's decision absolutely?
5. Do you win without swank and lose without grousing?
6. Would you rather lose than do anything which you are not sure is fair?

Then you are in the way to become a sportsman.

As a spectator:

1. Do you refuse to cheer good play of your opponents?
2. Do you boo the umpire when he gives a decision you don't like?
3. Do you want to see your side win if it does not deserve to?
4. Do you quarrel with spectators for backing the other side?

Then you are no sportsman. Try to become one.

CHAPTER XVI

Nazi Olympics

I. "It Was a Nice Armistice"

DURING a recent visit to Chamonix I was shown a small museum on the walls of which hung the skis used by the pioneer of ski-ing in Chamonix. It was with a shock that I realised that he had only antedated my own *début* as a ski-er by one year. I put on my first pair of ski at Chamonix just before Christmas, 1898. Since then I have seen the development of Alpine ski-ing from the sport of a few enthusiasts to its all-conquering popularity in the last winter before the present war. The pioneers of Alpine ski-ing were uninterested in racing. We regarded ski as a passport to the winter Alps, as a means rather than as an end in themselves. The exploration of the High Alps on ski began in the late nineties, and it was my good fortune to take part in pioneer ski expeditions during the first decade of this new development of mountaineering. In 1903 I won a race which subsequently became the Roberts of Kandahar, but I never raced again until the Kandahar Ski Club was founded in 1924.

Ski-ing originated in Scandinavia, where the terrain is in the main undulating and gentle and thus unsuitable for downhill racing. The classic Northern form of ski race is the langlauf, or long-distance race. The courses vary in length from about ten to thirty miles. The Blue Riband of Norwegian ski-ing, victory at Holmenkollen, is won on the combined result of a langlauf and jumping competition. It was perhaps not surprising that the Swiss should adopt the Norwegian form of race and set their courses along the valley floors instead of down the mountainsides, for the prestige of the North was immense and it seemed impious to experiment with new types of ski competition; but, of course, the downhill race is as naturally adapted to Alpine terrain as the long-distance race to Scandinavian terrain.

The first published plea for the recognition of downhill races as the obvious criterion for skill in Alpine ski-ing appeared in my book *Ski-ing*, published in 1913. After the Great War the Ski Club of Great Britain inaugurated a campaign to persuade European ski-ers that Alpine ski-ing could only be tested by Alpine races. Downhill races are of two kinds. First there is the downhill race proper, in which competitors start from one point and race downhill by the shortest line to the finishing posts; and secondly there is the slalom race, an old Norwegian name for a new kind of race which in its modern form I may claim to have invented. The course for the slalom race is defined by pairs of flags through which the competitors must pass, and the flags are arranged to provide an exacting test of turning. At the beginning of our campaign we had to face the routine "expert" argument. The Norwegians, we were told, had ski-ed for centuries, and the Norwegian Vice-President of the International Ski Federation asked me: "What would you say, Mr. Lunn, if the Norwegians were to suggest revising the laws of cricket?" To which I answered: "I wish to heaven you would; we might have fewer draws."

British downhill racing is one of the few delightful things

which began, and have perhaps ended for ever, in the twenty years of armistice between European wars. "It was a nice Armistice," as a Frenchman remarked in a tone of regret, and even if those days never return they will live in our memories.

Downhill and slalom races were included for the first time in the Olympic programme in 1936, when the Summer Games were held in Berlin and the Winter Games in Garmisch-Partenkirchen. I shall not inflict on the reader a detailed description of the ski races at these Games, but the social and political atmosphere there was so interesting and in some ways so ominous that I propose to devote this chapter to my impressions of a great Nazi sport festival.

II. A Dream

We sat and shivered in the stands waiting for the opening ceremony of the Winter Olympic Games. Suddenly through the driving snow a procession appears, headed by the Greek team. The Greek standard dips in salute to one who would have been more at home in Sparta than in Athens. Hitler returns the salute, and the Greeks are followed by the Belgians, the Bulgarians, and so on in alphabetical order to Turkey. A German reads the Olympic Oath, which was not an oath but an affirmation, and from the brazier, decorated not with a Greek frieze but with that modern vulgarism the Olympic rings, a fitful flame burns up into a flurry of snow, and the Olympic beacons on the hills repeat the Olympic fire.

Fire, driving snow and wind.

And then suddenly Greece comes back in a wave of memory.

The blue Mediterranean awakening to her summer dreams; a rocky creek in Delos and a dive through a shimmer of warm air into the Ægean; the wind sighing through the pines of Olympia; the aridity of Greek hills in August and the sunset which softens and subdues them; the web of twilight which makes of tawny cliffs a mystery of changing tones, and the immense depth of the purple night, pricked with the same stars which guided Odysseus over this tideless sea. . . .

And there is the Olympic fire feebly flickering through a smother of falling snow.

The nostalgia of the South had asserted its power over me, and I rebelled against the absurdity of linking these parvenu games with the "glory that was Greece." What was there of Greece in Garmisch?

There was a Greek banner in the place of honour and a Greek team, but the compliment to Greece began and ended with the place accorded to the Greek competitors in the procession. The Garmisch *Tages-Programm* lies before me as I write: no hint of Greece in its pages. The Greeks disliked mountains and detested snow, but the cover of the *Tages-Programm* was adorned with a snowscape, and the Olympic Medal was a relief of the Altspitz. Why not a reproduction of Myron's Discobolus for the former and any one of a thousand designs from Greek coins or amphora for the latter?

The main link between the old and the new Olympic Games is an occasional sentimental reference in after-dinner speeches to the truce which was preserved throughout Greece during the Olympic festivals. This is the sort of thing which, in the genial atmosphere engendered by a good dinner, is sometimes mistaken for (*a*) thought and (*b*) humour:

"It has often occurred to me that if only our politicians could be persuaded to leave a certain Assembly which shall be nameless [laughter] and join in these Games, not as competitors, of course [loud laughter], but as onlookers, they would discover the true Locarno spirit of sport [cheers], and learn more about peace in one day at Warmesluft than in a month at Geneva [Bravo!]. The true League of Nations is the league of international sportsmen [deafening chorus of Bravos!]."

The past history of the modern Olympic Games lends some colour to the view that they are valuable as a rehearsal for Armageddon. International sport helps to foster friendly relations between the sportsmen of different countries in inverse ratio to the importance of the event. The more important the event, the greater the determination of the Press to treaty victory as a contribution to national prestige, and the tenser the consequent atmosphere of fierce competition. As to those friendly events (such as the Anglo-Swiss University Ski Races) which undoubtedly promote good feeling between the ski-ers of different countries, the social consequences of such events are all to the good, but their influence on the great issue of war or peace is negligible. Young athletes marched in the war when mobilised by their elders in spite of friendly relations with the athletes of other countries. It is not by imponderables such as these that war is averted.

"No, whatever happens, we can't fight those Ruritanians. Their ski-ers are such jolly good chaps. Sportsmen in every sense of the word."

Does any sane man think that some such speech as this is conceivable in a war cabinet? "Think" is the operative word, but thought is not the operative influence in international sport.

With these thoughts in my mind I fell asleep one night. I awoke next morning from one of those vivid dreams in which one accepts everything without question. It seemed natural that the date should be A.D. 3036, that the river by whose shores I was standing should flow through Tokio, and that I should be watching the procession of boats which inaugurated the Henley Regatta which the Japanese Emperor had recently revived. Why Henley? Well, I knew the answer to that one too. And at this point the dream became a nightmare.

I knew that England had been conquered by Germany in the year 2000, but that English ideas had not died with the British Empire. England had conquered her conquerors. English culture, which the decadent English had forgotten, had become fashionable in the German Empire. English tutors were engaged by German aristocrats, much as Greeks had been engaged by the conquering Romans. The fact that

Führer Adolf III had won the Diamond Sculls as a young man helped to make Henley the great fashionable event of the year. The German Empire had lasted for five centuries before Germany had been conquered by Japan. Once again the culture of the conquered held the conquerors captive. A classical education – that is, an education of which English and German literature and philosophy were the backbone – formed an integral part of the education of the Japanese gentleman. In the thirty-first century the Henley Regatta had been revived, and it was this revival which I was watching.

The procession of boats was headed by a pair of Englishmen, greeted with sympathetic cheers, and wearing Leander scarves. Naturally nobody expected England to enter an eight, and everybody thought it very sporting of the English to send two competitors for the Diamond Sculls.

The Henley Committee of Japan were more imaginative than the Olympic Committee at Garmisch. A Japanese translation of the Eton Boating Song was sung as the procession passed the Emperor, and nothing could have been more appropriate than the Henley Gold Medal with a picture of Fujiyama and the classical motto, *Die Wacht am Rhein.*

III. "The Fight Begins"

"The fight begins; the Olympic spirit lives on." These encouraging words provided the perorating slogan to the inaugural message of the German Olympic Committee. But the fight began long before the opening parade. The controversy over the exclusion of ski-teachers from Garmisch threatened at one time to result in the withdrawal of the Swiss, Austrian, French and British teams. Protests and counter-protests had already been lodged by the ice-hockey players, and an objection against the alleged amateur status of a well-known lady skater had provided a minor sensation in the autumn.

For more than a year the question of American participation

in the Olympic Games had been vigorously debated. The final favourable decision was carried by a narrow majority – 52 per cent.

The movement to boycott the Olympic Games, which all but succeeded in the U.S.A., received no support in Great Britain from any representative leaders in the world of sport. I had more sympathy with those who wished to break off athletic relations with Germany than with amiable people who repeated with bland assurance the slogan, "Sport has nothing to do with politics." In Nazi Germany sport was a branch of politics. The old German ski association was disbanded and ski-ing was controlled by the Government Department for Bodily Exercises (*Fachamt Ski-lauf*). German sport was not only controlled by but infected by the Nazi political ideals. Sport admittedly should have no connection with politics. As sportsmen we are not concerned with the political constitutions of the countries in which we compete, but sportsmanship which is derived from chivalry is concerned with ideals which are beyond politics. In civilised countries political parties are not divided into those who do and those who do not approve of religious or racial persecution. The question as to whether a man should be clubbed to death or tortured merely because you disapprove of his religious views or dislike the shape of his nose is not a political question. It is difficult to exaggerate the prestige of sport in the modern world, or the prestige of Great Britain as the arbiter of sporting ethics. Words such as "unfair" and "unsporting" have been adopted by the Germans (*Es ist* unfair . . . *es ist nicht* sporting). Had British sportsmen chosen to define certain humanitarian standards and refused to compete in countries where those standards were defied, I am inclined to suspect that the blow to Hitler's prestige might have been fatal. Be that as it may, such a gesture would at least have proved that we regard sport, not as an end in itself, but as a means to an end, the maintenance of chivalric ideals.

In 1936 I was not prepared, officially at least, to advocate excommunicating the Nazis from the sport. Indeed, I accepted an appointment, not from the Nazis, but from the International Ski Federation, to act as referee in the Olympic slalom, but I declined all invitations to official banquets, and neither my son, who was the captain of the team, nor I, as manager, took part in the official procession at the opening of the Games. Nothing would have induced me to salute Hitler, whom I regarded as a thug responsible for a system of assassination and torture. My view was that if the Olympic Committee were to organise the Winter Games in the Cannibal Islands I would referee one of the events, but I would not eat missionary chop as the guest of the cannibal chief.

None the less my conscience was uneasy, with the result that, six months before the Winter Games were held, I drafted a letter which I asked the Archbishop of York to sign and send to the Governing Bodies of all British sports represented in the Olympic Games, summer and winter. These Governing Bodies were to be invited to ask the Olympic Committee to write to Hitler in the following terms:

"The British Olympic Committee have resolved to appeal to Your Excellency to follow the precedent of the ancient Olympic Games, which were, as Your Excellency is aware, inaugurated by a general truce.

"We appeal to Your Excellency to show yourself no less generous than the Greeks, and to issue a general act of amnesty for the benefit of all those who are suffering imprisonment for religious or racial reasons.

"International sport may either conduce to friendly relations or exasperate unfriendly relations. If the Olympic Games in Germany are to fulfil their historic mission, they must, as Your Excellency will agree, open in an atmosphere of friendship and reconciliation. Your Excellency will readily understand the special reluctance of sincere Christians to compete in a country in which religious papers are being suppressed, and in which Christians are being imprisoned or interned for loyalty to their faith."

Shortly after drafting this letter I was driving down Piccadilly in my car and noticed the Archbishop of York standing on the pavement. I offered him a lift to Lambeth. My secretary, Miss Holt-Needham, was unkind enough to suggest that anybody who had been driven by me would be ready to sign anything before the journey's end. Admittedly I remember the Archbishop remarking once or twice, "You've driven through the red lights again," but it was from the calm and security of his study that he wrote to me a few days later agreeing to sign, with some modifications, the letter which I had submitted for his approval. I quote the fact of our collaboration with the Archbishop's permission.

The Ski Club Committee endorsed the Archbishop's appeal, but I do not know how many other clubs urged the International Olympic Committee to accept his suggestions. In some cases, I am told, bewildered committees asked the advice of the Foreign Office and were recommended to do nothing which might aggravate relations between Britain and Germany. The Olympic Committee declined to write in the terms suggested by the Archbishop, but they sent to the Reichssportsführer (Reich Sport Leader) a mild letter in which they embodied discreetly some of the Archbishop's points. The Sport Leader was invited to put the case to Hitler, but he was so terrified of provoking the great man's rage that he kept the committee's letter in his pocket for several weeks and then, as he told a friend of mine, quietly destroyed it.

Though our letter never reached Hitler, I am glad that the letter was written, for I should have been sorry to have taken part as an official in these Nazi games without making some attempt, however ineffective, at a protest. It seemed to me more important that the influence of British sport should be exerted in the effort to mitigate, however slightly, the misery of Hitler's victims than that British sportsmen should do well in the Olympic Games.

It was undoubtedly the background of political conflict which gave a special interest to the Winter Games at Garmisch, and which explained the curiously tense atmosphere at the beginning of the Olympic parade. These facts cannot be omitted from any true history of the Games. In modern Europe a great athletic contest is a political and social, no less than a sporting event, and those who are ambitious to write true history must sometimes sacrifice discretion to historical truth.

No account of the Olympic Games would be complete which ignored the problem of the salute. The Olympic salute consists in extending the arm out to the side. The Nazi extends his arm to the front. The Fascist raises his arm. The friendly Communist thrusts a clenched fist upwards. The Englishman with his old-school tie feels rather lost in this world of new-school gestures. He is embarrassed when the courteous foreigner begins moving his arm about. To make no response is impolite. To reply with a corresponding gesture is disloyal to the Mother of Parliaments. Nobody has yet solved the problem of combining courtesy with an affirmation of unshaken confidence in nose-counting as the only sound basis of government. At Innsbruck I tried to please everybody by opening my speech with the International Windmill Salute, combining the Nazi, Fascist and Communist arm movements; but this is a little showy for general use, and perhaps the democratic ideal of surrender to the dictates of the majority might best be indicated by raising both hands smartly above the head.

At Garmisch we resolved that our salute during the Olympic parade should be most unmistakably Olympic lest the correspondents of the *News Chronicle* and *New Statesman* might accuse the British teams of secret Fascist tendencies. So the teams were coached in the Olympic salute, right arm well to the side. One member of our teams was particularly anxious to make this clear, and flung her arm sideways with such force that it landed on the nose of the young woman marching beside her.

The atmosphere of the Olympic Stadium during the March Past was electric. There were rumours that some of the competitors had decided not to return Herr Hitler's salute. The teams that were most warmly welcomed by the crowd were the Austrians, some of whom gave the Nazi salute, turning towards Hitler as they passed him, and the French, British and Americans, who gave the *Olympic* salute. At least, that was the scheme. But our careful rehearsal was wasted so far as the enthusiastic broadcaster was concerned. "The British," he informed the listening world, "greet the German Führer with the German salute."

The most tense moment in the parade was when the Swiss marched in front of Herr Hitler. First came the competitors for the Military Ski Race in uniform, and these, of course, saluted, and a few individuals in the Swiss contingent followed their example. A momentary hesitation, and then suddenly the Swiss ranks seemed to stiffen, and the descendants of the men who had fought for democracy at Sempach and Morgarten walked past Hitler, eyes to the front, arms stiffly to the side.

No cheers from the crowd.

No comments from the broadcaster.

IV. The Background of War

Occasional visits to the skating championship provided an entertaining interlude between the ski-ing events. There were five judges for each skating event, and these judges wore numbers like competitors, and the spectators were provided with a programme giving the names of the judges, their numbers and the countries which they represented. "Represented" is the right word.

At the conclusion of each figure the judges indicated by holding aloft numbered squares what marks they had allotted.

The competition between the judges aroused more interest than the competition between the competitors. Judges whose decisions were approved by the crowd were heartily cheered, whereas those who were deemed to have overmarked their own countrymen or to have undermarked a popular favourite were greeted with jeers of ironic laughter. Some of the judges appeared to be easily influenced by the crowds, but there was one stubborn old gentleman who seemed to delight in outraging the feelings of the spectators. There certainly ought to have been an Olympic Gold Medal for the most popular judge.

Competitors believe that the judges are influenced, consciously or unconsciously, by tumultuous applause, and the consequent anxiety of the competitors to have the crowd on their side had one interesting result. I have explained that the British team, skaters no less than ski-ers, had all agreed to confine themselves to the Olympic salute, and were resolutely determined not to let down the Mother of Parliaments by moving their arm in an anti-democratic direction. But their resolution weakened at the Skating Competition when a U.S.A. competitor elicited from the crowd a tremendous cheer by giving them the Nazi salute. Every British competitor followed his example.

I was, of course, mainly interested in the downhill ski races, for which we had entered a complete team, men and women. The great Norwegian jumper, Birger Ruud, won the downhill race, and his compatriot, Laila Schou-Nilsen, secured a surprise victory in the Ladies' Race, for Christel Cranz of Germany, who is almost unbeatable, slipped below a control. But on the combined result of the downhill and slalom Franz Pfnur of Germany won the Men's event and Christel Cranz the Ladies' event. Incidentally, the first slalom that Christel Cranz ever saw was set by my son Peter in the Black Forest. For the British, Peter was best, finishing twelfth on the combined result, out of sixty starters. Dick Durrance, the finest amateur ski-er that America has produced, was tenth, but Peter had his revenge a week later in the World Championship. Jeannette Kessler (eighth) was the best of our ladies, a good performance, for she had smashed her leg badly in the previous World Championship.

Peter told me that the Games suffered from over-organisation, and that though the German organisers had battalions of soldiers at their disposal, the organisation did not work as well as at the World Championship in Mürren, where we depended almost entirely on voluntary helpers.

A Swedish friend of mine saw a parade of a labour company with shovels who had been at work on the slalom course. The officer walked up the line and asked two hundred and fifty men the same question: "Did you work well?" He received two hundred and fifty reassuring replies.

"I get very tired," Major Oestgaard remarked to me, "of being asked to admire the organisation of these games." And I agreed. I had just picked up a German paper with the heading in large black letters to the effect that *only* Germany was capable of organising the Games with such clock-like efficiency. And in spite of Peter's criticism there were aspects of that organisation, particularly those aspects which involved military co-operation, which were not only impressive but rather disquieting. I remember lunching with three French officers. "I am reminded," I said, "of that story of Moltke going to bed for twenty-four hours after he had pressed the button for mobilisation in 1870. I have the feeling that these Games are only a rehearsal for war." The French looked uncomfortable, as well they might, for I had failed to observe the presence at their table of a German officer attached to them for the period of the Games. He replied at once: "You are mistaken. Our Führer loves peace. He has himself been a front-line soldier. He knows the horrors of war. Our army is for defence."

"Against whom?" I asked. "Who is threatening you with invasion?" But to that question there was no reply.

Garmisch Partenkirchen is in Bavaria, and the Bavarian sense of humour was beginning to rebel against the strain of humourless Nazidom. A friend of mine who was in Garmisch for the Games had witnessed an incident which suggested that the Nazis were not having things all their own way. A polite Bavarian arose and offered his place in the tram to a lady whom he addressed as *Gnädige Frau.* A Nazi brownshirt barked: "*Im Dritten Reich gibt es keine Gnädige Frau.*" "*Und auch kein Butter,*" was the reply. The Nazi swung round. "Who said that?" Everybody tittered, but nobody gave away the humorist, and the Nazi, sensing his unpopularity, got out at the next halt.

I did not enjoy the Winter Games. I dislike the pomposity of the Olympic atmosphere, the processions, the parades and the platitudinous speeches. There was much talk of international friendship and the "Olympic ideal," but the talk did not ring true. Those young Nazi athletes, mobilised by the Government, trained for months at Government expense, did not conjure up a reassuring picture of peace-time sport. The snows of Garmisch were flecked by the shadows of war. I contrasted the grim seriousness with which the Nazis trained for these events with the happy-go-lucky attitude of the British team, and on my return in 1936 I wrote as follows:

"Thucydides was my travelling companion last winter. I do not think that I am particularly superstitious, but I was often disconcerted by a weird feeling that I was reading the history, not of Athens, but of the decline and fall of the British Empire told in the form of a Greek parable. There is a disconcerting analogy between the Athens of Pericles and modern England.

"All our English pride is paralleled by the Periclean confidence that even the enemies of Athens were not humiliated by defeat against so great a foe. Very English, again, is the Periclean emphasis on the wealth and power of Athens, and his disregard of her culture. Nowhere in his speech is there any mention of the dramatists, the sculptors or the architects who laid the foundation of Athenian immortality. Pericles justifies his panegyric of Athens, not by her contributions to art, but by her imperial power and by the freedom she allowed to her citizens. 'We have no sour looks for our neighbour if he enjoys himself in his own way.' Again and again Pericles contrasts liberal Athens with the disciplined militarism of Sparta. 'We do not imitate the institutions of our neighbours; on the contrary, we are a model which others follow. . . . We Athenians decide public questions for ourselves.'

"These might almost be the words of an English politician complacently contrasting British democracy with Continental Fascism. 'If, then, we are ready to meet dangers by living at ease rather than by a severe training, and if we depend on the courage which is derived from a manner of life rather than legal compulsion, the gain is ours.' Why bother to train? The amateur spirit will muddle through somehow. Clearly, many of our own ski-racers are Athenian rather than Spartan in their outlook.

"The Fascists and the democrats will both find much to their taste in Greek history. The Fascist may argue that it was the vacillations of a democratic foreign policy, shifting with every shifting mood of the electorate, which brought about the downfall of Athens; the democrat can retort that though Athens was beaten by Sparta, it was the freedom-loving culture of Athens which established the empire of Greece over the minds of men, and those who believe that the problems of social justice have not been solved by either Fascism or democracy will find abundant justification for this view in Greek history." *

By quoting these rather gloomy forebodings I invite criticism as a pessimist. But I had some excuse. The England of 1936 still trusted to peace ballots and "collective security," and was still reluctant to face the brutal fact that a Great Power

* *The British Ski Year Book for 1936*, p. 426.

must be ready to defend by the sword the possessions which its ancestors have taken by the sword.

I often recall a chance remark of that gifted soldier General Fuller in the spring of 1938: "I don't know whether Hitler will save Germany, but I'm inclined to think that he will save England."

CHAPTER XVII

Rehearsal for War

SKI accidents are very seldom fatal, but there can be few sports where the risk of a broken limb is greater. It is unusual for international racers to reach their fifth season of first-class racing without breaking a leg. Speeds approaching eighty miles an hour have been electrically recorded on the special Flying Kilometre course at St. Moritz, and races have often been won at an *average* speed of over forty miles an hour. The motorist does not expect to crash and is lucky if he survives his first racing crash; but the ski racer falls as a matter of course during training and is fortunate if he does not fall during the race. A no-fall descent is the exception rather than the rule. During the long training period he must expect to strike the ground not once but several times at speeds which vary but which are in the neighbourhood of sixty miles an hour. As manager of the British team I used to calculate on a third of my best racers falling out through injury during the training period. Provided that a race course is intelligently set, and that the racers are deflected by means of controls from hidden rocks and stones thinly masked, fatal accidents are very rare, for a fall on snow, however hard, at speeds however high, is seldom fatal. Of the nine world championships in downhill racing which were held during our twenty years of uneasy peace, the Battle of Innsbruck was the most memorable; and as the hope of avoiding the repetition of such a tragic blunder depends on keeping alive the memory of our mistakes I am devoting this chapter to an experience which none who were present as either competitors, officials or spectators are likely to forget.

The Innsbruck meeting took place a week after the Olympic Games at Garmisch. Ski teachers had been excluded from the Olympic Games but they were entered as usual for the World Championship, which is in effect, though not in name, an open championship. It was an immense relief to escape from the pomposity and over-organisation of Garmisch into the old familiar atmosphere of dear casual Austria. Peter and Jeannette Kessler, the ladies' captain, turned up at the first meeting of the race committee. None of the important Austrian officials had arrived. Nobody present understood the group draw (a method of starting the competitors to prevent collisions between overtaking champions and the poorer performers). The official in charge turned to Peter and asked him and Jeannette to group the competitors, which they proceeded to do. Peter was a little hurt that he wasn't asked to set the slalom for himself and his rivals.

When I arrived at Innsbruck I learned to my dismay that the course chosen for the 1933 World Championship, of which I had written in unsparing condemnation, was to be used again for the championship of 1936. The finish of this course was far too low, less than 2,000 feet above sea-level, and I had the most vivid memories of tree stumps and stones protruding through the thin snow of the 1933 course. The weather, which had been perfect at Garmisch, broke as the games ended, and a heavy thaw removed most of the snow from the Innsbruck course. On the evening before the race a sharp frost transformed the wet snow into sheet ice. I had never seen such conditions on any race-course. The ice was so hard that a spectator walking up the course fell, slithered down the slope, and sprained an ankle on the projecting tree stumps. I was neither the referee nor the setter of the course, but as a member of the Race Committee I insisted that the race should be postponed until the sun had softened the ice. I should, of course, have been more explicit and demanded the immediate cancellation of the race. My position was difficult, as Peter was racing, but I should have ignored the possibility of being criticised as a fussy parent and used all my influence to prevent the race from being held.

The course started with about a thousand feet of comparatively open slope, and then came a glade which might be christened the Devil's Glade. This glade was not dangerous if one elected to follow a safe line, but the racer who gave the tree stumps a wide berth was forced on to bumpy snow, where he would inevitably lose time. If, on the other hand, he elected to follow a narrow little ribbon of smooth polished snow about two feet broad, and if he could hold this line, he could gain many valuable seconds. This ribbon was steep and fast and winding, and the slightest error of judgement entailed disastrous consequences. The snow was bordered by a long ugly line of villainous tree stumps protruding about eighteen inches above the snow. To do well in the race the ski-er had to shave these tree trunks, knowing well that the slightest mistake would involve an instant collision. Many of the best racers thought the risk too high, and preferred to lose time on the bumps rather than to risk a possibly fatal accident on the ribbon.

Some easy running led from the Devil's Glade to the top of the Ladies' Glade, described above, at the bottom of which the new course diverges from the old. I waited at the bottom of the Devil's Glade, for I believed that it was in this glade that the casualties would occur. Nor was I mistaken, for, though some of the most sensational falls occurred on the lower section, it was here that four out of six of the French team, and many other ski-ers, came to grief. I have never felt, as I did at Innsbruck, that a fatal accident was more likely than not, and Ruud's miraculous escape from death confirms rather than refutes the accuracy of predictions which made miserable the long, dragging hour of waiting at the bottom of the Devil's Glade. I looked from the sky to the snow and from the snow to the sky. There was little comfort in the clouds moving from the north or in the chilled gleam of the sun struggling through the mist, and there was no comfort in the snow, unrelenting in its unmelting hardness. There was one little bank of snow which faced due south. I turned to this bank again and again, prodding it hopefully with my stick. I can still shut my eyes and see every detail of its fretted surface, the feeble trickle of intermittent drops from a little icicle at the top of the bank.

I thought of poor Boswell's terror during a storm at sea.

"Piety afforded me comfort," writes Boswell, "yet I was disturbed by the objections against a particular providence which Dr. Hawkesworthy has recently revived, but Dr. Osborn's excellent doctrine on the efficacy of intercession prevailed."

All very well in a mere storm at sea, but I doubt if Dr. Osborn would have proved very reassuring at Innsbruck.

A shout – *Bahn frei* – and a stir of sudden excitement among the crowd.

And here comes Willy Steuri, lurching rather than ski-ing down the course, blood streaming down his face, the first victim of the Devil's Glade. Peter had drawn No. 3. No. 2 was a Jugoslav, and I might have spared myself much anxiety had I known that he had scratched. I set my stop-watch when Steuri appeared: 70 seconds – 80 seconds – and still no sign of the Jugoslav – visualised a collision in the Devil's Glade – 100 seconds – and then came Peter. He had taken the ribbon straight and held it. He disappeared out of sight.

For the account of what happened below I depend on the reports of eye-witnesses.

Just below the Ladies' Glade there were two sharp turns and then a ledge. From this ledge a winding glade had been cut down through the trees, involving four fast turns. The last turn brought the racer on to a sharp icy traverse on which snow had been plastered during the days before the race. If he lost control at this point, as Ruud did, he was shot sideways past the snow-plastered earth down a steep slope dotted with tree stumps. The traverse ended with a tremendous *schuss* leading to the finish, interspersed with tree stumps.

The first ski-er to appear down these last slopes was Willy Steuri. He saw one of the tree trunks just too late. On that appalling ice his steel edges refused to bite, he struck a trunk at a fantastic speed, was hurled head over heels, and thrown with tremendous violence on the corrugated surface. He tried to get up and then collapsed. No bones were broken, but he was seriously injured, and the flesh was torn off his face and hands. He lay there saying, "*Es ist leid. Es ist sehr leid*," in a quiet tone until at last the stretcher-bearers removed him.

Then came Peter. Othmar Gurtner, who thinks that straight racing should not be decided by speed alone, but by good ski-ing, summed up his views as follows:

"Peter did not want to die, and so he did a turn, and so, poor fool, he could not win."

Unfortunately he fell on the last *schuss* and was thrown among the spectators, and thereby lost all chance of being placed in the first three. He finished ninth out of fifty-seven, just ahead of the well-known Swiss runner, Schlunegger. Sörensen, the Norwegian, who shared Peter's distaste for death, put in a turn at the right moment and got down uninjured. Zanni lost control after a tremendous *schuss* and was thrown into the spectators. Rudi Matt also crashed after an involuntary leap into the spectators.

Incidentally, this race made ski-ing history, since the casualties among the spectators numbered three stretcher cases, including one broken leg. By this time people were getting hysterical. Women were fainting, men were shouting imprecations on the organizers. Frau Simon, the wife of the President of the Swiss Ski Association, was weeping quietly, and a small Austrian boy said to her, "Gracious Lady, shut your eyes tight and I will tell you what happens to the Swiss as they pass." Some members of the public seized flags wildly and waved them at the approaching competitors. When people fell they were cheered loudly, as men might be cheered who had escaped catastrophe. When they started to move again people shouted to them to go slowly. "*Es ist nicht so wichtig.*" Suddenly Graf, the Swiss reserve, got on to a tree trunk and shouted to the public to keep quiet. Immense cheers.

Now comes Sigmund Ruud, ski-ing as Norwegian jumpers ski. He tries to traverse at a fantastic speed, his steel edges fail to grip, he slides sideways at a speed faster than the speed of most straight *schusses,* strikes a tree stump, is hurled into the air, and down a steep slope studded with stones and tree trunks, and performs five somersaults, striking the ground again and again with his head. Groans from the crowd. Many people had shut their eyes at the first somersault and did not dare to open them for some seconds. Nobody thought he could possibly have survived, but as the stretcher-bearers leapt to his aid, he staggered to his feet with both ski broken off at the bindings, his face bleeding, mild concussion, but comparatively unhurt. The public went mad, and Gigilione leapt on the course like a wild dervish and screamed, "This isn't a race. This is a circus." A Swiss competitor staggered through the finishing-posts and shouted, "The organizers ought to be hanged." A Viennese answered him, "Young man, if you've lost your nerve, go home to your mother. *Hier wird gekämpft.*" He was right, for the slopes near the finish were beginning to look like a battlefield. Out of the fifty-four competitors no fewer than seventeen were too seriously injured to finish at all, and of those that did finish a large number were badly hurt, cut about the face and more or less concussed. Some of them just held out until they had passed the finishing-post, and then fainted. The hero of the day was Hermann Steuri, the climber of the North Face of the Matterhorn, who dislocated his shoulder, slightly concussed himself near the top, fell heavily again on the same shoulder, and none the less finished high up. I asked him whether he had been more frightened on the Matterhorn North Face or on this course. He said he was far more frightened in the race, and added, "I shan't race at Innsbruck again without my ice-axe."

Of the French team of six only two finished. One of them struck a tree stump in the Devil's Glade, somersaulted head first into another stump, fainted, staggered down on foot to the finish and once again lost consciousness. His friends thought he was going to pass out altogether.

The race was won by Rominger, the Swiss. A few days before his leg had been X-rayed, and he had been informed that there was a slight splinter on one of the ankle bones, and that he must run carefully. To this cautionary advice he possibly owed the fact that he won. He was one of the few who arrived at the finish comparatively fresh.

Meanwhile the wretched women were waiting at the start. The casualties were reported by telephone, and announced by the starter in a voice of ever-deepening melancholy. Grossly exaggerated accounts of Willy's injury sent poor Erna Steuri, his cousin, into a flood of tears. Conflicting messages added to the nervous strain. First the ladies were told that the race was cancelled, then that the American team had been withdrawn, then that the finish had been moved higher up, an alteration which was largely due to the initiative of Mrs. Wolfe, the American manager.

The Ladies' Finish was just below the Ladies' Glade. Finishing-posts were placed on each side of the glade, and below the finish there was a steepish slope covered with a quarter of an inch of snow. Meanwhile the crowd had been climbing up to the finish, and the air was full of imprecations. Somebody came up to me. "I hope you'll raise a stink about this."

There was no lack of expert stink-raisers without any assistance from one who was himself in the dock.

The Ladies' Race provided nothing as sensational as Steuri's crash, as none of the women tried to take the ribbon straight in the Devil's Glade, and there was only one serious casualty, a member of the Italian team, but it was a nerve-racking race for the women, for their friends and for the spectators. Only one competitor succeeded in stopping beyond the finishing-post without a pretty severe toss, and those who fell continued to slide helplessly down the ice, sometimes feet first, sometimes head first, while gallant volunteers leapt on to the ice and interposed themselves between the flying *Damen* and the tree stumps. I contented myself with placing the field, appointing Kessler wicket-keeper, Bracken longstop, and so on. The ground work was good, and few catches were dropped. On one occasion I counted the wicket-keeper and three fieldsmen all lovingly wrapped round the same tree stump.

One of the first to arrive was Jeannette Kessler, who finished seventh, a fine performance for a ski-er whose broken leg had not made a completely satisfactory recovery. Nini Zogg *schuss*ed the Ladies' Glade from a higher point than any other competitor, thus maintaining worthily the great traditions of her family. She finished barely a second behind Fräulein Osirnig, who ran beautifully.

Now came Evie Pinching. Her control on the top bumps was faultless, and now she put her ski together and prepared for the final *schuss*. "Hold it, hold it!" shrieked Bill Bracken. "My God! She's going to," said Duncan Kessler. Through the posts she came erect, ski well together, and finished with a superb Christiania in front of the long row of waiting fieldsmen, the only competitor to swing to a standstill without a fall.

Suddenly it dawned on us that nobody was likely to beat her time. As the time of each competitor was announced the little group round Evie cheered wildly, while Peter thumped her vigorously on her back. Lunn chivalry is intermittent and vigorous rather than graceful. I was amused by the puzzled faces of the spectators.

Es scheint eine Engländerin hat gewonnen – Kaum möglich.

Miss Pinching finished second in the slalom next day and won the world championship, which is decided on the combined result of the downhill and slalom races. This was a great triumph for Miss Pinching and her coach, Bill Bracken. Peter was tenth on the combined result and Dick Durrance was twelfth. Had ski teachers and others who would be professionals under British and American rules been excluded, Peter and Durrance would have been first and second respectively.

The most prized memories of the mountaineer are not those of easy victories beneath cloudless skies, but of mountains stolen from storms and of the reaction of relief following tormenting anxiety, and I think those who were present either as racers, organisers or spectators will look back to the Innsbruck F.I.S. with a curious and paradoxical pleasure.

As the train steamed out of Innsbruck Station, bearing with it poor Willy Steuri swathed in bandages, I knew that we should never hold another meeting at Innsbruck. Time, which is selective and sanguine in its treatment of the past, was already at work, softening in retrospect the memory of the grim hour of waiting below the Devil's Glade, without in any way lessening the pleasurable memories of Innsbruck, most lovable of Tirolean towns, or the grateful recollection of that warm welcome which we received from our Austrian hosts.

CHAPTER XVIII

Impressions of the States

I PAID the first of four long visits to the United States in 1935, since when I have lectured in more than fifty cities and have crossed the continent from New York to San Francisco and from Montreal to New Orleans in the deep South.

At the end of my first lecture on American soil Father Purcell, who used to edit *The Sign*, a well-known American Catholic paper, made a few remarks. "I'm surprised," he said, "to find that Mr. Lunn can talk. Most of the English who come over here don't talk. They just gurgle at us. I was pleased to meet Mr. Lunn, not only on his account but because he is the son of his father. Sir Henry Lunn is not a Catholic, but he has written one of the best devotional books in the language and some very beautiful prayers."

I quoted Father Purcell's remarks about English "gurgles" to Padraic Colum, the Irish poet. "The American," he said, "has a genuine respect for your country, which must be deep-rooted to survive the behaviour of some of the Englishmen who come over here. Lecturers who demand and receive big fees return to England to tell their fellow-countrymen that the Americans worship nothing but the dollar. Many of the English lecturers have no real reason based on achievement to put on airs of superiority, but do so none the less. Some of them make astonishing *gaffes*. X, for instance, was dining with one of the oldest families in New York, with an English pedigree going back to the Conqueror, and X remarked blandly, 'The thing that impresses me about your country is your success in getting rid of classes. You have only one class, the middle class.' But any man," added Colum, "who has done anything and who can talk and takes trouble to prepare his lecture will find that there is no audience to compare with an American audience for friendliness and appreciation."

"I'd go anywhere to hear the English accent," an American girl remarked to me. "There wasn't an English film here this week, so I came to your lecture."

A taxi driver who drove me, more than once, from South Bend to Notre Dame University, gave me some good advice. "You've a swell dialect, Professor. Don't lose it racketing about with those college boys. It's an asset, believe me, Professor."

There would be fewer misunderstandings if Americans realised that the standoffishness of Englishmen is due to shyness. Perhaps because I am half Irish, I am not as shy as most of my countrymen and I have therefore little difficulty in being classified as "easy" rather than "high-hat," a distinction the implications of which may be illustrated by an experience in the Middle West.

I had arrived in the early morning and was to be met by two ladies who had, as I subsequently discovered, fortified themselves for the ordeal of meeting an English "high-hat" by consuming a double Scotch. Even so I had to pass them twice before they summoned up courage to speak. However, duly fortified by the double Scotch, they at last summoned up the necessary courage to introduce themselves.

I was going on that night and so I decided to leave my luggage at the station. They told me that I should not be expected to wear evening dress. I fingered my collar. Would it do? Miss H. said she thought it was a little "edgy," so I unpacked my bag to discover another collar, a process which involved turning out on to the platform a pair of pyjamas and two pairs of pants, before the missing collar was discovered. By the time my friends had helped me to repack these indelicate garments they felt happier. "If we had known you'd be so easy," remarked Miss H., "we wouldn't have wasted all that money on whisky."

Sometimes my publics overlapped. Two young Benedictine seminary students called on me after a lecture. They explained that they often had snow in winter, that they'd heard of ski-ing and had consulted the *Encyclopædia Britannica,* and as I was quoted as an authority in the *Encyclopædia* perhaps I could help them. This was their problem. They'd found a picture of ski and built a pair in the carpenter's shop. They'd fixed up a loop through which they had stuck their toes, but they had no idea that ski could be reliably attached by heel straps, and they were not in the least surprised when their ski came off at the bottom of every run. This they assumed to be normal. The question of technique on which they wished to consult the expert mentioned in the *Encyclopædia Britannica* was this: What was the best method of leaping from the ski to avoid a fall at the moment when the ski detached themselves at the bottom of the slope? They were agreeably surprised to discover that the connection between the ski-er and his ski need not be broken even at the end of the run.

I travelled down the West Coast from Seattle to Los Angeles in a double rôle – as a defender of the Spanish Nationalists and as a ski-ing enthusiast. The bouquets which I received as a ski-ing pioneer were nicely balanced by the brickbats which were hurled at the champion of General Franco. Thus the Seattle *Daily Times* led off in big black letters with an outsize bouquet: "Have you heard of Arnold Lunn? He really is the man who put 69,000 folk into Rainier National Park last winter;

who sent more than 85,000 ski-ing into the national forests last year. His name to ski-ers old and young is – well, revered." And on the same day the "Young Communists of Seattle" provided the compensating brickbat: "Lunn is the 'father of ski-ing' and a professor of theology. What qualifications other than Spanish birth does Mr. Lunn have for the rôle of political commentator? By what right is an exponent of Fascism allowed to attack the democracy of Spain in the democratic country of America? Free speech? Fascism is the complete negation of free speech and all democratic traditions. Permitting it to have free expression is a direct blow aimed at the maintenance of free speech."

I am not a professor of theology, a Spaniard by birth or a Fascist, and it was not clear to me why in the name of free speech I should be prevented from speaking freely.

I did not find it easy to bring home the true significance of Communism to American audiences, for those who have never crossed the frontier which separates civilised security from the no-man's-land in which Caliban is unchained are apt to discount as "propaganda" even expurgated accounts of Communist activities. I have listened in Helsinki, Thalin, Budapest and Bucharest to men describing first-hand experiences of the Red terror, and I know that there is an all but insurmountable barrier between men who have lived through such experiences and people like a benevolent old lady in the Middle West who remarked to a friend of mine, "Surely Lenin meant to help?"

I never met or heard of a well-known American professor in the States who was a member of the Communist Party, but the Communists' penumbra was well represented in most of the universities. The detestation of Nazism was the chief asset to the Communists and their friends. If the relations of our intellectuals of the Left were determined through reason they would either applaud both Nazis and Communists or condemn both Communists and Nazis, for Nazism is merely a Prussian form of State Socialism which is practised in Russia.

But we need not be surprised that so many intellectuals should sincerely detest the Nazi and sincerely admire the Communist system, for men tend to think well of political systems which bring their own type to the top. The only distinction of importance between Communism and Nazism is that the former represents the dictatorship of crooks and the latter the dictatorship of thugs. The old Bolshevik guard was composed almost exclusively of intellectuals, and it is therefore hardly surprising that Left-Wing intellectuals should prefer a system under which they have hopes of blossoming out as commissars to a system under which they would be forming fours under the command of a promoted sergeant-major. Of course, the intellectual is living in a world of illusions, for every Socialist revolution from the French to the Spanish has begun by attacking the aristocracy and has ended by sending the intellectuals to the gallows; but as Santayana somewhere remarks, those who cannot remember the past are condemned to repeat it, and if America ever goes Communist the intellectuals will follow the priests to the electric chair.

I spent most of my time in the States lecturing to people who were in agreement with my views, but we shall never make progress until we can force the opposition to give us a hearing. The best method of reaching the opposition is by debate, in book form or on the platform. At least half of those who read my controversy with Professor Joad,* or my controversy with Professor Haldane,† were only lured into reading the case for Christianity because these books bore the names of distinguished opponents of the Church.

While I was in the States four hundred Protestant clergymen signed an anti-Franco manifesto. I circulated to them an invitation to nominate one of the signatories to debate this issue either in New York or in Chicago and was disappointed that my challenge was not taken up. I succeeded, however, in ar-

* *Is Christianity True?*

† *Science and the Supernatural.*

ranging five debates on the Spanish War and two on Communism, but that was the best I could do in the course of four visits to the States. In default of debaters I was at some pains to discover hecklers, but hecklers are not encouraged in the States. Indeed, one has to work overtime to produce even the faintest echo of a good British "boo." I neglected no opportunities for searching out heckling talent. When the Communists of Pittsburgh arrived at headquarters on a November morning, they found this notice pinned to the door: "I called at 8 A.M. and again at 9.30 A.M. and should be glad to be informed what time Communists get up." I signed this notice: "Arnold Lunn. A hard-working Catholic" – attached two tickets for, and a pressing invitation to, my lecture. The tickets would probably have been disregarded had not the Press taken a hand in the game. "Author scores first heckle by beating Communists out of bed," was the headline to an article urging the Reds to get even. In England the heckler who is scored off is on his mettle, and returns to the charge; but in the States hecklers subside after the first rebuff.

Heckling develops as the duel disappears. The transformation of the formal courtesy of the eighteenth century, as mirrored in Chesterfield's letters to his son, into the smart and witty rudeness of the young people so brilliantly portrayed in Evelyn Waugh's novels is due to many causes, of which, perhaps, the disappearance of the duel is not the least important. Our own century supplies evidence on this point drawn from a different social milieu. A friend of mine enjoyed wandering round Limehouse disguised as a proletarian. "I suppose you find Limehouse pretty tough," I asked him. "On the contrary, I find it difficult to tolerate the hearty rudeness of my friends on my return. It is the greatest mistake to associate physical and verbal violence. Manners in a Limehouse pub are formal and precise, for rudeness is uncommon where discourtesy lands you on the back of your head. Irony and sarcasm are particularly dangerous." Americans are two generations nearer to the duel than we are, which is one of the factors responsible for the greater courtesy of American audiences. In the Far West, when orators carried six-shooters, you could either listen in silence or duck for cover. Natural selection took care of the heckler.

The apathy of Conservatives is the greatest asset to the Communist. "It can't happen here" is the slogan which ensures its happening here, but a hostile opposition will often serve to kindle that latent *esprit de corps* which still unites those who feel, however vaguely, that the values of Christian civilisation are being challenged by subversive forces. Indeed, enthusiasm seems to vary directly with opposition. A striking example of this fact was my experience at Glasgow during the Spanish Civil War. The Friends of Nationalist Spain applied to the City Corporation for the use of a hall. Labour was in power and the Labour majority refused to let the hall on a Sunday. I postponed my visit and my friends applied again for the hall on a weekday. I attended the debate, which was held in the early afternoon. Until the last vote had been recorded the issue was in suspense. The Independent Labour Party spoke up valiantly for the right of free speech. "Free speech!" exclaimed a Socialist. "Pah! It was by allowing the Nazis free speech in Germany that the Nazis got into power." The hall had been let to several speakers for the Spanish Republicans, and the democratic principle of free speech ultimately triumphed by one vote.

We were warned to expect trouble, and the mounted police were called out. Half an hour before the debate began I was ushered by the police into a committee room behind the platform, but I managed to elude my protectors and slipped out with a friend into the square, where the Communists were organising a demonstration. We joined the demonstrators, an ineffective crowd led by a dispirited little man who urged the bystanders to rally to the defence of democracy.

"There's no pep about this show," said my friend; "let's wake them up." So he uttered a piercing scream, "Join up for democracy and peace before it is too late." Two apathetic bystanders were galvanized into enthusiasm by this appeal. They joined up just behind us. "That's better," said my friend. "Now then, boys, step on it. Down with Lunn, the baby killer!"

"Down with Lunn!" I shouted.

"Down with Lunn!" the crowd repeated. More mounted police arrived to protect Lunn from Lunn. "Paid agents of Fascism," I hissed. The police looked contemptuous. "These chaps," said my friend, "would follow us anywhere. Let's tell them to storm the hall."

Eluding the police I reached the platform just in time to see the champions of democracy surging through the door. Thanks to their co-operation the meeting was an outstanding success.

Pittsburgh ranks in memory with Glasgow, for the Community Forum of Pittsburgh provided me with two splendid evenings. In 1937 the Forum induced Earl Browder, who had stood for President on the Communist ticket, to debate Communism with me at Pittsburgh. Browder put up a member of the party to debate with me in the Middle West, and subsequently decided that he would not appear in person at Pittsburgh. He informed my agent that he was ill and that he would send a substitute. I heard of this defection at Chicago and travelled a thousand miles to New York to investigate this sudden sickness. I employed a detective, who traced Browder's movements and proved that he had travelled to Washington by air on the day when he announced that he was too ill to go to Pittsburgh. I communicated to the Press the details of Browder's yellow fever a few hours before my debate with Browder's melancholy substitute.

Communists are humourless folk, and though they can stand invective, and indeed expect it, they cannot bear genial badinage. I am so grateful to hecklers and interrupters that I feel nothing but affection for those who are co-operating to make the party a success, but for some reason or other my gratitude, which is sincere, does not have a calming effect.

I am only too well aware of the fact that many good Christians, and many people who detest Communism, will be disedified by the fact that I enjoy a stormy evening with the Reds. The Communists have been very successful in reinforcing the defeatism of the Christian by establishing a double standard of controversial morality. I do not believe in the modern technique of dismissing an opponent with a label, and I hold that invective usually defeats its own objective, but an opponent of Communism is entitled to say why he regards Communism as an evil, provided that he documents his charges. Now my book *Communism and Socialism* was carefully documented by about five hundred quotations, most of them from Left-Wing sources. My old Balliol friend G. D. H. Cole referred contemptuously to my "mud-slinging," and added that no doubt some of this mud would stick. As the mud in question had been gathered from Left-Wing mud banks, I am inclined to think that it will prove as adhesive as Mr. Cole seemed to fear. But I should be interested in his definition of mud-slinging. To accuse an opponent of mud-slinging merely because you are unable to meet his case is my conception of slinging mud.

The Communist assumes that he is entitled to attack Fascism and Capitalism with vituperation and abuse; but if we reply by a documented criticism of Communism and its works, he whines that we are "Red-baiting." I should be intrigued to discover why White-baiting should be considered legitimate and Red-baiting caddish; but I suppose the answer to this question has already been provided by Yaroslavsky in his famous apophthegm: "Whatever coincides with the interests of the Proletarian Revolution is ethical."

CHAPTER XIX

Notre Dame

MORE than a hundred years have passed since a French missionary of the Confraternity of the Holy Cross pitched his camp beside a miniature lake in the Middle West. To-day that lake is within the grounds of the great University of Notre Dame. Notre Dame is just outside South Bend, which is little more than two hours' run from Chicago.

I remember listening in to a broadcast of a Notre Dame game from the bar of an American Pullman. My *vis-à-vis* seemed to be feeling the strain, and when Notre Dame drew ahead he ordered a stiff highball. "I'm not a graduate of Notre Dame," he said, "but it tickles me to see them put it across those Protestant colleges."

I asked him if he was a Catholic.

"Oh yes, I'm a Catholic, I guess. Leastways I'll be buried as one." And then he added reflectively: "Anyhow, I'm a Notre Dame rooter. When Rockne's Fighting Irish swept from coast to coast without losing a match, I guess that was the first thing that made Catholics stick out their chests in this country."

There are, indeed, thousands of American Catholics to whom the Church Militant is represented by the Fighting Irish, many of whom, incidentally, are Poles or Italians. The hero of one of the greatest come-backs in football history, Notre Dame's victory in the last few minutes against Ohio State, bore the good old English name of Shakespeare. Millions listen-in every Saturday afternoon to the football broadcasts, and many are the stories that are told of nuns and other devout "fans" who sit round the radio fingering their beads. A well-known nun, when the opponents of Notre Dame were leading by 14 points, removed the statue of Our Lady from the top of the radio and substituted a statue of St. Joseph. "After all," she remarked philosophically, "it's a man's game."

Another nun removed the statue of her Founder from the radio and placed it on the sill outside the window. It was snowing at the time. "You don't come in if Notre Dame doesn't win," she remarked grimly.

There is always a short service the evening before the match to ask the intercession of the saint who is the patron of the match in question, and on the morning of the game the team receive Communion. Knute Rockne was so impressed, not only by the piety of the Notre Dame footballers, but also by the practical results of that piety on the field of action, that he became a Catholic. I have heard Catholics criticise prayers for football, for prayers, so they argued, should not be overloaded with such trivialities. I disagree. The Catholicism of Notre Dame is nearer to the primitive Christianity than the Protestantism which believes in prayers only for spiritual benefits. Our Victorian grandparents were much exercised by the problem of praying for fine weather. Was it really sensible to believe that the weather, which was determined by cyclones and anticyclones, could be affected by prayer? "Please make Tommy a good boy" was not an unreasonable request. "Please make Saturday a good day" was absurd. Our Lord said, "Ask, and ye shall receive"; he did not say, "Ask for spiritual benefits, and ye shall receive them, but don't ask for most of the things you really want."

I remember a "pep" meeting on the campus just before the Pittsburgh game which would certainly have disedified a reverent agnostic. A crowd of about a thousand undergraduates marched in procession round the campus carrying coloured lights and making strange noises. They were addressed from a balcony by a series of orators. The speeches were diversified by the "cheer leaders." A cheer leader is an important official whose duty it is by Corybantic movements and Bacchic cries to whip the supporters of the team to frenzy on the day of battle, and thus incite the team to its ultimate efforts. A middle-aged man who had played in the team just after the war said that some people thought that the boys weren't tough enough to beat "Pitt," but they were getting tougher and he was hopeful.

Then the captain spoke, and he said that he knew he could count on the support of the boys. He expected them all to offer their Communions for the team next morning, and if they had any difficulty about getting up – well, there were a lot of husky guys who'd come round at six and help them. And he knew that, when the game was being played at Pittsburgh, they'd be listening on the radio and praying for the team.

And the cheer leaders said, "Ra . . . ra . . . ra . . ."

All of which will shock refined people who think of religion as a discreet emotion to be turned on in church. The spirit of Notre Dame is reactionary. It is out of touch with the modern world, for it has its roots in the past. The Olympic Games in Greece and the knightly tourneys of the Middle Ages and the Notre Dame football team have one thing in common, the close association of religion and sport. The captain of the Notre Dame team asking the crowd to offer up their Communions for victory was as free from self-consciousness as a Homeric hero soliciting assistance from the gods before battle, or a mediæval knight praying before a tourney. Prayer becomes self-conscious when the faith in the supernatural weakens. When the favours and the frowns of Heaven are alike discounted prayer tends to be regarded as merely a display of virtue or moral courage. The Sunday-school story of the good boy who knelt down to say his prayers in a dormitory full of mocking young infidels would have puzzled the Greeks. Why should this sensible youth be praised for his "moral courage"? The Greek would have been impressed, not by the "moral courage" of the boy on his knees, but by the reckless audacity of the boys who refused to placate the gods by prudent worship.

But the principal object of Notre Dame is neither academic nor athletic, but spiritual. Notre Dame spells football to the average American, and its prestige in university circles is based very largely on its excellent mathematical and scientific schools; but to those who are responsible for its welfare the principal object of the University is the salvation of souls. Every evening a bulletin is distributed to the students, and this bulletin carries on a high-pressure campaign directed to that end. Here is a characteristic extract from a bulletin issued at the beginning of the semester: "Above all, if for the last week or month or year you've headed straight for destruction at the bottom of the sea, don't try to kid yourself and others that everything's O.K. – get the point? Notre Dame exists primarily to help you through a swingy, thoughtless, sinful world to heaven. . . .

"For the sake of thick, stupid fellows who can't think and act for themselves, this attendance at all the services (of the Mission to Freshmen) is expected of you if you're enrolled as a freshman. . . ."

There is nothing academic about this bulletin, and its literary style was often criticised by the intellectuals of the University, who would have preferred spiritual exhortations to be modelled on the writings of Christopher Dawson or Maritain. But the bulletin speaks to its readers in a language that all its readers understand. The use of slang in lay sermons is only offensive when it represents an attempt to play down to an immature audience. There are, indeed, occasions when colloquialisms attain a dignity unattainable in more academic dress. A boy who had been fatally injured in a football match, and who had been warned that he could not live through the night, replied: "That's O.K. by me, Father." The Catholic Church, uncompromising on matters of faith and morals, has always shown a readiness to adapt itself to its environment.

Notre Dame and its bulletin carry on the traditions of primitive Christianity. The methods of publicity are American, but the high-pressure campaign for daily Communicants is directed towards the same end as the Pauline publicity of the first century. Careful statistics of daily Communicants are kept, and when the graph shows a downward tendency the bulletin renews its drive. A special feature of Notre Dame is the spiritual questionnaire. The alumni are invited to answer certain questions by post, the students dropping their answers into boxes kept for this purpose in the halls. The answers are anonymous, and are summarised in the annual report. Here are some of the bulletin answers.

Question: If you are not a daily Communicant, mention your reasons for not going to Communion daily.

Answers: I'm what J. B. Priestly terms a "highbrow." When everyone does one thing, I do another. . . . Habitual sin used to keep me away. Now the habit is gone. . . . I don't believe in Christ, hell, heaven. . . . It's too bad the non-daily Communicants don't wake up. It's impossible to talk to them on the subject. They want to be radical, independent, or just plain stubborn. . . . I sin too frequently. I don't like to go to Communion until I go through a couple of days without sinning. . . . If I have a date for Saturday, why should I go to Communion when I have the idea that I am going to sin? . . . I would feel lost and lonely without this great aid. It's iron in my spine. . . . I no longer go to Mass if I can get out of going. . . . I started off with a bang in September, but have gradually fallen away.

Question: When you go to Confession do you give much thought to your purpose of amendment?

Answers: If God gives you one chance for forgiveness, you are a rat to ask for it habitually for the same sin. . . . I have to, for I have a pet sin I have to lick. . . . I'm so unhappy, and discontented that I don't think much about it. I just want to feel great again. . . . I will not make any statement, as it may incriminate me.

Though the authorities were mainly concerned with the spiritual welfare of the alumni and undergraduates, the faculty were not neglected. I remember an address by the President at a faculty meeting. "You earn your salary," he said, "on the average students. Your reward is the brilliant students. You save your souls by taking a real interest in the stupid students."

I was always grateful for such time as Father O'Hara could spare me, for he was delightfully direct in his approach to a problem. A newcomer to an old institution is always in a difficult position if he has any suggestions to make for varying the programme assigned to him. The chances are that his suggestions are impracticable, but the odd chance that they may be acceptable is often worth taking. I never hesitated to take this odd chance with Father O'Hara, for I knew that he would neither resent suggestions nor camouflage his poor opinion of silly suggestions. It is an immense relief to deal with people who not only say what they think, but who also expect other people to be equally candid. I made firm friends with Father Cavenaugh, who was Prefect of Religion during my first two semesters, and with his successor, Father Lynch.

Father Cavenaugh's day began with Mass at 6 A.M. He remained in his room on the ground floor till noon, and from 5 P.M. to 11 P.M., with an hour off for dinner. During these hours he was accessible to all and sundry. I loved his broad humanity and wide knowledge of men. He had left a brilliant business career to take Orders, and he knew many sides of life. But he was not an easy man to talk to; for just as he had warmed to the subject, the bell in his room would buzz, and he would dash out to give Communion or to hear Confessions. I remember one evening he was very sad, for he particularly wanted to hear a lecture. "I don't think I can go," he said. "I'd love to, but a boy might come round who was in a jam of some kind, or who was losing his faith; and if I wasn't there, he mightn't come back."

His hobby was collecting small sums to distribute among the poor of South Bend. He never pestered people for money, but those who knew his tastes sometimes added to his store of small coins. And when he had collected enough to buy food or clothes, he would go down town to call on his friends among the down-and-outs. "A priest," he once said to me, "has to fight against the temptation to become arid and self-centred. After all, we've little to worry about. Three square meals a day. No family responsibilities. And sex is less of a difficulty to a priest than to many a young Catholic married couple who have to limit their families by self-control and abstinence. Our Lord never meant us to think of nothing but ourselves and our own salvation. That's why He insisted so much on the corporal works of mercy. We're meant to contact the poor, share their sorrows, see the lives they lead. . . ." Of the many good things which I owe to Notre Dame, I value none more highly than my friendship with Father Cavenaugh.

CHAPTER XX

Wandering Journalist

MY colleagues at Notre Dame were very kind to "the wandering journalist," as they described me. I certainly wander, but I have no right to describe myself as a journalist, a skilled calling for which a man must serve a proper apprenticeship. I have always regretted that I allowed my father to overrule me, for he discouraged my youthful ambitions to seek a career in journalism. I enjoyed editing the *Isis*, the Oxford undergraduate journal, and I have seldom been happier than when serving as a special correspondent in Spain; but I am only an amateur journalist, and a still more amateur professor. Yes, "Professor," though it was a shock to be greeted as such on my arrival at Notre Dame, even when this formidable title was abbreviated to "Prof."

I am always happy among mountains, and I do not feel homesick for the mountains at Oxford or at Bruges, but Indiana is flat, and South Bend is not very like Bruges, and there were moments when I suffered from nostalgia for the Alps, and for the legacy of mediæval Europe. In such fleeting moods of depression I used to wander over to visit the General of the Order, or that very gifted poetess, Sister Madaleva, the President of the sister College of St. Mary's.

The General of the Order was a man of wide culture and compelling charm. He had spent many years in Rome and he shared my passion for Italy. I remember a long talk which began when I quoted those beautiful lines of Hilaire Belloc's:

> But, ah! With Orvieto, with that name
> Of dark Etrurian subterranean flame
> The years dissolve. I am standing in that hour
> Of majesty Septembral, and the power
> Which swells the clusters when the nights are still
> With autumn stars on Orvieto hill. . . .

"Orvieto," said my friend, and a nostalgic look came into his eyes. "I shall never forget that polychrome façade of the Cathedral. Father Miltner and I had just finished our exams and we went off to Orvieto to recuperate. And we had dinner in a charming little inn somewhere near the Cathedral. Yes, 'the years dissolve' when you mention Orvieto."

The General's term of office ended at the end of my second semester, but I met him by chance two years later in Milwaukee. I have never been more delighted to see an old friend again.

Sister Madaleva's room was hung with pictures of Chartres and Oxford, where she studied for two years. She loved Oxford as I do, and as she spoke I could see again Magdalen tower on a May morning. Her room was a veritable House of Loretto, a fragment of the Europe I love transported across the Atlantic. She had the knack of collecting some very charming girls. I used to meet a group once a week for an informal discussion, and one of this group came to dinner with my wife and me at home. My wife was impressed by the discerning enthusiasm with which she spoke of the places in England which she had visited. We hear too much about the American tourist who remarked, "Naples! That's where we bought those stockings, isn't it?" I can speak with authority on tourists, and I am convinced that the average American visitor to Europe takes a great deal more trouble to understand what he is about to visit than the average Englishman.

I enjoyed my work at Notre Dame. My class were, in the main, picked students, most of whom had won scholarships at Notre Dame. They were easy to teach and appreciative of my efforts not to bore them unduly. They were very charming to me, and I hope one day to have the pleasure of seeing them in Europe.

My subject during my first semester was "Hellenism and Christianity." It is impossible to understand the philosophy and culture of Christendom without some knowledge of the Greek legacy, and even an elementary acquaintance with the Greek philosophers is useful as an antidote to half-baked political panaceas. "It is not the absence of communism," said Aristotle, "but the wickedness of the human heart that makes men unhappy." And yet there are still people who construct Utopias on the assumption that sin and selfishness can be eradicated by political revolutions. Most of our modern political problems are anticipated by Plato in the sixth book of *The Republic.* My subject was "Apologetics," but the President left me a free hand, and it was not difficult to fit Hellenism into an apologetic framework. Now, it is little use to confine one's teaching of apologetics to a class-room. One does not learn to swim from a book or by attending lectures, and one does not learn to defend one's creed if one never defends it against sceptics. If St. Paul had founded a college near Corinth he would not have been content to include a course of apologetics in his curriculum. He would have sent his boys into the streets of Corinth. But in those days Christianity had the crusading spirit that Communism has captured to-day. Christ did not say: "Now, remember that though I should like you tactfully to insinuate in the minds of your friends a hint that there is a lot to be said for loving one's neighbour, I do not want you to ram your religion down other people's throats." What Christ said was: "Go into the world and preach the gospel to every creature." The Apostles were so controversial that many of them died violent deaths. For the Church militant is always unpopular. It is only a Church dormant which can hope for toleration.

My class thought it would be rather fun to collect some non-Catholics to meet us in discussion. Waddell, a veteran of three semesters in my class, and Wurtzbach, a jolly militant controversialist, backed the idea, and in due course we collected a Rabbi (who, however, failed to put in an appearance), a very nice Methodist, an Atheist, a near-Communist, and representatives of other schools of thought.

The star turn at our first meeting was a real wandering journalist who had spent most of his life wandering round the world. "I'm not a scholar," he began, "and all your scholarly boys and profs get me skeered. 'What I love about you,' a friend of mine remarked, 'is that you're so Gawd darned ignorant.' Maybe; but I've knocked about the world a bit, and I wasn't too particular about my amusements – get me? – but I tell you I'm skeered when I see the way this country is going. A young girl came to me the other day and said she'd like me to take her on a picnic. In November. Not the month for picnics, I guess. So I said, 'Quit stalling. It's not a picnic you're looking for. I'm old enough to be your father.' And she said, 'I've knocked about with a lot of guys older than you.' I tell you I admire the boy who can keep his hands off these young girls to-day. I wouldn't mind if I hadn't a lovely girl of my own, but these modern girls make me sick."

The Methodist said that we would have to do a lot of profound thinking about sex. It was a problem which had to be thought out. I disagreed. We can continue to think about this problem without arriving at anything more profound than the old truth that chastity is extremely difficult.

Meanwhile the journalist continued to talk sense, which was

not intended to appear profound, but which was anchored on fact. "The other day I was out in the country with my boy. He'll learn a lot more horse-sense in the country than he'll ever learn in schools. We passed an old gander doing sentry-go for his dame who was brooding near by. And a young gal from another flock was preening herself and trying to attract the old gander's attention. And I said to my boy, 'We'll be back in a few days, and you'll see that the old dame will kill that gal'; and sure enough when we came back the gal that had tried to break up her home was stretched out dead. The old goose had given her the works. You can't fool old Nature without paying for it sooner or later. . . . I'm not a religious man, but I tell you that I'd like to go round this country and preach one sermon, a short one. I want to tell them they're going to hell because they've turned their back on God. I'm not a Catholic or a Protestant. I'm nothing, but I know that this won't get right again until we get back the old American mother. When I was a boy what helped me to keep my hands off a nice gal was the thought of what my mother and hers would think of me if I didn't. Let me tell you this. I'm twenty-five years older than most of you, and I've seen a lot. Your fathers looked up to American womanhood, your brothers look at American womanhood, and, if you don't get back to God, your sons will look down on American womanhood."

I think the wandering journalist has missed his vocation. As a wandering preacher he would certainly have at least one good sermon to fall back on.

CHAPTER XXI

Battle in Spain

I NEED not repeat in this chapter the reasons which I gave in my book *Spanish Rehearsal* for believing in the justice of General Franco's cause, nor my experiences, described in that book, during my first journey through Spain at war. The war and the controversy which it provoked have both come to an end, but to those who are still interested in the background of the Spanish struggle I commend one of the most interesting autobiographies of our day, Douglas Jerrold's *Georgian Adventure*. It was Jerrold who made the arrangements for the aeroplane which carried three British tourists to the Balearic Islands, and which left (without the tourists) with General Franco for Morocco on the day before the rising began.

Franco's final victory was rendered possible by two decisive battles, the first of which united the armies of Franco and Mola in 1936, the second of which, in 1938, separated the defenders of Barcelona from the defenders of Madrid.

I returned to Spain at the beginning of April, 1938, and saw the final phases of the battle for the sea.

On arriving at Saragossa I met an officer who greeted me with the words, "To-day our outposts saw the sea." I shall never forget the mystical enthusiasm with which he said these words.

Thalassa! Thalassa! But the sea meant more to those who had to fight every yard of their advance than it could have meant to Xenophon's army.

On Wednesday, April 13th, we returned to Morella. We left our cars within a few yards of a battery of big guns. Other batteries were in action half a mile down the road. The violence of their dispute echoed from the mountain walls. Their immediate objective was the Republican artillery which had been shelling our road in an attempt to locate our batteries. A noise of angry wings above and a flight of thirty bombers swept across the sky to administer the *coup de grâce* to the Republican artillery.

The Republican anti-aircraft spluttered an indignant protest, and the blue heaven was flaked with white cloudlets through which the eagles of Spain dived disdainfully. The hills re-echoed to the continuous thunder of their bombs.

Three friends of mine with whom I was to pass the Easter week-end took part in this attack. I knew that they were at the front. The planes dived perilously near the artillery, which they silenced, and returned unscathed across the lines. An hour later they were back again.

We left our cars and started up the hillside towards an artillery observation post above the valley. Many a time I have scrambled in a crescendo of excitement up the last yards leading to an Alpine pass, but never with a greater sense of expectancy than on the final slope of this nameless hill. I broke into a run on the last incline of limestone boulders, and suddenly the ground fell away from my feet. Beyond the plain and the ultimate hills was a thin blue strip – *Thalassa! Thalassa!*

The artillery observation officer spoke fluent English. He was sixteen when war broke out, and spent the first six months of the war in London. This was not the first day on which outposts had seen the sea, but it was the first day on which artillery observation posts commanded the Mediterranean. "To-day for the first time," said the boy, "I saw the sea." *For the first time.* I knew what he meant. I, too, felt as if I had never really seen the sea until I saw it from this Spanish hill.

The battle was dying down. Through glasses we could see the Nationalists occupying a ridge from which the Republicans had retreated, and a long line of tanks going into action against a burning village, the outskirts of which were still defended by the enemy. A Russian tank – we photographed it next day – had just been put out of action in a road the Nationalists had not yet occupied. Another tank could be seen cautiously moving up the road towards its disabled companion. A few shells burst; the rescuing tank hesitated, paused, turned tail and fled.

We spent three lazy hours watching the dying battle. The air was fragrant with spring and the ground on which we lay was graced by April flowers. The soft outlines of these southern hills melting into a blue mist, the Mediterranean, recalled indolent hours among the mountains of peace. The war seemed curiously unreal. Even the sights and sounds of battle seemed to translate themselves naturally into mountain terms – the white puffs of bursting shells into clouds, the thunder of distant avalanches. But the war broke through this mountain reverie when the Republican planes came over.

"Red aeroplanes," said the artillery officer; "we know they're Red because we can't see them."

Which was true enough, for though we could hear the aeroplanes as they swept over us, they were flying so high they were invisible. They must have been flying at a height of over 20,000 feet. "Their best fighters have been killed," he continued, "and the pilots who have now replaced them are not properly trained and their morale is bad. That's why they fly so high."

We regained our cars as the sun set, and on our return journey we met lorry after lorry bringing the troops that were to fight next day. A vivid memory of a memorable day is the silhouette of a lorry full of sombre, hooded Moors seen against the last glow of the evening sky.

Morella, where we slept, is a small town in which the one hotel had been commandeered for the General. We arrived at nine, and at eleven our Press officer returned with the good news that the Mayor had placed at our disposal three beds in a private house, beds which had been vacated by cavalry officers who had left that afternoon for the front. Their soldier servants had remained behind, and refused to permit us to occupy the beds allotted to us by the obliging Mayor. So the Press officer went off in search of a military patrol, while we paced up and down outside the gates of a somewhat dingy paradise. Along the distant mountain line the camp-fires were burning, and the lowering clouds inspired a proper feeling of gratitude for the prospect, however dubious, of a shelter, however poor.

The Press officer returned with a corporal and two military policemen. The faithful servants of the departed cavalry officers surrendered the fort at discretion, and we marched in and took possession of three beds for four people. There was a fourth bed, but it had no mattress, for the Republicans had removed most of the mattresses and every available blanket from Morella. It was excessively cold, and my companions did not sleep until dawn. I was more fortunate, and woke thoroughly refreshed. The threatening storm had passed, and the sky was cloudless. I paid a short visit to the beautiful little church, which had miraculously escaped destruction, as had its priest, who spent eighteen months in a mountain cave with the Mayor of Morella. As I came out of the church I saw a flight of bombers pass over the town on their way to the last defences of the Republicans in this battle for the sea.

Few experiences are more exhilarating than to follow the day-by-day advance of a victorious army. We drove rapidly down the road to the sea, left behind us the ridge which had been captured from the Republicans when I first visited this front, drove through a village from which the Republicans had been driven on the previous day, and emerged in a pleasant little valley on to open ground where only one low-lying ridge still separated us from the redemption of the sea. We turned a corner to find the artillery in action. The batteries were firing from a point just behind an abrupt ridge, from the summit of which we watched the battle for the last and lowest of the hill barriers which separated the Nationalists from the low ground leading to the sea. Through our glasses we could just see the reserves moving up to the slopes on which the front line had been established. We could follow every phase of the offensive. The preliminary bombardment had already been in progress for more than an hour, and the big shells were still bursting beyond the ridge, hurling vast sulphurous clouds into the sky. Then followed the shrapnel barrage, which burst, not on the ground, but in the sky, so that the ridge was rimmed with thunder clouds. A pause and the hills re-echoed to the vicious splutter of machine-guns punctured by the staccato of hand grenade and bomb, as the infantry advanced to storm the front lines. The duel between machine-gun and grenade lasted for about twenty minutes, and then suddenly the clamour faded into silence. Had the attack succeeded or failed?

"We shall soon know," said the Press officer. "If the attack has failed the bombardment will begin again."

We rejoined the car and drove down the road leading to the ridge which had just been captured, and entered Chert three hours after the village had been captured by the Nationalists. Three tanks had halted in the main square, for a Russian tank was round the corner. "They've sent for an anti-tank gun," said the Press officer, "to put the Russian out of his misery."

A woman came out of a house and blinked timidly. And then she smiled. It was true, it was really true. The Republicans had gone. The nightmare had passed. There were the soldiers making a bonfire of those monotonous Republican posters – "*No passeran*" going up in flames. A group of villagers gathered round our Press officer and overwhelmed him in a flood of cheerful babble. A girl just on the edge of this group kept on chanting a kind of lyrical refrain: "They *said* '*No passeran*,' but they have passed [chuckle]. They *said* '*No passeran*,' but they *did* pass [more chuckles]."

An old lady explained that she had not tasted bread for a month, but she had managed to get a piece of meat and had hidden it very carefully. But not carefully enough. That morning the Republicans had come round on a last looting foray, and had found the meat. The Republican planes returned, and the anti-aircraft imprinted its pattern on the sky, and the old lady repeated her moan about the meat.

As we left Chert the Republicans started a counter-offensive on the ridge which they had lost. We were near enough to see the infantry without glasses. I remember a group near the top of the ridge huddled against a stone wall as the shells exploded just below them. War in Spain retained something of the colourful pageantry of the Middle Ages. The infantry went into battle behind an immense banner which was planted in triumph at every stage of the advance, and which marked the frontier between the Spain that had been saved and the Spain which was still unredeemed. The colours of Nationalist Spain are the same as those of the M.C.C., and the familiar red and yellow glimpsed between the clouds of exploding shells awoke very different memories – idle hours at Lord's, M.C.C. flags drooping listlessly in the summer haze.

The bombardment ceased. We saw a wave of little figures stumbling over the skyline. Some fell. We went back to our car, and round the next corner met the anti-tank gun towed by a car at racing speed. We passed in rapid succession three lorries crowded with reinforcements, but the counter-attack was already dying down. The Republicans were irrational fighters, for it is unreasonable to abandon positions of great natural strength if you feel yourself strong enough to attempt their recapture within an hour of losing them. Forces which are not strong enough to hold can hardly be expected to recapture the crest of a mountain ridge.

Two days later the Nationalists reached the sea.

Our journey back to Morella was slow, for we were driving against the stream of traffic – infantry, cavalry, big guns, and a long procession of pack mules loaded with ammunition. *And there with the rest were the lads who would never be old.* I thought of Housman's lines as we passed lorry after lorry of young men, their faces turned towards the sea. Many of those we saw on those memorable days were destined to

> Carry back straight to the coiner the mintage of man,
> The lads that will die in their glory and never be old.

Barcelona made most of the shirts worn in Spain, a fact which might have been deduced from the appearance of the Nationalist army. Anything in the nature of a shirt was welcome, and no questions were asked. I saw one soldier with a loud check pattern protruding cheeringly through a sheepskin coat. A few officers in smart khaki set a tone which the troops made no attempt to maintain. They reminded me of old pictures of the Confederates during the last stages of the American Civil War. I liked the hats, ranging from a magnificent straw hat, which would have pleased a Mexican cowboy, to Carlists' berets. Nor was there any drab uniformity about the lorries, particularly those of the Moors. An incongruous effect was produced by the mascot of a large inane doll dangling just beneath a fierce Moor stretched out on the top of a van, the roof of which he shared with a Mickey Mouse, a dead calf, a live hen and a mattress. For the Moor likes to lie soft if he can, even on the field of battle.

Halfway to Morella a German officer in the car ahead jumped out into the road, shouted "*Avions!*" and made for the field. "Get out," said the Press officer. So we got out. The bull's-eye is the safest part of a target when aeroplanes are flying at the height favoured by the Republicans, so I decided not to follow the Germans into the field, and before lying down in the ditch, to minimise the danger of flying fragments of anti-aircraft, I cautiously searched the heavens; for I was wearing the less disreputable of two disreputable suits, and hoped to see General Franco within a few days. I could neither see nor hear the aeroplanes, which was not surprising, for it had been a false alarm. I climbed back into the car, composing my own epitaph on the assumption that my reluctance to spoil my suiting had proved fatal:

He died as he lived
A martyr to Good Form
Keeping up Appearances to the Last.

From the small pass which we descended to Morella two roads diverge, to reunite lower down. The authorities had naturally made these one-way roads. In the morning we met three lorries coming down the road for ascending cars, and it was nice to round off the day by dodging two lorries charging cheerfully up the road reserved for the descending traffic. Spaniards have no sense of motoring sin. A few days before our driver had passed a car on the bend of a mountain road and met a lorry which obligingly took to the ditch. In England our driver would have been the target for colourful abuse, and would have been properly contrite. But the lorry driver was not perturbed, and our driver was not penitent.

Night fell as we left Morella. The hills just beyond were full of Republican stragglers, who sometimes held up cars and sometimes strung a row of bombs across the road wind-screen high; but the trivial risk of such playful pranks was more than offset by the relief of seeing the lamps of the oncoming lorries before we met them round a bend. I confess to these fears with shame, and am consoled by the reflection that a Spanish general noted for his personal bravery remarked that the one thing in this war which really frightened him was the return from the front against the stream of unending lorries driven by light-hearted Spaniards.

I spent Easter at Epila, the headquarters of the Spanish Air Force, with the Infante Alfonso d'Orléans Bourbon and the Infanta Beatrice. Our friendship began in Mürren a few months after the King had left Spain. The Infanta Beatrice is the daughter of the late Duke of Edinburgh, and thus a granddaughter of Queen Victoria on her father's side. Her mother was the daughter of the Tsar, Alexander II. The Infanta has had her fill of revolutions. She was in Russia when the Grand Duke Cyril was blown to pieces by a bomb, and she travelled from Nice to Moscow during the 1905 revolution. During her journey the governors of the different provinces met her at the stations, and five of these governors were subsequently murdered before the revolution was finally suppressed.

The Infante accompanied the King when he left Madrid. It was a perilous journey. "I used to play Rugger," said the Infante, "and a Rugger back is often in a dilemma. If he tackles too soon, his man passes, and if he waits too long he may be accused of funking. I sat beside the King with my revolver ready, and decided that I wouldn't shoot if we were held up by a large party, as in that case I couldn't save the King, and should expose him to inevitable vengeance; but if those who challenged us were not more than four or five I decided to shoot."

The Infanta volunteered to stay behind to bring out the old and beloved Infanta Isabella. The old lady was at the point of death, but was determined not to die in Republican Spain. She was popular with the Republicans, who shouted outside her house, "Long live the Republic! Long live Snub Nose!" which was their name for the old Infanta. One of those who saw the Infanta during those days spoke to me of her amazing courage and calmness. After the King left, a well-known journalist called on the Infanta. "Do tell me," he said, "how the Queen took it. I've got to send a telegram to London." The Infanta replied: "I was proud of her. She behaved as I should expect a British princess to behave. She shed no tears, and she kept her head high and behaved with undiminished dignity." "Oh, that won't do at all," said the journalist. "I'm going to say that she broke down absolutely"—which he did. This person was not a professional journalist, but an amateur with no respect for the code which all good journalists observe.

The Infanta's three sons, Alvaro, Alonso and Ataulfo, raced for Spain in the World Ski Championship of 1935. When they arrived at Mürren they found the Spanish Republican flag flying, and promptly hoisted the old flag of monarchical Spain on the hotel in which they were staying. Their most outstanding performance as ski-ers was in the Parsenn Derby, an event which attracts the best Alpine runners, amateur and professional. They entered not only for the individual event, but also for the team race held in connection with the race. More than twenty teams entered, and the three brothers, representing the Kandahar Ski Club, finished second.

A little scene comes back to me as I write: New Year's Eve at Mürren in 1934. An objectionable and semi-inebriated young man was pestering a beautiful Swedish girl for a dance. The Swede, who was the daughter of a man who had been imprisoned in connection with the notorious collapse of a famous Swedish firm, rebuffed the young man, who murmured something to the effect that girls with her background could not afford to be so particular. I saw the girl in tears and learned what had happened, and, moved by some curious telepathic instinct, left the hotel and walked towards the ice rink. There I saw two shadowy figures rolling in the snow. I separated them. The inebriated young man had a black eye. Alonso was full of bitter reproaches. "Here I've spent five pounds on boxing lessons and you come along and spoil the first fight I've had."

The three boys enlisted in the Air Force at the outbreak of

the Civil War. Alonso was killed during his first month in Spain, but Alvaro and Ataulfo and their father survived the war.

During a debate at Windsor, Ontario, my opponent referred contemptuously to the degenerate Royal Family of Spain. Windsor is the other side of the river from Detroit, where the Infante had worked for some months in the Ford works. He had held a responsible position in the Spanish Air Force before the revolution. After he left Spain he asked Mr. Ford, who was a friend of his, if he could join the firm. Mr. Ford replied, with a smile: "You know my rule. Everybody starts at the bottom." "I know your rule," said the Infante, "and I only ask to start at the bottom."

For six months the Infante worked as an ordinary workman, at Detroit, and he spent the next year as a commercial traveller trying to sell agricultural motors to French farmers. Shortly before the Civil War he was appointed to an administrative position with an assured future, and he would have been at the front as soon as his sons but for the opposition of both wings of the Nationalist movement. The Carlists are conservatives and traditional, but they have never reconciled themselves to the present dynasty, though the last of the Carlist pretenders had died, with the result that King Alfonso is the legitimate king on any theory, Carlist or otherwise. The Phalangists were anti-monarchical – in part, at least. Whereas the Carlist motto was "For God, King and Country," the Phalangist motto was "For Country, Justice and Bread." So the Infante fretted his heart out in England while his sons fought, and then one day he wrote and told me the good news that he had been accepted for service in the Air Force.

"You will rejoice to know that to-morrow," he wrote, "I leave for Salamanca, as I am back in the Air Force! I owe it all to my wife, who has persuaded them to waive their scruples and accept me. God bless her for her self-sacrificing courage, which shames us mere fighting men.

"You can imagine how pleased I am – for three main reasons!

"(1) It shows how much stronger the Franco side has become and how united all anti-Communists are now.

"(2) I feel I may be useful to the cause.

"(3) I can look men and my sons in the face again, and when God ordains I should meet Alonso I can tell him I did my best for my country and for a cause which knows no frontiers."

On the eve of Good Friday the son of General Kinderlen, commander of the Air Force, drove me out to Epila. He and his friend had been brought down by the Republican anti-aircraft, but had managed to land in their own lines. "When we heard," remarked the Infante next day, "that the Reds had brought down the General's son we felt that something ought to be done about it, so we bombed their anti-aircraft good and proper. We came down to within 300 metres, and put three out of four guns out of action. Their anti-aircraft, which is in the main in the command of French and Russian officers, is exceptionally good."

The old ducal palace had been assigned to the Infante and his family. The Infante showed me to my room. "I shall be leaving at 6 A.M., and I am afraid Alvaro and I will be busy until the evening. We shall have to leave you to your own devices until we return." His manner was that of a courteous host at a country-house who has suddenly been summoned to town on business. The war seemed remote, and it was difficult to believe that my host and his son might never return, and that my hostess, who was organising relief for the sick and destitute in Lerida, was also under daily shell-fire.

"I am afraid," said my host, "that the Infanta won't be back to-morrow. She is at Lerida. But she will be here on Saturday evening, please God, so that we can all spend Easter together." The Infante spoke casually of his own plans, but a sudden note of anxiety came into his voice when he mentioned the Infanta.

I had the palace to myself next day. I had coffee in the sombre dining-room, hung with portraits of grandees. They seemed slightly contemptuous of the intruder lounging about in security. I felt as if I were living in one of those queer dreams in which scenes from different lives are inexplicably mixed: war and a week-end in a country-house. We expected the Infante back for tea, and at six-thirty there was a little group of anxious servants hanging round the doorway. I wondered how the Infanta stood the daily ordeal of waiting for her husband and sons to return from the front. I happened to be at the gate when the Infanta arrived on the following evening.

"Well, are all my family still alive?" she said.

It was on Easter Saturday that the Nationalists captured Vinaroz, on the Mediterranean. The Republican armies to the north and south were finally separated and the battle of the sea had been won. Never have I heard on the radio a voice more vibrant with emotion than the voice of the Nationalist broadcaster when he announced that the vanguard had reached the sea. Three pilots staying with the Infante grasped each other by the hand and gambolled round the room with delight. Much might yet pass before the final surrender, but the war had been won.

"And now for Daventry," said the Infanta.

"We regret to announce that Mr. Mills, the great entertainer, has died. There was a heath fire in Shropshire and the report of this fire ended with the tragically significant words: 'The fire was perhaps caused by somebody dropping a lighted cigarette end.' The weather shows every prospect of continuing fine over the week-end, so that Easter holiday-makers may count with confidence on sunshine. Will Mr. John Tomkins go at once to 74, Smith Street, Manchester, where his mother is lying seriously ill."

These placid happenings seemed as remote as if they were taking place on another planet, but it was interesting to learn that the "insurgents" claimed to have reached the sea.

I spent the morning of my fiftieth birthday (April 18th) gossiping with the Infanta in a charming little courtyard full of colour and peace. The Infanta's official work was to follow up the advancing army and to organise relief for the wretched inhabitants. Lerida, from which she had just returned, had been one of the black spots in Republican Spain. The Bishop and every priest but two in the town had been murdered. The Infanta's first task was to reorganise a large asylum for the aged. In the general disorganisation of the final phase these old people had been left to fend for themselves.

The Infanta told me that the nuns had been much edified by the piety of an altar boy of seventeen. He had put in an appearance the first day that they had arrived at Lerida, and had been most helpful in unearthing vestments, altar linen and sacred vessels for Mass. As a server at Mass he was a model of attention and devotion.

And then one day a lady of Lerida came into the big dining-room where all the destitute refugees were fed, and caught sight of the altar boy. "That's the little brute," she said, "who came round to see me a few weeks ago and bragged that he had helped to kill four priests and threatened to kill me." The pious altar boy was led away tearfully protesting that he had been very young at the time and had been misled by his elders.

"I do object," said the Infanta, "to people being arrested when I am feeding them. I think they might wait till they leave the refuge. Next day they arrested two men who came to us because they were hungry, and who were identified as Reds who had buried people alive."

Spain is a country of extremes. Its climate is congenial to the development of great sanctity and violent sin. The Vicar of Bray, whose doctrines were discreetly adapted to the dominant fashions of the day and who remained well-bred and well-behaved through all variations of belief, is perhaps a classic type of the English opportunist. But he is not a type that matures easily on Spanish soil. The Spaniard steers a middle course with difficulty. Oscillations as violent as those of the altar boy at Lerida are, of course, uncommon even in Spain, but I doubt if any other European country, during a revolution, would have produced a greater host of heroic martyrs or a longer tale of Satanic atrocities. Those who do not understand Spain are often puzzled by the intermittent violence of these anti-Catholic outbursts. "How can you explain the fact," an American Methodist once asked me at the end of a lecture on Spain, "that in a Catholic country so many priests should have been murdered and so many churches burnt? Isn't that rather a pitiful reflection on Catholicism?"

"I should feel much happier," I replied, "about the future of American Methodism if there were the least danger of anybody ever wanting to burn down an American Methodist chapel."

In the heroic age of Methodism, John Wesley was interrupted in his sermon by an excited intruder who rushed into the room in which he was preaching and exclaimed that the house was surrounded by a mob who intended to burn it down. "Then our only way is to make use of it while it is still standing," said John Wesley. Methodism at its best had the sign-mark of authentic Christianity. It inspired hatred. "And ye shall be hated of all men for my name's sake."

In Spain the burning of churches and the massacres of priests were, in the main, the work of small bands of itinerant gangsters. There, as in Communist Russia and in revolutionary France, the unorganised majority proved defenceless against an organised minority of terrorists.

We motored into Saragossa for lunch, and paused for a few moments to visit the famous cathedral, through the roof of which a bomb fell without exploding, since when Our Lady of Saragossa has been informally adopted as the special patron of the Nationalist airmen. The Infanta gave me a statuette of Our Lady of Saragossa as a memento of my fiftieth birthday.

We had lunch at the hotel with General Kinderlen and Señora Kinderlen. General Kinderlen had been in the movement from the first, and had left his children in Madrid, as he was making preparations to join Franco. It had been a point of honour with the generals who were privy to the plot not to move their families from Madrid, for a sudden exodus would have aroused the suspicions of the Republican Government. I can conceive of no sterner test of devotion to a cause than to expose one's children to the certainty of capture and the probability of execution. His elder boy had been in prison for a year, and had been sentenced to be shot on more than one occasion, but was eventually exchanged for a prisoner in Franco's hands.

The General made a courteous allusion to the gallantry of our sailors who had rescued the survivors in the Nationalist man-of-war, the *Baleares*, which had been sunk by the Republicans. Our seamanship on that occasion was the object of universal admiration in Nationalist Spain, for it had proved by no means easy to get alongside the sinking *Baleares*, and the operation was dangerous; for the Republicans had continued to shell the *Baleares*, and inflicted three casualties, one of which proved fatal, on the British who were attempting to rescue the survivors.

In the village of St. Luca, where the Infante has a house, people went about saying, "We will never hear a word against the English again."

"The English are wonderful," a Nationalist said to me; "we have always liked the English, and get on with them. It is only your politicians who are Red."

The Cabinet was in possession of documented reports of the Republican régime in Madrid and Barcelona, and were under no illusions as to the alleged "democracy" of the Republicans. They had to consider the interests of Great Britain and the interests of their own party. The ineffective Opposition in Great Britain was still desperately searching for some policy with which to appeal to the electorate. Constructive policy they had none, but had the National Government betrayed overt sympathy for Franco, Labour would have raised the cry of "pro-Fascist," and on that negative issue might conceivably have won the next election; but I could not persuade my Spanish friend that it was unreasonable to expect the National Government to increase the electoral chances of the Labour Opposition.

It was impossible to persuade the Spanish Nationalist that the average Englishman was no more interested in a Spanish civil war than in a war between the South American Republics. I remember asking a member of the British Ladies' Ski Team whether she had ever heard the war mentioned during the winter season. This lady was a Catholic, and, as such, a mild supporter of the Spanish Nationalists.

"Well," she replied, "I did happen to remark the other day, 'I wonder how Franco is getting on,' and somebody at once replied: 'Pretty well; he finished third yesterday in just under five minutes.' There is a racer, you know, with a name rather like Franco."

When we returned to Epila we found Alvaro and Ataulfo examining some photographs taken in the course of Alvaro's bombing raids on a railway junction. In spite of improvement, accurate bombing is still difficult, and accuracy is largely a question of morale. We are apt to think of aerial war too much in terms of machines and to forget that the relative importance of the man behind the machine is greater in flying than in any other branch of the service. Unwilling troops may be held in the front line and even forced to advance, but no discipline can transform an airman who has not got his heart in the job into an accurate bomber or a dangerous fighter. Few things demand more cool and calculating courage than to dive down through an anti-aircraft barrage, and nothing is easier than to dump one's bombs overboard anyhow and then make a beeline for home.

It was the harbour of Barcelona and not the town which was the object of bombing raids, and bombs which struck the crowded part of the town were, so I was told, dropped by non-

Spanish volunteers who were not inclined to take the great risks of diving sufficiently low which were necessary to make reasonably certain of hitting the harbour.

Alvaro had motored into Vinaroz to examine the scene of action and the effect of his bombing raid. He had amused himself by collecting various specimens of explosives, the handling of which gave him the most unaffected pleasure.

"Do leave those horrible things behind," said the Infanta as we went in to dinner; but Alvaro refused to be parted from his trophies, and brightened my fiftieth birthday party by planting down an Italian hand grenade just in front of my soup, and a little Spanish bomb just beside my bread. He fished out of his pockets a handful of bullets which the Republicans had left behind, and proceeded to explain their finer points. I was not interested. I prefer as my dinner neighbours people who collect stamps.

"It wouldn't look too well," said the Infante thoughtfully, "if Arnold were blown to smithereens on his fiftieth birthday. We haven't got too many English visitors to our side of the lines, and we can't afford to be extravagant."

CHAPTER XXII

Easter, 1938

"YOUR English Catholicism," a Spanish friend remarked to me, "always seems to me to have a sort of Protestant veneer. It is so decorous. I was at Mass in a London suburb last Sunday and the priest astonished me by stopping before reading the Gospel to rebuke a young man who was trying to creep unobserved to his seat. 'It is very wrong,' said the priest, 'to arrive late and to disturb people at their devotions.' "

"That does not strike me as very unreasonable," I said.

"No, of course it wouldn't strike you as unreasonable," my Spanish friend continued, "but then, you are English. If you were a Spaniard you would know that devout people are not so easily disturbed."

I recalled this conversation in the church at Epila on Good Friday, 1938.

I wandered up after breakfast to the village church. A large notice on the door recalled the ladies of Epila to their responsibilities. "Women. Modesty is the key to victory. There is no place in the new Spain for bare arms, bare legs and short skirts."

So much for the ladies. But the men were not neglected. Inside the church there was the routine notice, which always makes me feel at home, inviting the faithful to refrain from spitting, as a mark of respect for the House of God.

On Good Friday the Saints and images which adorn the church at Epila have a day out, and are taken in procession to see the sights of the town. When I entered the church I found them all parked expectantly in the north aisle. I was glad to see St. Ignatius, and was impressed by the local saint – I forget his name – a fine, strapping, bearded Spaniard whose services as an honorary colonel of the local A.R.P. were highly spoken of by the inhabitants. Thanks to his intercession, Epila had been undamaged by hostile aircraft. In the next carriage to the saint there was a jolly marble skeleton supporting his head on his hands as if he had a headache.

Bells were silenced on Good Friday, but rattles were distributed at Epila as a symbol of mourning. The sunny court in front of the church was full of small boys waving these lugubrious rattles. As mourners they were not very convincing, and the cacophony of their choral efforts could be heard all too clearly in the church. Sometimes a small boy pushed his head through the doorway, and tried a tentative rattle in the church itself. If he persisted, somebody would murmur a mild "Shoo," and the small boy would fade away; but nobody seemed to mind very much, for the Catholics of Epila are, as my Spanish friend would say, Catholics of the unreformed variety.

Many women were kneeling on the stone pavement with outstretched arms. Some were old enough to have sons at the front, others were perhaps praying for husbands or lovers. Some of them remained kneeling without lowering their arms throughout the entire Mass of the Presanctified. And the rattles did not seem to worry them. The devout Spaniard, as my friend remarked, is not easily disturbed, which is perhaps as well.

The church swarmed with children. Small boys scrambled

up into the carriage containing the skeleton and sympathetically stroked its head. A little girl tiptoed to reach the holy-water stoop, and looked puzzled when she withdrew her dry finger. Her sister murmured a gentle rebuke. Did she not know there was no holy water on Good Friday? Children jostled each other all the way up the steps leading to the pulpit, and after the priest had carefully picked his way down the children swarmed into the pulpit in order to get the best possible view of the proceedings. They were at home, which was as it should be in their Father's house.

The side-altar, which was to serve as the Altar of Repose, had been transformed by local talent into a passable imitation of what local talent imagined to be a Roman tomb. An impression of receding perspective had been ingeniously obtained by a succession of Corinthian colonnades. The Church was warm and the glue was beginning to run, and the Roman arch at the entrance sagged lugubriously. Two Roman soldiers stood guard before the tomb, armed with tin spears and protected by cardboard shields. To their chins were attached the blackest and bushiest of beards, which seemed to me to violate that fine old tradition in which I was reared, the tradition which distinguished so carefully between the legions of ancient Rome, composed of clean-shaven Nordics, indistinguishable in appearance from modern Englishmen, and the swarthy little "wops" who began to swarm in Italy when the best people left with Julius Cæsar and settled down in Great Britain. That Roman tomb at Epila reminded me of E. M. Forster's charming description of the little theatre at Monteriano: "There was also a drop-scene, representing a pink lady lightly clad, and two more ladies lay along the top of the proscenium to steady a large and pallid clock. . . . There is something majestic in the bad taste of Italy; it is not the bad taste of a country which knows no better; it has not the nervous vulgarity of England, or the blinded vulgarity of Germany. It observes beauty, and chooses to pass it by. But it attains to beauty's confidence."

The priest left the altar and led the procession to the Altar of Repose. The Roman soldiers clanked their tin spears, and one black, bushy beard began to droop, revealing the pink and chubby face of a boy of seventeen.

Epila, even in peace-time, is remote from the tourist route, which is just as well, as I suspect that the Easter services might tend to reinforce the usual prejudices against Latin Catholicism. I should not like one of those reverent agnostics, who generally behave more correctly in Catholic churches than Catholics, to have been my companion at Epila. Professor Julian Huxley, who writes with such nice feeling about the God in whom he does not believe, and who takes off his hat with the same gentlemanly gesture to a funeral and to a creed, would have been disgusted by the rattles and irritated by the little children swarming in the pulpit – and, above all, disconcerted by the vitality of a creed which is "such an unconscionably long time dying."

The painted tomb, the bushy beards and the rattles are no doubt distressing to a severe taste, but at least they are the by-products of an organic and living religion. I found the same note of undisciplined vitality in the Anglo-Catholic Church of St. Saviour's, Hoxton. There, too, little children swarmed in and out of the church with imperturbable unself-consciousness. True religion, as Tyrrell somewhere remarks, cannot be manufactured; it grows. It is the product, not of committees who are agreed on a formula, but of life which is impatient of formulæ. The fantastic colonnades of the painted tomb at Epila have their own place in the scheme of a living faith, and fit as naturally into the outward expression of that faith as the Porte Royale at Chartres or the glories of Seville Cathedral.

I went out into the April sunshine and I remembered Mattins in the days of my youth. *Paterfamilias* breathing decorously into his top hat while the vicar tuned in for the "Dearly beloved." A few nervous late-comers tiptoeing timidly into their pews. No rattles, no cautionary advice to the spitters, and no devout women kneeling with outstretched arms in the aisles. And I saw the Catholic Church as the natural home not only of those who feel no temptation to spit in their own drawing-rooms, but also of those who can with difficulty be prevailed upon not to spit in church. And I was glad to remember that within that household there is a friendly welcome, not only for the devout minority, but also for the undevout majority who begin to edge out of church at the *Ite Missa est*, and who seem to think that the response *Deo gratias* should be translated, "Well, thank God, that's over."

II

Corporate prayer is little more than a phrase in times of peace. It is difficult to pray and easy to let the mind wander. Even in congregations which are exceptionally devout, corporate prayer, in the proper sense of the term, is exceptional. Different people pray for different things.

I well remember the first time on which I was really conscious of the authentic atmosphere of corporate prayer. It was in a cathedral at Munich at a time of grave anxiety for Catholics. Priests had been imprisoned, and the Catholic schools had been threatened. A good many of that congregation in Munich would have been present at a Sunday Mass because it was their duty, but this was a weekday Benediction, and every one of those who passed in from the streets to the cathedral had come to pray. And in their responses one heard the convincing accents of anxious prayer. I have heard those accents since – many times. In Burgos and Seville during the Spanish War, in London since the outbreak of hostilities, I have felt this moving sense of a congregation held by a common grief, a common determination and a common hope. *When the Devil was sick, the Devil a saint would be*. I know. But is it really surprising that children at play should forget their mother, or so shocking that a child who falls and hurts himself should run to his mother for comfort? *Illos tuos misericordes oculos ad nos converte.* Which she does.

Persecution is the native air of the Church, a fact which we forget because we wish to forget it. There is no century in the Christian era which has not enriched the Christian martyrology, no country which has been wholly free from persecution. At the best the Church can only hope for an uneasy truce.

There was a time when I was perplexed by the fact that there are so few prayers of thanksgiving in the Catholic liturgy. The mood of sorrow and anxiety dominates the prayers of the Church; but is this really so surprising? The first Mass was said on the eve of Calvary, and our liturgy developed in the ages of persecution. Sorrow is the native climate of the Church. Prayers of thanksgiving are seldom as convincing as prayers of supplication. Only a saint could have written St. Francis's lyrical song of gratitude for the visible beauty of the world, but a great sinner wrote the greatest of penitential psalms. Prayer flowers most easily in a climate of sorrow. The greatest prayers and the noblest hymns, Protestant and Catholic alike, are those which were written for times of trial—as, for instance, "Abide With Me," or Charles Wesley's hymn, "Come, O Thou Traveller Unknown."

The Mass, which contains so few phrases of thanksgiving and so little recognition of human happiness, might have been written for times such as these. *Quare me repulisti? et quare tristis incedo, dum affligit me inimicus* (Why dost thou repel me, and why do I walk in sorrow while the enemy afflicts me?) . . . and then the note changes from despair to hope. *Spera in Deo, quoniam adhuc confitebor illi* (Trust in God, for I will yet have faith in him). There is something very human in that "yet."

I was in Seville Cathedral for High Mass on Easter Sunday. It was not only for the Resurrection of our Lord that we gave thanks, but for the survival of one of the noblest shrines in

Christendom. One hundred and eighty-three determined men had held Seville against 2,000 enemies, and, by a miracle of courage and faith, saved the town and cathedral from the destruction which had already transformed some of the loveliest churches in Seville into gutted ruins. When I returned from Spain I wrote: "Burgos, Avila, Salamanca and Seville have a power over the mind of man more potent than the spell of Chartres or St. Mark's. One loves Chartres as Martha loved Lazarus before he died, but one loves Seville as Martha loved Lazarus after he had been raised from the dead. We are always in danger of taking beauty for granted, as if we had a right to Chartres, but in tragic Spain one takes nothing for granted. There is a spring-time freshness about the churches which have been saved, a blended beauty in which the wonder of the past is married to the surprise of a new discovery. For in the things one has almost lost one finds a loveliness which is hidden from the eyes of secure possession."

But to-day it is Chartres and St. Mark's that are in danger, and Seville that is secure. When I heard of the German-Soviet Pact I knew that war was certain, and I went to Venice for four-and-twenty hours to say good-bye to St. Mark's; for though I still hoped and believed that Italy would remain neutral, God alone knows what will remain of Europe's heritage when peace returns to a distracted world.

On the day that war was declared an American priest, Father O'Brien, and I went into Westminster Abbey to say a prayer before the tomb of the Unknown Warrior. "It's tragic to think," said my friend, "that we haven't even evolved a method of insuring shrines such as this from a chance bomb."

III

In the English-speaking world the word "Christianity" is losing its old precise meaning. "You're a Christian" is a compliment to a man's character rather than a definition of his creed, for we are losing all sense of the distinction between "Christian" and "Christ-like." A man who unhesitatingly believes that Jesus Christ was true God and true Man is a Christian, however badly he behaves. Many evil men repeat the creed with conviction and many good men have stumbled over the first article, "I believe in God."

Now, the Church is not only the nursery of saints, but a hospital for sinners, and few errors are more disastrous in their consequences than the attempt to restrict the word "Christian" to the Christ-like. The Catholic Church gives rise to scandal because Neapolitan brigands and Chicago gangsters are often seen at Mass, and a gangster with a Methodist background is never seen at a Methodist class meeting. In her intolerance of fashionable sin, and in her reluctance to repel unfashionable sinners, the Church is in the tradition of One who came to call not the righteous but sinners to repentance. As long as a man continues to believe there is some chance that he may return to the practice of his religion and to the obligations which that religion involves.

The Latin Catholic is more logical than the Anglo-Saxon Christian. He does not cease to believe merely because he has ceased to behave. The Spaniard knows that Christianity does not cease to be true because he himself has ceased to be true to his wife. He cannot understand why he should withhold intellectual assent to a creed because he cannot withhold physical assent to a temptation. A Spaniard whom I knew well once paused during a walk and pointed to a shadowy grove haunted with romantic memories. "I often came here when I was young," he said, "and I can tell you that when spring blossoms, April breezes and the insinuating lilt of that little brook are combined with no mean powers of persuasion, the result is all but inevitable." And then he added regretfully: "But the trouble with us Catholics is that we can't kid ourselves. Sin is sin. Now, your English intellectuals not only seduce their friends' wives, but persuade themselves that their actions are enlightened and progressive and in accordance with the dogma of the new morality. We think that hypocritical."

The Englishman, on the other hand, writes down the Spaniard as hypocritical if he continues to attend Mass while making love to another man's wife. As if there were any reason why a man should disobey those commandments of God which are easy to obey because he finds it difficult to obey those which are difficult. Spaniards are often slack, not only in so far as their code is concerned, but also in the matter of religious observances. The national motto, *Mañana* (To-morrow) is their attitude to the Church. They will return to the *practice* of the Faith – *mañana*. Meanwhile Santiago will put in a good word for them. After all, it is mainly his fault. It was he who asked God that Spanish women should be the loveliest in the world.

"By their fruits ye shall know them." Spanish Catholicism does not fail if judged by this criterion. The Spanish Church has been the nursery of some of the greatest saints in Christendom. It has produced, and still produces, thousands of men and women who have modelled their lives on Christ. It has succeeded in imposing upon Spain a high standard of honour and intellectual integrity. The courage of the Spaniard is related to his vivid sense of the supernatural. As one reads the stories of the Spanish martyrs, laymen no less than priests, one is impressed by their radiant confidence that death is only a door from this life to the next.

I like the story of the Spanish colonel who was waiting with a captain for the firing-party. The executioners, being Spaniards, were late. The colonel turned to the captain with a smile, and said: "They have robbed us of half an hour of heaven."

High standards are of immense value to a society, even if few men live up to them. There is an inevitable lag between the ideals of a society and its average standard of conduct. If those ideals are lowered to adjust them to this average standard, the inevitable lag soon reappears, and the average man falls as far short of the debased as of the lofty standards.

The average Spaniard does not practise what the saints preach, but, unlike our progressives, he does not preach what sinners practise. When he begins to do this he degenerates very rapidly into the sort of thug who murders priests and rapes nuns.

There are few Catholics who find it more difficult to uproot the Catholicism in their souls than the Spaniard. Do what he will, he remains a child of the Catholic culture.

The Church has learned by experience that a Catholic who retains nothing more of his faith than a mere reflex action, such as a genuflection, is more likely to return, if only in the hour of death, than those who have retained nothing.

Most of the Republicans asked for priests before they faced a firing squad, and such requests were not inspired by cowardice, but by that intuition of truth which comes to all men in the hour of death. The lamp of faith may burn low in the Spanish soul, but it is seldom extinguished, and it is often rekindled by persecution into an heroic flame.

CHAPTER XXIII

Shadow over Austria

I WAS in Rome when Hitler marched into Austria. That night I dined at the English College. During dinner I was asked to take a personal call from St. Anton am Arlberg.

"It's Mrs. Wolf," said an agitated voice. "I've got to be very careful. Please be careful what you say. They've arrested Schneider. Isn't it terrible? Be careful what you say because I'm sure there is somebody listening in who will report everything we say. I've told them that I'm sure you will cancel the Arlberg–Kandahar, but do be careful. . . ."

I took Mrs. Wolf's advice, and confined myself to saying that I would leave Rome next morning for St. Anton.

Hannes Schneider, the founder of the famous Arlberg School, was perhaps the most outstanding personality in the world of ski-ing. I first met him in 1928. At that time I had not yet carried to a successful conclusion the campaign for the international recognition of downhill and slalom racing, and I realised that Schneider's personality and co-operation would ensure the success of an international meeting of downhill ski racing. In 1929 I founded the Arlberg-Kandahar at St. Anton, one year before downhill racing had been recognised by the Congress at Oslo. The Arlberg-Kandahar achieved instantaneous success, and victory in this event was regarded as the blue riband of Alpine ski-ing.

In the *British Ski Year Book* for 1936 I wrote as follows of Hannes Schneider:

"And then, of course, there is Hannes. Perhaps it is the personality of Hannes which is more responsible than any other single factor for the A-K atmosphere. The ten years that have passed since Walter Bernays introduced me to Hannes have only served to deepen my respect and affection for this paladin of ski-ing. He dominates St. Anton, not only in virtue of his outstanding success as a teacher and his great record as an active ski-er, but by force of his engaging personality. His leadership is a leadership of character, and there is a granite-like integrity about the man which is unaffected by the vacillations of political fashion."

I stayed the night in beloved Innsbruck. I had known the imperial Innsbruck of the Hapsburgs. There was a mellow glory in the Indian summer of the Hapsburg Empire, and some afterglow from its autumn colouring lingered on in post-war Austria.

Externally Innsbruck had changed but little. The soft radiance of a full moon flooded the mountain background of one of the loveliest of European streets. The town was beflagged for its own funeral, for the swastika was omnipresent on the coffin of Austrian civilisation. Meanwhile the Tyrolese were learning the salute. I stopped for a few minutes to watch them pass two Nazi guards. A few, a very few, saluted them joyously and acknowledged their slave status with delight, but most of these salutes were awkward and perfunctory, and I was glad to see two Tyrolese stop when they had passed and laugh contemptuously and bitterly at the sorry spectacle. Hitler received a noisy welcome from Austrian Nazis, but where the opposition is cowed and silenced and driven behind doors, a minority demonstrating in the streets can convey the impression of a solid and enthusiastic citizenship.

The moonlit palace recalled an old memory. At the World Championship the officials and captains of the various teams had been entertained at a tea-party by the President. We sat down at a large table in a banqueting-hall, and suddenly the President rose to his feet. We all stood up respectfully as the head of the Austrian State left the room. We were perplexed by his sudden and abrupt departure. What was wrong? From where I was standing I could see him through an open door dash down the corridor, halt a retreating waiter in his tracks, remove a box of cigars which the waiter was carrying and return in triumph to his seat. We all sat down again while the President offered his next-door neighbour a smoke. In 1936 I travelled with the President in his private carriage from Seefeld to Innsbruck. He could not have been simpler or less formal. The Austrian Nazis explained contemptuously that Miklas had been elected president as the only way of providing for his vast family of twelve. He was a devout Catholic and an enthusiastic student of Thomistic theology. The main subject of his conversation during that journey was the best means of applying Thomistic principles to the social problems of his country.

We walked down to the river and looked at the moonlit mountains reversed in the flowing waters of the Inn. Somewhere behind those mountains lay Garmisch, where I had spent a happy summer in pre-war days. And as I looked at those mountains I remembered an evening in 1910, the scent of mown hay and the moon rising beyond the Zugspitze, and singing voices from a neighbouring inn, and I was overcome by an intolerable longing for the old Germany, the Germany that gave us words like *Wanderlust* and *gemütlich*, the Germany in which there was room, not only for Prussian officers, but also for dreamy idealists and unpractical professors, the old type of *Gelehrter*—poor, but immensely respected, unlike the new type of *Gelehrter*, the unwilling exponent of Nazi history, who is even poorer and who is losing the respect, not only of his neighbours, but of himself.

I still take with me on my travels a little pocket Goethe's *Faust* which used to live in my rucksack, and which evokes memories of quiet evenings outside Alpine huts, and of old walled cities in Germany, such as Nuremberg, which once whispered from their towers the last enchantments of the Middle Ages, and which now re-echo to rococo rhetoric of the Nazi Party days. I looked at the swift-flowing river and consoled myself with the thought that all things pass, and that death comes, not only to what we love, but to what we hate. Hitler is not the first conqueror to have crossed the bridge of the Inn, and will not be the last. Others before him have created some commotion in the imperial valley. The Romans have gone, the Corsican has gone, the Hapsburgs have gone. The Nazis will go.

Of these our strong posterity will say,
Lord Jesus, what are these to us?
The wind has blown them all away.

I caught an early train to St. Anton next morning, and called a meeting of the British and American members of the Kandahar Ski Club who were present at St. Anton. The proposal to cancel the race was carried without opposition so far as the members of the Club were concerned. The only criticism emanated from a non-member who could not understand why a race in which he wished to compete should be cancelled.

"Cancelling the race won't do Schneider any good," he remarked plaintively, to which Palmer-Tomkinson, the captain of the British team, gave the entirely adequate reply:

"No; and it didn't do the King any good when we cancelled the Duke of Kent's Cup on the death of King George, but it would have done us a lot of harm if we hadn't."

After the meeting I called on poor Frau Schneider. I did not, of course, ring the bell and walk in at the front door. One does not do that kind of thing in Russia or in Germany. I crept in at the back door. She was relieved to learn that we had cancelled the race, and that removed my last doubt as to the wisdom of our action. She told me that Hannes had been arrested in the early hours of the morning and taken straight from his bed to the prison at Landeck. "I am glad he is not here," she added; "he had such pride in the school which he created. It would have broken his heart to have to continue working in the school if somebody else had been put above his head."

I looked through the window and saw the Nazi flag flying from the house across the road – the swastika on a red background. There had not been time to buy or manufacture enough swastika flags to go round, so the Arlbergers just cut the old Austrian flag (red and white) in two pieces, discarded the white half and sewed a swastika to the red half.

"I would not fly that flag from my house," said Frau Schneider.

I crept out of the back door and walked down the street to see my old friend Gomperz. In pre-war days he rendered immense services to the Mid-European Ski Association, to which he gave a thousand pounds and of which he had been president. Gomperz and Bernays, another Jew, had devoted themselves with single-minded enthusiasm to the Arlberg School. Bernays was a genuine fanatic with a dog-like devotion to Schneider. He had no financial interest whatever in St. Anton, but had proved a generous donor to the Club.

I walked into the Kurverein office and found Gomperz hard at work. "My poor old friend, these are tragic times," I said.

"Oh, that's all right," he replied in a flat tone; "it's not too bad, thank you. Everybody has been most kind to me. They say: 'You are a Jew, but you have worked for St. Anton for twenty-eight years and you are still a poor man. Of course you must go, but we shall pay you a month's salary, and we want you to stop on for the Arlberg-Kandahar race, for you know the ropes. Only, of course, you must not put in a public appearance at the race or at the prize-giving.' That is all right, because I would not wish to stop on in St. Anton if I could possibly get work in another country. You see, I have been here so long, and it is not nice for me to think that my two sons, of whom I am very fond, would not be allowed to bathe in the bathing-pool, and would have to sit on another bench in the school from the other boys. That would make me unhappy. But now we must get down to our work together and discuss the organisation of the Arlberg–Kandahar."

I told him our decision, and he made a protest.

"All right," I said, "I will tell everybody that you did your best to persuade me to hold the Arlberg-Kandahar as if nothing had happened."

He shook me warmly by the hand. "Thank you; that is most kind – thank you."

On the way back to the Post Hotel I saw a sight which saddened me. Two Arlberg ski-ers met in the road, sheepishly murmured "*Heil Hitler*," and gave each other the Hitler salute. I knew those boys. They had been ardent Austrian patriots and bitterly anti-Nazi. But they did not quite trust each other, so, though they were friends, they submitted to the humiliation of greeting each other with a lie on their lips.

I have followed down the mountainside a stretcher on which lay the body of a friend killed among the mountains, and I have seen wounded men in dressing-stations. Neither death nor wounds rob the body of dignity, but there is no dignity in a wounded soul. There is, indeed, a squalid nastiness about the climate of terrorism which must be experienced to be believed.

The Nazis confuse two things which are totally different – power prestige and quality prestige. Power prestige is imposed and quality prestige is conceded. The bully, the Russian Ogpu and the Nazi Gestapo have power prestige. The Italy of St. Francis was full of petty tyrants, but who remembers them today? Power prestige is ephemeral, but St. Francis is a living force to-day. Periclean Athens and the Germany of Goethe had quality prestige, but Sparta and the Germany of Hitler had power prestige. Aristotle and Plato and Goethe will endure; Hitler's power will go the way of Sparta's.

No man who had any sense of ultimate values would derive the least satisfaction from those robot movements of the arm which are the tributes paid by the terrorised to the terrorist. The Nazi régime can compel the Austrian peasants to move their arms in salute, but it is in the power of no dictator to compel that very different type of arm movement which provided the central incident in one of the stormier episodes of John Wesley's life.

An angry mob had seized Wesley, for this was in the days when Methodism was almost as unpopular in England as Catholicism was in Republican Spain during the Spanish War, and when he asked leave to speak they cried out: "No, no; knock his brains out! Down with him! Kill him at once!"

A "lusty" man struck at Wesley and a "turbulent rascal" forced his way through the press, raised his arm to strike and "on a sudden let it drop, and only stroked my head, saying: 'What soft hair he has!' "

A prize-fighter rescued Wesley, and was converted instantaneously from a thug to a chivalrous knight. "Sir," he exclaimed, "I will spend my life for you; follow me and not one soul here shall touch a hair of your head." The prize-fighter became a Methodist. According to his own words, he knew that Wesley was "a man of God; and God was on his side, when so many of us could not kill one man."

Which is the greater tribute, the arm raised to salute Hitler or the arm raised to strike and dropped in unconscious homage to Wesley? Unlike our modern dictators, Wesley had no need of a bodyguard, or of that bullet-proof glass through which Hitler addresses his faithful subjects. Wesley was protected by the armour of quality prestige.

* * *

After lunch I interviewed Herr Moser, the new Burgomeister of St. Anton. Moser had been a ski teacher under Schneider, and had been expelled from the Arlberg School for Nazi propaganda. Schneider himself was no politician and did not take an active part in the anti-Nazi campaign. He was first and foremost a ski-er, and he did not tolerate the intrusion of politics into his ski school. Moser, whose personality did not attract me, began by reproaching me for mixing up politics with sport.

"I hear you want to cancel the race. Your only reason for cancelling it is political."

I asked him if Schneider was in prison because he ski-ed badly or because his politics did not commend themselves to the authorities, and then Moser became abusive.

"You have no right to cancel this race. We have spent a lot of money on it. It is your duty to hold it."

He was puzzled, poor man, by my odd reaction to the fact that the man with whom I had founded this race had been ejected from his school and thrust into prison. I explained to him that I understood his point of view. "Nazis race out of what they call *Pflichtgefühl* (sense of duty), inspired by keen sense of duty and loyalty to their Führer. We English still race for fun. We came to St. Anton in the old days because we liked the old atmosphere, and we propose to leave," I added, "because we don't like the new atmosphere. It was fun to race here when St. Anton was Austrian. It would not be fun to race here now that St. Anton is German."

He scowled. "You are trying to bring pressure to bear on us to release Schneider. We shan't yield to pressure. On the contrary, if you cancel the race the consequences will probably be very serious for Schneider."

The hostage argument. There are, as I pointed out, some things which weigh with us even more than the effect of our action on Schneider. We owe a duty to our Club, to the tradition of British sport and to ourselves. To hold the race when one of its founders was in prison for no reason would be an indecency.

"Well, anyhow," Moser continued, "you can't prevent us calling the race the Arlberg-Kandahar, and we shall do so."

"No, I can't prevent you," I said. "If you raced three donkeys round a field near St. Anton and described the event as the Derby, the Jockey Club would be powerless to interfere."

After our discussion I telegraphed to Reichssportsführer von Tschammer und Osten and asked him to prevent the Arlberg Club from appropriating the name of a Kandahar race for one of their local events. The German sport leader was an old type of Prussian aristocrat, rather uneasy in his present surroundings, who could be relied upon to be correct, and he gave the necessary instructions that the races which were to be held next Saturday were to be described as the "First Arlberg Race," and the winner received a thermos flask decorated with a swastika.

I left next morning, and I was glad to go. The train was detained for three hours at the frontier while suspects were searched for smuggled money and jewels. We were all turned out of our carriages and formed up into a queue to wait our turn for examination. A Nazi with two days' growth of beard was standing in front of a big poster on which was written *Der Deutsche Grüss heisst Heil Hitler.*

"You people," I said to him, "may be pleased about the *Anschluss*, but you are not half as pleased as the Swiss hotel-keepers. They are delighted. There is nothing like making English ski-ers stand for three hours in a queue in order to ensure that they will not return to your country."

This pleased the crowd, but it did not please the Nazi. I began to sing the famous Grindelwald song, and I sang it very loud and clear. The enjoyment of the crowd was highly offensive to the officials, who were alarmed, for they did not know exactly what to do. The Nazi system cracks when confronted by a situation which cannot be solved with a prod of the bayonet. At least I saved myself a long wait in the queue. I was hurriedly taken into a little room for examination. The first question was characteristically inept — in fact, a museum piece of Prussian officialdom: "Jews have been smuggling jewellery in the train lavatory. Have you seen anything of this?" Such is my love of solitude that I never share that part of a train with anybody. I allowed a remark to this effect to sink in, and then added that even if I had seen Jews smuggling *valuta* I should not have reported them.

"Even if you had seen Jews smuggling," he repeated with solemn astonishment, "you would not have reported it. Why not?"

The bewilderment of that *Warum nicht* was rather touching. The existence of people who were not ready to co-operate with officials in the discharge of their official duties perplexed him.

I came out of that little room and he did not seem anxious to detain me. I caught sight of some people who had been detained, and I shall not easily forget their expressions of blank despair. As the train steamed out of Feldkirch even those who had nothing to fear sighed with relief. In the old days I had always left Austria with regret, but in this new Austria the very air that one breathed seemed infected by cruelty.

As the train drew into Buchs we saw a flag which, like the Nazi flag, had a red background, with, like the Nazi flag, a cross in the middle; not the swastika cross, the symbol of oppression, but the cross with an older tradition which will still stand for freedom when Hitler and all he stands for has passed away.

After a long period of "protective arrest," Hannes Schneider, thanks to the intervention of influential friends in England and elsewhere, was allowed to leave the country for the States. It is only fair to state that he was treated with consideration by the high officials in Berlin, and might perhaps have been allowed to return to St. Anton but for the attitude of the Austrian Nazis. He was succeeded at St. Anton by Salcher, a university graduate who had failed in more than one profession before devoting his energies to the nazification of Austria. Salcher is a fine ski-er who has won the coveted A–K badge.

In the course of 1938 the Kandahar Ski Club decided that the race should be re-christened the Alpine Kandahar, and that the famous A-K badge awarded to those who finished in the first three places should be retained. I had designed this badge, which was bordered with the Kandahar colours. Early in 1939 Salcher wrote and asked if I would meet him on my way through to the World Championship in Poland. I replied that if he craved to travel with me from St. Anton to Innsbruck I would be glad to give him my views.

As the train drew into St. Anton I caught a glimpse of the slope on which Hannes and I had set the first slalom ever seen in the Arlberg, and I saw the corner of a road on which I had met Audrey Sale Barker, radiant with happiness, for she had just learned of her victory in the Ladies' Arlberg-Kandahar. And the ghost of dear old Hannes Schneider still haunted the platform where he had so often welcomed me in the days when St. Anton was Austrian.

Salcher boarded the train wearing an A-K badge.

I knew that St. Anton had been virtually boycotted by British and American ski-ers, and that Salcher would make every effort to persuade the Kandahar to hold the Arlberg-Kandahar in St. Anton. He hoped that the restoration of friendly relations between the Kandahar and Arlberg clubs would be accepted as a symbol of ski-ing appeasement, in which case British pounds and American dollars would return to St. Anton, to be converted, no doubt, in due course, into guns. Salcher was friendly but critical. It seemed he was disappointed in me. He had always regarded me as a man who did not mix politics with sport, and yet here I was allowing political considerations to ruin the greatest of all races. Salcher had forgotten that *Das Schwarze Korps* * had referred with contempt to *Diesen guten Leute die noch mit einem Beinem in dem liberalischen Glauben stecken, Sport habe mit Politik nichts zu tun* (These good people who still have one foot in the liberal faith that sport has nothing to do with politics).

Our conversation took place in a crowded restaurant car. Our fellow-travellers at other tables seemed interested in my views of the Nazi régime, so I was at some pains to say what I had to say as clearly as possible. I repeated the substance of our conversation in a letter from Mürren dated March 2, 1939, in which I wrote as follows:

"You tell me that you are anxious that ski-ing at St. Anton should not be political. But words cannot alter facts. As your own Goethe has said:

> *. . . Eben wo Begriffe fehlen*
> *Da stellt ein Wort zur rechten Zeit sich ein.*†

Schneider has been driven out of St. Anton by political opponents. You owe your position not only to your merits as a ski-er, but to the fact that, as a member of the S.S., you played a prominent part in transforming what remained of Imperial Austria into *Gau* 18. The Arlberg Club, as I knew it, no longer exists. In the old days it was a club, as we understand the term, which controlled its own fixtures and elected its own officers. To-day it is a section of the German Imperial Association for Bodily Exercises (*Fachamt Skilauf*). You told me that Baron Le Fort would postpone the date of this year's Arlberg races if I would agree to hold the A-K in St. Anton. The dates of your fixtures are thus determined, not by your club, but by a German whose head office is Berlin. The old atmosphere of the A–K, unpolitical and light-hearted, can be preserved if the race

* October 27, 1938.

† This may be paraphrased: "Verbiage helps to conceal a failure to understand."

alternates between Switzerland and France. All that would remain would be the name if we held it at St. Anton. The Arlberg–Kandahar, like the great German universities and the Salzburg festival, would join the melancholy list of lifeless ghosts:

Sie waren lang gestorben,
*Und wussten es selber kaum.**

I hope I may still quote without offence the greatest of German lyric poets, the Jew, Heinrich Heine.

"You attributed my views to my alleged hatred of Germany. My father was knighted by the King and decorated by the Kaiser for his work in connection with Anglo-German friendship. I went into Germany just after the Armistice and wrote against a vindictive peace. As a boy I never travelled or climbed without a pocket 'Goethe.' I loved the old Germany, and I admire many aspects of the marvellous recovery which Germany has made under Hitler's leadership. And there is nothing in this letter with which the overwhelming majority of Germans, who are sick and ashamed of *Der Stürmer* and all that it stands for, would not agree.

"You were good enough to pay me compliments as the creator of the world's greatest downhill race, and you reproached me for imperilling its future. But even if the A-K were to come to an end, I should not for one moment regret the decision of our Club. All evil, a great thinker once remarked, comes from mistaking means for ends. Sport is not an end in itself, but a means to an end, and that end is the promotion of friendship, tolerance and that spirit which your Christian forbears called chivalry, and which the Greeks called *aidos*. '*Aidos*,' writes Mr. Gardner, 'is the direct opposite of *hubris*. It is the feeling of respect for what is due to the gods, to one's fellow-men, to oneself – a feeling that begets a like feeling towards oneself in others. It is the spirit of reverence, of mod-

* "They were long dead, and did not know it."

esty or courtesy. Above all, it is the sense of honour, and as such inspires the athlete and the soldier and distinguishes them from the bully and the oppressor.'

"It is because ski-ing in Germany is controlled by a government which encourages the bully and the oppressor, a government which has no *aidos*, and far too much *hubris*, that I, for one, would have only agreed to return to St. Anton under present conditions to help an old friend, Hannes Schneider.

"One's decision in such matters is determined by one's scale of values. I do not attach any particular importance to the fact that I founded a successful race. If that race were to disappear I should feel less proud of having created it than of having sacrificed it on the altar of ideals which belong to the heritage of European civilisation. You are, in effect, inviting me to sacrifice my principles to my vanity, and I can only reply in the words of one who led an earlier German revolution: *Hier stehe ich und kann nicht anders.*

"The Arlberg Club has degenerated into an Arlberg section of a German government office, and yet you still use the same badge. I recently met an English scientist who was studying at a famous German university which included Nobel prize-winners on its staff. The Nobel prize-winners had been expelled and the presidency offered to a brown-shirted philistine whose contribution to culture was an attempt to impose on the university those racial theories which provoke the derisive contempt of every scholar outside Germany, and fill with shame those German scholars who have not succeeded in escaping to countries where culture is not in chains. And yet the German universities have not yet changed the Doctors' robes which once inspired respect throughout the world. If we do change this badge we may perhaps substitute for the symbolic mountains an outline of Mont Blanc. Shelley's lines might serve as a motto:

> Thou hast a voice, great Mountain, to repeal
> Large codes of fraud and woe. . . .

"I am anxious not to break all bridges to St. Anton. Things are changing in Germany. The German kindliness and chivalry is reasserting itself. And the day may come when the Kandahar can again co-operate with an emancipated Arlberg Club in the Arlberg–Kandahar. But that day has not yet come. I recently met, not far from Bern, a German paying a short visit to this country. He held a position of some importance in Germany, and at first he was cautious and reserved. And then suddenly he broke into passionate invective against the Englishman who supports the present system in Germany by continuing to visit Germany. 'Your young people,' he said, 'are often very naïve. They admire our police and the order in our streets, and have not enough imagination to see the horrors of Dachau behind the façade of friendly welcome to any foreigner who brings money into the country. We still have effective laws for the prevention of cruelty to animals, but no law for the prevention of cruelty to Jews. The Jew is an outlaw at the mercy of any young hooligan. The fact that the English stayed away from Austria last winter is producing a reaction in favour of humanity. Believe me, you can best help those of us who are trying to save what can still be saved of the Germany of Goethe by staying away from the Germany of Goebbels.'

"Hannes is in exile, Niemöller in prison, and Streicher at liberty. Why, then, should we return to St. Anton? But nothing lasts for ever, not even *Der Stürmer*, and one day I shall come back to the country I love, and Hannes and I will once again set an A-K slalom in St. Anton. Till then, *Au revoir*."

The Arlberg–Kandahar controversy had its lighter side. I was pleased by an article in the leading Viennese newspaper to the effect that I had removed the cup from St. Anton because I was jealous of Lord Londonderry for giving a cup to the "German ski sport"; and flattered by the paragraph which appeared in a French paper, announcing that "*Lord Arnold Lund avait décidé que les courses de chevaux pour la Coupe Kandahar n'auraient plus lieu à St. Anton am Arlberg mais à Chamonix.*"

CHAPTER XXIV

"The Switzers Last Well"

We see the Switzers last well in spite of their diversity of religion and of canton. For utility is their bond and not respect.

— BACON

MY wife wanted to join us, but I thought we had better dine alone, as we have so much to discuss."

My friend, a member of the Swiss Nationalrat, spared me the customary ritual of polite protest. "You are a half Swiss," he said, "and you understand."

Nearly fifty years have passed since I first visited Switzerland. As a boy I spent all my summers and most of my winters in the Alps. As a man I lived there continuously for many years, and I am just beginning to understand this inscrutable mountain race. If I had spent a week or two in Zermatt, or two or three weeks on the shores of Lake Lucerne in summer; if I had had three or four seasons of ski-ing on the Parsenn or in the Oberland, I should know the Swiss very well indeed. If I had, in addition, visited Vienna and had ski-ed at pre-Nazi St.

Anton, I should know enough about the Austrians to contrast their charm with the more prosaic and worthy virtue of the Swiss. If I had any ambition to make an impression on the intelligentsia, I should, of course, avoid the gaucherie of discovering beauty in any view accessible to trippers. To Goethe, Schiller, Byron, and Shelley, Lucerne was as romantic as Pæstum or Argos to a modern poet. Indeed, Shelley, when he ran away from his wife, could conceive of no spot more romantic than Brunnen for an illicit honeymoon, that same Brunnen, on the shore of Lake Lucerne, through which the modern poet hurries rapidly on his way to the Italy of his dreams. Fashions change, and it is no longer correct to admire Switzerland. Politicians, however, often refer to the "model democracy" of Switzerland. This little country where different races live together in harmony provides the ground-plan on which the United States of Europe will be constructed.

Few words are more loosely used in the modern world than "democratic." Britain is a democracy in the correct sense of the word, but the social structure is still feudal and aristocratic. Italy and Germany are dictatorships and anti-democratic, and they are also anti-aristocratic. Mussolini, indeed, has recently issued instructions that the popular *voi* should be substituted for the old courteous, aristocratic method of address, *lei.* "I bridle with rage," an Italian aristocrat remarked to me, "every time a douanier addresses me as *voi*, and I make a point of scrupulously replying with *lei.*"

Hereditary titles are still sometimes used by survivors of the old feudal aristocracy of Switzerland. They have no legal status, and there is an increasing tendency for such titles to disappear from social usage. Fifty years ago aristocratic families of Bern and Zurich intermarried within a restricted circle and were as exclusive as the grandees of Spain. An aristocrat of Bern was once presented to the last Austrian Emperor. "Our families," said the Emperor patronisingly, "were very good friends many centuries ago." To this the Bern aristocrat replied: "In the old days our family had no more faithful vassals than the Hapsburgs."

The old Swiss aristocrats, though they still take themselves seriously, have long abandoned all pretensions in their relations with their fellow-countrymen. There is not and never has been in Switzerland the equivalent of the social gossip-writers in our own press. The whole bias of Swiss life is against pretensions and display. No Swiss official may receive a decoration from a foreign government, and no provision has been made for any medal or other decoration in the event of war. This contempt for what Burke somewhere calls "the solemn plausibilities of this world" has its roots in Swiss tradition.

In the sixteenth century the ruling families of Davos and the district sent their proconsuls and prætors to administer the wealthy Italian provinces over which the Grisons ruled. The strategic importance of the Valtelline was recognised by Austria, Spain and France, and their diplomatists intrigued for the support of the republicans of the Grisons. Ambassadors left Davos to negotiate with crowned heads. The noble families of Davos, the Buols, Gulers and Sprechers, were knighted and ennobled by kings. Their portraits were painted in armour or in the dress of ambassadors. They were men of great culture, writing an elegant and easy Latin. All this we know from contemporary records, but Davos itself bears no witness to these ancient glories. We find none of the customary signs of vanished splendour which we expect to find in any country once ruled by a great nobility. There are no ruined castles or stately halls at Davos. The nobles of Davos, though they exercised the reality of power, were careful to mask it under a republican simplicity. "For a Buol, a Sprecher or a Guler," writes Symonds, "to display in Davos, at the centre of government, the luxury or elegance to which he was accustomed elsewhere would have awakened the suspicions of the jealous mountaineers."

Political democracy is not inconsistent with a profound if unformulated faith in the virtue of the aristocratic principle. Many Swiss peasants have coats of arms and pedigrees which can be traced back to the Middle Ages, and have more right to be described as aristocrats than the self-made millionaire who buys a peerage. The mountain peasant is the most conservative of men, and his democracy finds place both for tradition and for hierarchy. The hierarchy of the mountain valley may be instinctive rather than formal, but it implies, none the less, a profound respect for the representatives of families which have played their part in village life generation after generation. It would, indeed, be naïve to assume that, because the Swiss talk so freely of democracy, a Taugwalder at Zermatt, an Almer at Grindelwald or an Anderegg at Meiringen has no more influence in his valley than newcomers.

During the Boer War a meeting was held at Meiringen to collect money for the Boers. The Swiss naturally sympathised, as did many Englishmen, with the Boer farmers fighting for their independence.

Melchior Anderegg, the greatest guide in his day, listened in silence until all those present had signified their enthusiastic approval of the proposal. He then remarked quietly: "The idea is not altogether stupid, but if we collect money for the Boers we must first collect money to repay the English for helping to rebuild Meiringen after the fire." There was no more talk of collections for the Boers or for the English.

"We Swiss," said a friend of mine, a member of the Swiss Parliament, "love to talk about democracy, but a Socialist workman in Bern would never touch his hat to a rich shopkeeper, but would take his hat off to a surviving member of the old Bern aristocracy.

"Every adult inhabitant of Grindelwald has a vote, and in theory are all equal before the law, but if a newcomer to Grindelwald tried to treat a Steuri or a Borhen as an equal he would soon learn the limits of Swiss democracy. You have got to live in one of these valleys for at least forty years before they stop treating you as a stranger."

"I have been here nearly fifty years," I remarked hopefully.

"Yes, but even that wouldn't do you much good if a Swiss paper hadn't christened you the Ski Pope. As it is, if they see you running to catch the funicular with your hat falling off and your pocket-book falling out, they will bring back the funicular into the station if it has started, and wait until you find your pocket-book, because you are only a silly old professor who has made no money, but who has invented the slalom. But if the King of Spain arrived on the platform a second late they would take great pleasure in sending the train off on the stroke of time, so as to have the chance of telling him that in democratic Switzerland trains don't wait for kings."

A few weeks after this talk I was on my way to the Gornergrat, when the train stopped rather suddenly at a small station below the Gornergrat. I was thinking of something else and jumped out on to the platform, and did not realise my mistake until the train had left. Just as the train was disappearing round a corner, the guard put his head out of the window and asked: "Did you really mean to get out here?"

"No," I shouted back.

The guard stopped the train and brought it back to the little wayside station, and I resumed my journey. Such is the reward for having invented the slalom.

The Swiss are less affected by the glamour of royalty or of titles than any other people. I remember helping the Queen of the Belgians to choose a pair of ski. The owner of the shop was a friend of mine, so I took him aside and said: "When the Queen comes into your shop you might remove one of your hands from your pockets. I admit that to remove both would be undemocratic."

"Oh, I thought," was the delightful answer, "that the Queen

was travelling incognito, and I wanted to make her feel at home."

The Swiss are realistic in their attitude to royalty. They understand the value of eminent people as guests in an hotel, but in their personal judgement they draw the old feudal distinction between the man and his office. The Swiss who knew him loved and reverenced King Albert of the Belgians, not because he was a King, but because on every ground he merited respect and affection. They admired the heroic rôle which he had played in the defence of his country's independence. They thought of him less as a king than as a mountaineer, who was never happier than when sharing the risks and responsibilities of guideless climbing. His favourite companions among the mountains were Swiss amateurs such as my friends Walter Amstutz and Godi Michel. He was a discerning judge of men, and he knew and loved the Swiss. He was more at home with the peerage of mountaineers than in the atmosphere of courts. He enjoyed telling the story of an unsophisticated Swiss chambermaid who had looked after him when he had spent a night in Room 27 of an unpretentious mountain inn. Next year when he returned to the same inn he was welcomed with enthusiasm by the chambermaid. "You are – " she began; then she hesitated, for this big, genial-looking man was, she knew, a king, and she had not the least idea how she ought to refer to kings, and so she continued: "*Sie sind der Herr von Nummer sieben-und-zwanzig.*"

"How much easier my life would be if I were always known as the *Herr* from Room 27!" observed the King.

Prefixes such as *Herr Nationalrat* (Mr. Member of Parliament) are more common among the Swiss than among ourselves, but the Swiss are as little overawed by such prefixes as by foreign titles. Politicians have less power and less prestige than in any other European country. No Swiss paper would publish gossip about leading politicians, their wives and daughters, and if they did no Swiss would read such gossip. No Swiss legislator would ever think of referring to his Parliament as the "best club in Switzerland." The President of the Confederation draws a salary of about £1,000 a year, and this small salary is not compensated for by a great prestige. If you ask the average Swiss for the name of his President, he will scratch his head and murmur: "How silly of me! The name is on the tip of my tongue. . . . Oh yes, of course." And he will then probably give you the name of somebody who was President three or four years ago. There is no country where the business of government is carried on with so little pomp and ceremony, with so complete an absence of corruption and with so much quiet efficiency. Go into the Café du Théâtre at Bern any evening, and you will probably see two or three Swiss Cabinet Ministers puffing away at their long cigars and consuming their glasses of beer. Nobody pays them any particular attention. Their only reward is the consciousness of performing a public service in as unostentatious a fashion as possible.

The British Minister in Bern once remarked to me that he had just learnt that the Swiss President was spending his summer holidays in London. He sent a message to the President asking him if he wished to be received by the King, who would naturally be delighted to entertain him at lunch. The President replied that he was honoured by this invitation, but he added that – in effect – that sort of thing was not very much in his line, and he begged to be excused.

Pomp and circumstance were always suspect to the mountain Swiss. Not for nothing had they fought and defeated the Burgundians and the Hapsburgs. It would have been dangerous for a Swiss noble to assume the trappings of aristocracy. He would promptly have been suspected of the design for a personal or oligarchical rule. This democratic distrust of aristocracy survives unchanged in modern Switzerland. I remember joining a group of friends round a board in an hotel on which the results of an important international race had just been posted. The eighth name on the list was a certain "Bourbon,

Alf," who was known in official circles as H.R.H. Prince Alfonso d'Orléans-Bourbon. I was amused by the "Alf," and made a remark which my Swiss friend misinterpreted. "Of course we leave out the Prince's title," he said; "we are a democratic country."

"That's all right," I answered; "but even so, 'Alf' seems to me to be carrying democracy a little too far, and incidentally I see that Dr. Schmidt has been credited with his title. I am all for simplifying life, but to be logical you must drop all prefixes or allow people the prefixes to which they are entitled."

"The Doktor's title," said my friend, "has to be earned, whereas the Prince's title – *dass kommt aus dem Bett.*"

"But the Doktor's title also 'came out of the bed,' " I replied. "If Dr. Schmidt hadn't possessed brains he wouldn't have been a doctor, and if he had started life in a peasant's cradle he wouldn't have been sent to the university." Prefixes are, as it happens, far more common in Switzerland than in England. In our universities few graduates proceed to the doctor's degree, and few students leave a Swiss university without it. Doctorates are therefore proportionately as common as B.A.'s in England. Moreover, in Switzerland, as in Germany, the wives take their husbands' academic titles. The wife of a doctor is *Frau Doktor* and the wife of a member of Parliament is *Frau Nationalrat.* To the Swiss it seems strange that a Prime Minister and his wife could be known as Mr. and Mrs. Chamberlain.

Such readers as assume that the tourist industry is the most important of Swiss industries, and that the hôteliers are in consequence the most important class in the Confederation, may find nothing surprising in the fact that representatives of the hotel industry should believe themselves entitled to treat as equals a Swiss Cabinet Minister. But in point of fact agriculture ranks ahead of the tourist industry, and the hôteliers are for ever complaining that they have little or no influence in the government. Switzerland is controlled by a peasant oligarchy, by far the most important class in the state. It is, for instance, to the interest of the hotels that food should be cheap in order that the hotels may compete on equal terms with those of the surrounding countries, but it is in the interests, not only of the peasants, so I believe, but of the country as a whole, that agriculture should be protected and that the interests of the peasant should not be sacrificed to the interests of the urban population, or even of the tourist industry.

In our own country the policy of free trade broke down tariff barriers which hindered the payment of interest on foreign loans, interest which returned to England in the shape of foreign food and foreign goods. Free trade was therefore welcomed by the financiers, who cared little that agriculture should suffer as long as London remained the finance capital of the world. Free trade benefited the consumer by lowering the prices of food and of goods, but it depopulated the country-side. Now the Swiss have instinctively realised that it is possible to pay too high a price for cheapness, and they have accordingly protected their peasantry, and thereby arrested the flight from the country to the towns. The cost of living in Switzerland is far higher than in neighbouring countries, not only because the peasant but also because the urban worker is assured a far higher standard of living than in Germany, Italy or France. There is no country of which the Socialists have better reason to despair, for a strong peasantry and a reasonably contented urban population are the best of all guarantees against revolution. Moreover, Switzerland has no great towns, and most of the evils of modern civilisation are generated in the evil atmosphere of giant cities.

Switzerland is the finest example in the world of a Distributist state. "Distributism" is an awkward word for a fine ideal. That property should be widely distributed is, of course, the ideal of all social reformers; but whereas the ideal of the Socialist is a state in which every citizen shall draw a good wage as the employee of a bureaucracy, and shall own a small car, the ideal of the Distributist is a state in which the ratio of those who own their own land or their own small businesses to those who are the employees either of the state or of big businesses shall be as high as possible.

The foundations of modern Switzerland were laid when the first *Landesgemeinde* met in Schwyz in 1294. The assembled people of Schwyz agreed that it should be forbidden to sell land either to monasteries or to strangers outside the valley. This decree established for all time the principle of peasant proprietorship, and marked the first dawn of revolt against absentee landlords, and against the monopoly of land by ecclesiastical corporations.

In Grindelwald, the valley I know best, most of the grazing ground is communal. Every burger of Switzerland has the right to send a fixed quota of cows up to the cattle land. Cheese-making is in the control of a man appointed by the commune who lives throughout the summer in the Alps, and when the Grindelwalders bring their cows, he attends the milking of them by the communal Alp-herd. The amount of cheese to which a Grindelwalder is entitled depends on the amount of milk which his cow or cows produced.

For twelve centuries at least, and probably for longer, the Alps above Grindelwald have borne the names which they bear to-day and have maintained their old boundaries, unaltered and unchanged. During those centuries ministries have been overthrown, and the frontiers of great kingdoms have been thrust forward and driven back, but the Alp-herd has the same placid philosophy of life which he has inherited from the first settlers in these valleys. They know that emperors and kings are accidents of no ultimate importance, and that the fundamentals of life remain unchanged in spite of war and revolution. No revolutions affect the cow, for whatever happens she will return to her pastures in the spring and to the valley in the winter.

As the result of continuous agitation, a few states in America have abolished chain stores. The Swiss quietly, and as a matter of course, put an end to the activities which they instinctively felt were anti-social. The mountain man who has saved up his earnings as a guide to buy a small shop is not going to be deprived of his immemorial privilege of slightly over-charging the tourist by the employees of a chain store owned by foreigners in Bern or Zurich. The word "foreigner" is rather an elastic term in Switzerland, for I have heard the owner of a small shop in Mürren, who came from Lauter-brunnen at the bottom of the Mürren cliff, referred to indig-nantly as a foreigner.

I lived in Grindelwald for years and acquiesced uncomplain-ingly in the admirable system of prices. The highest prices were for tourists, the medium prices were for foreign residents such as the present writer, and the lowest price for the *einheimische*, and the *einheimische* are prepared to pay rather more to the local store than to tolerate the intrusion into the village of a chain store.

"It is the duty of the State," said my friend Mr. von Almen, "to help the poor, but not to run business." The Swiss are uninfected by the heresy that it is the duty of the State to run business and help the politicians. There is no European country which is more hostile to Socialism, and none which has been more successful in solving the problem of social justice or in equalising incomes. A Swiss engine-driver receives a salary equivalent to about four hundred and a Swiss District Judge a salary equivalent to six hundred pounds a year.

The word "democracy" is acquiring a most unpleasant flavour in the modern world. In the English-speaking world it is gradually developing into government of the people by the bureaucrats for the bureaucrats. Where Socialists are in con-trol, as in Soviet Russia, democracy meant government of the people by the crooks for the crooks, but in Switzerland de-mocracy still means the government of the people by the peo-ple for the people.

If the motto of Germany be *Ein Reich, ein Volk, ein Führer*, the motto of Switzerland might be *Ein Reich, vier Völker, vier millionen Führer.* Moreover, I have yet to meet the Swiss who does not feel that he is entitled to have some say in the control, if not of his country, at least of his native village. The Swiss, indeed, would prove the most intractable material for a Hitler or a Stalin.

The Socialists despair of Switzerland, for Switzerland is a country of small capitalists, and the trouble with capitalism in other countries is not that there are too many but that there are too few capitalists. In Switzerland the Socialist "initiative" for a capital levy was submitted to the entire electorate and was rejected by an overwhelming majority. One small Oberland village had exactly one hundred registered voters, of whom one was an old man in bed, and of whom the remaining ninety-nine voted against the capital tax. Many of them would not have been directly affected, but they were all shrewd enough to realise that the Socialists who began by taxing big capital would end, as Socialists have ended in Russia, by attempting to eliminate peasant proprietors.

Distributism is a great barrier against the tyranny of the Socialist, and for this reason all champions of the tyrant state, be they Socialists or Nazis, inveigh against the small man as "uneconomic." And of course the small man is uneconomic, for freedom is one of those imponderables which the science of economics does not recognise. We must be prepared to pay for freedom and, if necessary, to preserve freedom by paying rather more for our goods than we should pay in a servile state. If the prosperity of a state is deemed to vary inversely with the average amount of goods which it can procure in the course of one year, Distributism is still infinitely preferable to State Socialism, but probably compares unfavourably with the *laissez-faire* Liberalism of the Victorian Age. But there are still some people who are prepared to pay for freedom, and who are not prepared to sell it for a song in order to buy in the cheapest market. Freedom, indeed, is the crux of this controversy. Private property widely distributed is the basis of the free state. The

Socialist who is prepared to surrender to the state the right to determine what should be produced and who should produce it (each according to his capacity) must necessarily acquiesce in the tyranny of bureaucrats, and inevitably seek to liquidate the property-owning peasant as the main obstacle to the bureaucratic Utopia. Stalin's brutal attack on the Kulaks is the logical sequence of the Socialist creed. Private property widely distributed, a flourishing peasantry and small businesses adequately protected against the competition of chain stores provide the sure foundation of freedom. For there is indeed a spiritual quality inherent in the ownership of property, provided that the property be restricted to that which a man can properly control and manage with his own resources. "*Il y enterre*," writes De Tocqueville of the French peasant, "*son cœur avec son grain.** This little corner of the earth which belongs to him alone in this vast universe fills him with pride and independence."

And property is the basis not only of freedom but also of human dignity. The Swiss mountain men have a dignity and a reserve which is seldom found in big cities. The barriers of this reserve are not easily lowered. The Swiss like the English – indeed, they prefer them to any other visitors to their country, and easily welcome them to a superficial intimacy; but you do not gain a profound insight into local life from a yodelling party, or by drinking a glass of wine with a man you do not understand, even if you know enough to describe the wine as *Gluwein* and the pub as a *Wirtschaft*. "Their lives," writes Margaret Symonds in her novel, *A Child of the Alps*, "were governed by a sort of grim courtesy common to all old breeding . . . and so it came about that Linda grew up as a peasant. It is a free but yet well-ordered life – a life of open air and hard work, too; a life where class distinctions have no part, and breeding counts for more than birth. In it there was neither room nor reason for delicate frocks or expensive toys, still less

* "He buries his heart with the grain."

for the distinction of nursery and of kitchen company. Linda had only to go into the village street to find companions as self-sufficient and with as great a natural dignity as she herself possessed."

Pas d'argent, pas de Suisses is alleged to have been the old motto of the Helvetians. Now, the Swiss, like the Scotch and like all other mountain folk, know the value of money, and because they know the value of money they have money to spare when their friends are in distress. During the Great War there were hundreds of Swiss families in Zurich and Basel and the frontier towns who had no spare suit of clothes. They had given all that they possessed to the refugees who had poured over the frontier. At the end of the war thousands of Swiss working-men received into their homes without payment German and Austrian children who were suffering as the result of the blockade. There were, indeed, many war victims who might with justice have transposed the old proverb and have said, "*Pas de Suisses, pas d'argent.*"

The classic retort of the Swiss mercenary may be quoted in this connection. "You fight for money. We fight for honour," said the Frenchman. "Ah, yes," replied the Swiss; "we both fight for what we haven't got."

We live in an imperfect world, and there is no system of government, however good, which has no characteristic defects, but I am inclined to believe that the Swiss have evolved as good a political system as any in Europe to-day. I have no faith in that servile democracy which hands over the destinies of the people to "planners" and other varieties of the urbanised ideologists, with no roots in the soil and no respect for tradition. But I have great faith in the future of the free democracy of Switzerland. That democracy is based on peasant proprietorship and on small ownership, and my faith is not weakened by the fact that there is a price to be paid for freedom and for free democracy, for I think the price is worth paying.

The horizon of the mountain man is limited, and he is not

readily prepared to pay the price for brains. Switzerland in the past has lost many of her best men to other countries, a process which is facilitated by the fact that every Swiss speaks as his native language the language of the adjoining state.

Again, pure democracy does not provide a congenial climate for art. We must, of course, always remember that Switzerland is a very small country and its total population is about half that of London, and it has produced a proportionate number of artists who have attained to European fame, such as Hodler. Nevertheless, it would be idle to compare the contribution of Switzerland to culture to that, say, of Italy. In an égalitarian society where everybody has enough for the necessities of life, nobody has enough for luxuries and art seldom flourishes. Art naturally takes refuge in aristocratic societies, particularly in those in which wealth is concentrated in the hands of the few. For untold centuries the Vispthal leading to Zermatt has been inhabited by man. Life in these Alpine valleys was hard and frugal, but no doubt the mountain men had enough to eat and a roof to shelter them, and their condition was enviable compared to the lower strata of the London or New York proletariat. Now, the Vispthal had both the advantages and the drawbacks of an égalitarian society. There was no squalor and there were no extremes of wealth on the one hand and poverty on the other, and life, though hard, had its dignity. Men who lived in this valley were free men, owning for the most part their own means of production. That is one side of the picture, but we must also remember that since those centuries when man first penetrated up the long Vispthal to Zermatt no song and no books and no thought have come out of that valley, nothing to enrich the culture of Europe. We first heard of Zermatt when the mountaineers discovered Monte Rosa and the Matterhorn.

It would be unreasonable to expect the characteristic virtues of an aristocratic society in a pure democracy. Before the Nazis ruined Austria, English visitors often contrasted the charm and courtesy of the Austrians with the more prosaic virtues of the Swiss. Graciousness and charm belong to the courtly tradition of a society organised on the lines of a feudal aristocracy. The Swiss do not easily acquire the technique of the pretty speech, and their compliments have more matter than manner. I remember the proprietor of a railway hotel in Switzerland who had refused to present me with the bill for two poached eggs and a cup of coffee, disclaiming this gesture with the remark: "You have done more for Switzerland than two poached eggs." Now, *that* is the kind of compliment which I value, but an Austrian would have put it rather differently.

The Nazis, who have wasted a great deal of money in the attempt to organise a Swiss Nazi party, invite the reply which two young Spartans gave many years ago to the emissary of a Persian town, when he asked if they would assist him to conquer their country. "Speak of the things you know," replied the Spartans, "not of freedom, of which you know nothing. For if you had tasted freedom you would urge us to fight for it, not only with battle-axes, but with swords."

CHAPTER XXV

Poland before the Bombardment

AMONG the many good things for which I am indebted to ski-ing is the memory of Poland in the final phase before the bombardment, for the World Championship was held in Poland in 1939. Strictly speaking, this was not my first visit to Poland, for I had crossed the Corridor on my way to the Baltic provinces. I shall never forget the indignant reply of a Polish guard when I asked him in all innocence whether we had reached the Corridor.

"Corridor? If you want a corridor, walk up and down outside the carriage. *That* is a corridor, but *this* which we are crossing is the province of Pomerz."

The expression "Polish Corridor" was a propaganda name invented by the Germans. Even before the Great War the population of the ancient province of Pomerz was preponderantly Polish.

I travelled to Poland via Innsbruck and Vienna. As the train drew into beloved Innsbruck, an electric sign, a swastika, gleamed from a mountain slope, like the brand mark on the forehead of a slave. "I loved thee, Athis, long ago . . ." but I was glad when the train left Innsbruck.

I stopped for a day in Vienna.

"Is it going to rain?" I asked the chambermaid.

"That depends on the *lieber Gott*," she answered.

"But is the *lieber Gott* still *Führer* in Austria?" I asked. "They tell me there has been a change of government."

Glancing at the labels on my luggage, she said: "The *lieber Gott* is a great traveller like you; he is sometimes here and sometimes there."

Poor woman! She had some excuse for wondering if God had left Vienna. Gaiety had certainly disappeared from that once light-hearted city. I wandered sadly into St. Stephen's Cathedral, the deep gloom of which was only relieved by a few dim lights. The wooden boards which covered the stone floors provided miserable protection against the cold. One of the windows in the Archbishop's house, broken by the mob, was still unmended. The stone-throwing, so we were assured by the Nazis, was a spontaneous demonstration. I looked at the asphalt street, which was not a very hopeful quarry for stones. The stones, like the spontaneity, had come from many miles away.

Zakopane, where the World Championship was to be held, has very special associations for British ski-racers, for it was at Zakopane in 1929 that the British first entered an official team for a world championship. The British rules for downhill ski racing had been provisionally approved by the Congress of 1928, and, though these newfangled races were still suspect, the Poles decided that the World Championship programme should include not only the classic events, cross-country and jumping, but also a downhill race. Bill Bracken, the British captain, finished second to a fine Polish runner, Czech Bronislav, and two English girls, Doreen Elliott and Audrey Sale Barker, created a tremendous sensation, for they entered for the men's downhill race, finished thirteenth and fourteenth respectively, and beat no less than forty-six men. A few days later when they entered a restaurant at Cracow everybody stood up and cheered.

I had not been in Zakopane very long before I sensed that the atmosphere was electric. The Poles begged me to accept the chairmanship of the committee for the downhill races and to referee both events, the downhill and the slalom. "We don't want that German, Le Fort," they confided, "running the races."

My relations with Baron Le Fort, the Nazi representative on the International Federation, have always been cordial. I have known him for years. In the old days before Hitler assumed power he was comparatively unaggressive, but I well remember the first committee meeting after the Nazis came into power. Le Fort's chest measurement had increased by three inches. Still, we have always got on well with each other, for Le Fort, unlike most Nazis, can take as well as give hard knocks in controversy, and he enjoys a joke at his own expense.

At our first committee meeting at Zakopane he brought forward a proposal, sponsored by the Berlin Foreign Office, to the effect that Germany should have a second vote, since the Austrian association had disappeared. We countered this with the motto *Ein Reich, ein Führer, ein Stimmrecht,** and that particular try-on was abandoned.

At the end of the first committee meeting one of my Polish friends came up and whispered dramatically in my ear: "Le Fort has forgotten to book a room at the Pension Halama, so when he arrived he walked into your room and insisted that he should have it."

I was not prepared to admit that my bedroom was part of the German *Lebensraum*, so I took a taxi back to the Halama, but as I opened the door of my bedroom I was fully reassured. There had been, to quote a favourite phrase of my wife's, no

* "One country, one leader, one vote."

slum clearance. The room looked exactly as I had left it, and as nobody else would be likely to leave it. Le Fort had walked into my room before my own luggage had been put into it, and had withdrawn at once on learning that the room had already been allocated to me.

Next day Le Fort was accused of having annexed a car which was to convey me, as referee, to the course. A libel, as Le Fort had walked into the town. At a cocktail party that evening a Pole in the Foreign Office came up to me and took me aside. "I hear," he said, "that Le Fort began by annexing your room and then proceeded to steal your car, and that you and he were discovered exchanging blows in the passage. We want you to know that we are on your side. We are determined to stand no nonsense from the Nazis."

The downhill race was held under trying conditions. As referee I had to postpone the start, for the summit slopes were covered by driving mist. I stationed myself at the telephone at the third control . . . the bell rang. I heard an anxious voice, the voice of the starter. Everybody was getting terribly cold; the President of the Republic was at the start. The storm wasn't so bad. Wouldn't I let the competitors start? Now, there are two views of international sport. The first that the competitors are the bricks who build the temple of fame for the middle-aged gentlemen who function as important officials, with blue rosettes, and who make eloquent speeches at prize-givings. According to the second view competitors alone matter, officials are necessary nuisances, and spectators unnecessary nuisances. It seemed to me more important that the competitors should be alive that evening than that the spectators should be insured against frostbite, but I did not enjoy the next half-hour. A radio commentator was broadcasting to the spectators and to the world: "Mr. Lunn still won't let the race start . . . Mr. Lunn still won't let the race start." Refereeing a world-championship straight race is seldom exactly fun, but I have never paid so high a price for this high honour as at Zakopane. But I remembered Innsbruck and waited for the storm to clear.

The Nazis scored a tremendous triumph at the World Championship in winning not only the Downhill Races, but, for the first time in the history of this event, the classic * Northern events.

On leaving Zakopane I visited Cracow and Warsaw. In Warsaw I called on our ambassador, Sir Howard Kennard. "The most impressive thing about these people," he said, "is their cheery courage. They don't in the least realise the danger of their position."

I returned to Switzerland via Prague. A few weeks after the September crisis I listened with interest to a lecture by an American professor who assured us that Chamberlain had been bluffed at Munich, and that Hitler would never have dared to invade Czechoslovakia. My Czech friend in Prague smiled sadly when I quoted this view. "But the war had actually begun," he said. "There was fighting all along the frontier, though the fighting was unofficial. The corps of Sudeten volunteers was already in action and there were many casualties. Hitler could never have left the Sudetens on the Czech frontier without fatal loss to the German prestige. I do not blame England," he went on, "for refusing to fight in September, for you stated again and again that you could not guarantee our frontiers. But I wish we had known for certain that France would not march, so that we should have had time to come to a reasonable agreement."

But in justice to England it is only fair to add that we did, in point of fact, warn Czechoslovakia of the dangers of the Beneš policy. A high official in the Foreign Office told me that he had conveyed a warning more than once to the Minister of Czechoslovakia in London. "I know you are right," the Minister replied. "We ought to do everything possible to placate the genuine grievance of the Sudeten Germans. But it is no use advising Beneš. It's time you stopped giving advice and started

* Langlauf and jumping as opposed to downhill and slalom races.

issuing commands. *Tell* us what we have got to do. The trouble is that Beneš relies on the Freemasons. He is confident that they will see him through."

"Are you expecting war this year?" I asked him.

"I fear not," he answered sadly.

There was something tragic about his evident sincerity. The universal catastrophe which Europe dreaded is the only hope for the Czech of salvation from an intolerable tyranny. But there was no repining. The Czechs bore their fate with dignity. They waited and hoped. Never once was I reminded of the thousands of Czechs who had deserted the Austrian Army to fight our battles in France or in Russia.

Before leaving Prague I visited the War Memorial. Light rain was falling. From the torches that flanked the memorial rose the undying flames which symbolise the unconquered courage of a race that has refused to die. And through the drizzle and failing twilight of a February afternoon I could see just one word – the one word VERDUN.

CHAPTER XXVI

St. Remigio

Ego te per omne quod datum mortalibus
et destinatum sæculum est
claudente donec continebor corpore
discernar orbe quolibet,
nec ore longe, nec remotum lumine
tenebo fibris insitum,
videbo corde, mente complectar pia,
ubique præsentem mihi.

— Paulinus of Nola

THERE are hundreds of Italians to whom this war between England and Italy is the supreme tragedy, and to none more than to my two friends to whom this book is dedicated, the Marchesa Sophie delle Valle di Casanova and her daughter the Contessa Etta Bonacossa. The Marchesa is Anglo-Irish by birth and her husband was half Irish. Etta Bonacossa is therefore three-quarters Irish and one-quarter Neapolitan – a lively mixture. I have never met anybody with a more passionate love of England (and Ireland) than the Marchesa. It was in her home, the Villa St. Remigio, that the British and Italian diplomatists met in the autumn of 1914 to discuss the treaty which was to confirm in war the traditional friendship between the country which was the Marchesa's by birth and the country which claimed her at marriage. "We used to sit out on the terrace after dinner," said the Marchesa, "and watch the moon rise beyond Laveno. Mr. Runciman, who was one of the party, was so enchanted by the beauty of the lake that he declared he would buy a villa on Maggiore and spend all his spare time there during the long years of peace that would follow the war." Lord Runciman little suspected that those years of peace would pass all too soon and that he himself would spend a summer, not on Maggiore, but in a desperate attempt to prevent the outbreak of a war in Czechoslovakia.

We spent the summers of 1938 and 1939 in the Villino St. Remigio, which was lent to us by Etta Bonacossa. Nature and Art have combined at St. Remigio to produce a supreme masterpiece. The garden is laid on the terraces of a hill above Pallanza which commands the Simplon range to the north and Maggiore towards the south. St. Remigio is the creation of the Marchesa and her husband and bears witness to the marriage of minds, for St. Remigio combines the classic stateliness of the Renaissance with the informal grace of an English garden. Palm and pine meet on this frontier between two kingdoms, the austere Alps and the tenderness of the Italian south. I have seen St. Remigio in all its changing moods. It is loveliest in the prodigal splendour of May, but autumn at St. Remigio is my favourite season. I remember the gold of larches on Mottarona, set against the sombre background of evergreens, and the last November roses entwined round the baroque statues on the terrace, statues which are the expression of the November mood of a declining culture. "It is in rare and scattered instants," writes Santayana, "that beauty smiles even on her adorers, who are reduced for habitual comfort to remembering her past favours." In war-time, more than ever, one is grateful for those "scattered instants" which transform the dreary present so that it seems less real than the uncorrupted memories of the golden past. And in these moods of escapism I return to the terraces of St. Remigio. I see again the steel-grey waters as the darkness ebbs, and the rumour of colour on the lake. Slowly the eastern hills define themselves against the radiant sky, as the dawn unshadows the dark campanile of the little church below the terrace and lights her Sanctus candles on the Simplon snows. To the north the great wall of the Alps is faintly pencilled by the outlines of shadowy ravines in which man feels himself imprisoned and confined, but there is space and air in the blue immensities of the southern lake, and freedom in the sunlit surges of the hills that lean towards Lombardy. I remember the transient temper of the lake, deep blue when the north wind blows, masked in pearl haze in the noontide heat. I remember the glow of sunset which softens the asperity of serrated crests, and confuses the outlines of separate and successive ridges. And perhaps, as I write, the full moon is rising beyond Laveno and building its bridge of shimmering silver across the dark waters of the shadowed lake.

The garden takes its name from the Romanesque campanile of St. Remigio, the oldest church on the lake, which stands between the Villa and the Villino St. Remigio. The bells of St. Remigio summoned the faithful to prayer when the invading armies swept down on to the Italian plain. Tyrants, less ignoble than Hitler, crossed the Alps and gloried in their little hour of pride and dominion, but they have gone, as Hitler will go, but the Church of St. Remigio still stands, a symbol of that Power against which the Gates of Hell shall not prevail.

St. Remigio is, for me, a symbol not only of the beauty of nature and of art, but also of a beauty more impressive than these. "The nobility which in life we call 'moral' is itself æsthetic. There is a true analogy between ethical and æsthetic values . . . the 'dignity' of architecture is the same dignity which we recognise in character." These are the words, not of a theologian, but of the late Geoffrey Scott, whose *Architecture of Humanism* is a classic in the literature of æsthetics. The verdict of the art critics is endorsed by one of America's greatest scientists, Alexis Carrel. "Moral beauty is more impressive than the beauty of Nature and Science. It gives to those who possess it divine gifts, a strange inexplicable power. It increases the strength of intellect. It establishes peace among men." Carrel's book, *Man, the Unknown,* shocked old-fashioned scientists who still clung to the faith in the dogmas of Victorian secularism, but even a materialist would not quarrel with the passage which I have quoted, had he known the Marchesa.

The Villino, which was our home for two summers, was inhabited just before we arrived by a party of Jewish refugees from Germany, and the garden staff included another melancholy exile. People are easily moved to indignation by persecution of those of their own race, religion or political party, but the rarity of any but partisan protests against cruelty provokes an uneasy doubt. Is the hatred of injustice, as such, less common in the world of to-day than in the world of our grandfathers? At such moments of doubt my faith in human nature is strengthened by the memory of St. Remigio. I have met few people with a more passionate hatred of cruelty than the Marchesa and her daughter. Their compassion recognised no difference between Jew and Gentile, Catholic and Protestant. They have found work for Austrian monarchists and German Jews, and extended their hospitality to a Pole who was too Radical for Poland and to an Austrian too Conservative for the Nazis.

"Fritz," the refugee in the garden, had left behind him in Germany a brother and the brother's wife. He used to wander down to the Villino to discuss plans for getting his brother out of Germany. He talked of the misery of his race in a queer, flat, unemotional voice, which was more impressive than any rhetorical denunciation. He seemed to accept Hitler as a cosmic and impersonal catastrophe, like an earthquake or a universal plague. In the matter of generous sentiments, I can compete on equal terms with other people, but only a powerful stimulus can incite me to generous actions. Fritz must have been unusually stimulating, for, after one of our talks, I sent a cheque for five pounds to Victor Gollancz and asked him to forward it to the Fund for the Relief of Jewish Exiles. On the previous day I had written to him in another connection, and asked him, as the founder of the Left Book Club, for some information which I needed for my book on Communism. He replied to my first letter before receiving my second, and the tenor of his remarks was that I, as a supporter of Franco, must necessarily be an admirer of Franco's ally, Hitler, and, as such, an enthusiastic supporter of Hitler's anti-Semitism. He had no sooner posted this letter, which would qualify for admission to my brother's anthology of *Invective and Abuse*, than he received my cheque, whereupon he generously admitted that he must have misunderstood me. Emboldened by his friendly letter, I asked if he could do anything for Fritz's brother. He offered to provide the necessary guarantee demanded by our Government, and thanks to his intervention Fritz's brother left Germany and spent several months in England as Mr. Gollancz's guest, before sailing for America with his wife. I mention this incident because I have found it necessary to protest against the widespread illusion that intellectuals of the Left are necessarily more altruistic and disinterested than Conservatives, but if anything which I have written, either here or elsewhere, is tolerant of the interpretation that Left-Wing intellectuals never translate their generous sentiments into generous actions, this story of Mr. Gollancz and Fritz's brother may serve to correct an impression which I do not wish to convey.

II

I left Pallanza for England a few days before war was declared, under the impression that even civilians in the early fifties would be useful if London was heavily bombed. After six weeks in London I returned to the Continent, and spent ten days at St. Remigio before proceeding to the Balkans as the occasional correspondent of the New York weekly *America*. After visiting Hungary, Jugoslavia, Rumania and Bulgaria, I returned to Rome for Christmas. I was impressed by the rising hatred of the Nazis in all classes and delighted by the fact that hundreds of young Italians had volunteered to fight in Finland.

During March I lectured in Malta, Palermo, Naples and Rome, and, after spending a few weeks in Switzerland, left for Italy on May 6 to lecture in Milan, Florence and Genoa. In spite of a violent Press campaign the Milanese remained resolutely pro-English and anti-German. During the spring Mr. Chamberlain had been applauded on the films, and Hitler hissed. An Italian from another part of Italy reported that her child's schoolmistress devoted an hour daily to reading to her class the history of the Italian campaign against Austria in the last war, and had displayed great activity in tearing down anti-British posters.

Germany invaded the Lowlands while I was in Florence, and the Government issued a violent manifesto on the subject of the British blockade. Many people believed that Italy would be at war within four and twenty hours, and I should have been delighted to have left forthwith for Switzerland, but I had still to lecture in Genoa.

On my return from Genoa I spent a few hours in Milan, and emerged from a side street to find myself walking beside an anti-British demonstration composed of students who had been released from their studies for this purpose. Not one passer-by joined in, or showed the least interest in the procession. A cheerful young tough rushed up to people who had not saluted the flag and forced them to salute, but made no attempt to cross-examine me on my neglect to comply with this ritual.

I waited for an hour in the Bonacossas' flat for my friend to return, and spent the time playing over old records, but even Mozart failed to open an avenue of escape from the misery of the moment. His enchanting arias seemed haunted by the premonition of parting. *Voi che sapete* evoked a vision of the Villino, and of many other things that are gone for ever, and the very words *Non andrai più* had acquired a new and melancholy significance.

And then Etta returned, saddened by the demonstration, which she had met on her way to the flat. It was a sad lunch and a sorrowful parting. I wonder if we shall ever meet again.

I spent the afternoon at Pallanza. The Marchesa and I sat together on the Upper Terrace, from which Mr. Runciman had watched the moon rise beyond Laveno, the terrace which overlooks the campanile, set in its framework of cypresses.

St. Remigio is the Italian variant of St. Remi, the great Saint of France, who founded the bishoprics of Cambrai, Arras and Laon. I was glad to remember this link between the Church and Garden of St. Remigio and the France for which St. Remigio is still interceding.

The Marchesa was convinced that Italy would be at war before many days had passed, and I remembered, with a sinking heart, the prediction of an anti-Fascist that I had met in Malta: "Mussolini will declare war, and Fascism will fall, to be followed by Communism." I thought of the desecrated churches in Republican Spain, and wondered whether St. Remigio would one day share their fate.

We talked of those who have fallen under the spell of St. Remigio, of Father Hohman, who spent a few days at St. Remigio in the summer of '39, and of two dear friends who helped me write this book, Phyllis Holt-Needham, who was my secretary up to 1938, and Blanche Bennett, who succeeded her. I owe them both a debt which I cannot repay, but I think St. Remigio has repaid that debt with interest.

"It is rare," said the Marchesa, "to find anybody who combines, as Phyllis combines, a passionate love of beauty with so critical a mind. In this she reminds me of my Etta."

"Father Hohman," the Marchesa continued, "wrote to me a week ago. He often writes. Those days he spent here remain in his memory. I keep on hearing from Phyllis and Blanche. It makes me happy to feel that in all this horror they do not forget St. Remigio."

I thought of Helen Waddell's exquisite rendering of the poem which Paulinus addressed to Austonius; and when I left the Marchesa to say good-bye to the Villino, I tried to console myself by murmuring the opening line:

Ego te per omne quod datum mortalibus.

I wandered down past the baroque statues, which seemed inhumanly aloof from the miseries of the moment, through the little path roofed with branches and bat-infested at night, past the great sweep of purple azalea which mantles the lower walls of the church to the little terrace beside the Villino.

I tried to convince myself that I should return some day, that the Marchesa would be there to welcome me when peace returns, and that St. Remigio would escape the devastation of war and revolution; but I was haunted by a tragic sense of irrevocable finality. "No man," says Heraclitus, "goes into the same stream twice." The perfect happiness of those summers will not return.

Maggiore had never seemed lovelier, her shimmering blueness flecked by a single sail. The dark campanili on the western shore showed up, firm and precise, against the soft colouring of May pastures. The declining sun picked out the white façades of a castle on the far southern shores of the lake.

And as lake and hill, colour and form, slowly asserted their power over my mind, I shook off the fetters of time. Vanished happiness rose again from the dead. Past and present seemed fused into one concentrated moment of ecstatic happiness and poignant misery. And I knew, beyond need of proof, that neither time nor space could wholly separate me from the beloved spirit of St. Remigio:

I, through all chances that are given to mortals
And through all fates that be,

So long as this close prison shall contain me,
  Yea, though a world shall sunder me and thee,
Thee shall I hold, in every fibre woven
  Not with dumb lips, nor with averted face
Shall I behold thee, in my mind embrace thee,
  Instant and present, thou, in every place.

Come what may, there are some things which even war cannot destroy.

CHAPTER XXVII

The Regrets of a Frankenstein

MY *vis-à-vis* in the Scheidegg train, a newcomer to the Oberland, was inquiring anxiously about the qualifications for the local Standard Tests. Apparently he travelled round the Alps in search of badges. He was wearing the famous "crash helmet" of Warmesluft and the King Boar of Lindenalp. "Last winter," he said, "they built three new *téléfériques* at Schmitzenheim. And they're putting in another next spring. Now, I call *that* progress."

And I dare say lots of people would agree with him. The great heresy of our age is this habit of equating spiritual and mechanical progress. They had no cars and no radios in Periclean Athens, but the Athenians sat for hours, unsheltered from the fierce sun of Greece, listening to the plays of Euripides, and remembered them so well that many a private soldier won his freedom in Sicily by reciting scenes from those plays to his captors. They had no aeroplanes in mediæval Venice, but they built the ducal palace as a convenient target for twentieth-century bombing raids. Every mechanical invention, from railways to radios, has conferred definite benefits on the human race, but it has sometimes been forgotten that there is no mechanical invention which does not entail some corresponding drawback. Mediæval Europe had no telephones, but it was far more united than modern Europe. It had its wars, but these, for the most part, were conducted by professionals, and were therefore less ferocious than the modern wars in which amateurs are conscripted. It is the amateur spirit which has ruined that ancient sport. I should have remembered this during the Olympic controversy.

"The professionals aren't so rough as the college boys," a taxi-driver explained to me in Washington. "They're not playing for the honour of the college like the college boys, so they don't need to get so excited, and they know that if they start rough stuff, it will be just too bad for the guy that starts that racket. After all, they're all playing for the pay-roll, so there's no sense in checking a guy any tougher than need be to stop him." The true *condottieri* spirit. In the pre-funicular age the phrase "International Ski Family" was not only a phrase, and in the Europe which had no railways there was a unity which has gone for ever, a unity derived from a common culture with its roots in the classics. All educated Europeans spoke Latin, and could therefore exchange thoughts when they met, and even as late as the eighteenth century Harvard undergraduates still debated in Latin. To-day if a speaker quotes Latin in the House, Conservatives are the first to scream "Translate." *O sæclum insapiens et infacetum.* Greek is in a worse plight. Even the Olympic Medal at Garmisch had a Latin motto. Hellas, like Athis, is a discarded mistress.

ὴραμαν μεν ὲγω σεθεν 'Ατθι παλαι, ποτα.

To quote Greek (even without newfangled Alexandrian accents) suggests an intolerable parade of bogus learning.

Mediæval Europe was a family and, like other families, it had its quarrels. Modern Europe, in spite of its modern facilities for communication, has lost all sense of European unity. The aeroplane annihilates distance, but you do not bring about a *rapprochement* between minds by accelerating the *rapprochement* between bodies. It is because space is not yet annihilated that America has some hope of keeping out of this war.

The truth is, of course, that King Boar is a little dated. His belief that progress can be measured in terms of *téléfériques* is Mid-Victorian. The *Illustrated London News* recorded the opening of the Great Exhibition in these noble words: "Who shall say if we had had a railroad system pervading Europe in 1780, whether Napoleon might not have become a great sculptor or a great cotton-spinner in 1810? Whether a thousand battles might not have remained unfought?" This majestic vision of Napoleon as a Lancashire cotton-spinner is as characteristic of Victorianism as the *Iliad* of archaic Hellenism. Tennyson, despite his Balaclava poem, was the inspired interpreter of the Victorian ethos, as is only too apparent in his translation of the Beatific Vision into a tradesman's dream:

> Saw the heavens fill with commerce, argosies of magic sails,
> Pilots of the purple twilight, dropping down with costly bales.

Every mechanical invention for speeding up communications from motor-cars to mountain *téléfériques*, breaks down barriers which are still some protection against the horrors of a standardised civilisation. A hundred years ago the United States was developing a score of attractive and sharply contrasted cultures, but to-day the Kentucky Colonel and the Boston Puritan and the Southern Planter all listen to the same radio and travel in the same cars down the same vast standardised arterial roads. In my youth I once heard an eloquent peroration to a speech by an eminent Free-Trader, which he had used with great effect in America. "I have travelled," he said, "from San Francisco to New York, a distance greater than from London to Constantinople. Had I taken the Orient Express I should have crossed seven frontiers between London and Constantinople, and been pestered seven times by officials who wished to know whether I had anything to declare, and been worried by seven different currencies, and had to struggle to make myself understood. But in the course of my three-thousand-mile journey across the American Continent my luggage was unopened, I spoke the same language throughout, and the 'Red Cap' at San Francisco was as glad to get two quarters as the porter in New York. America is the greatest Free-Trade area in the world."

Well, I too have travelled from San Francisco to New York, and I have also journeyed from Mürren to Finland, a shorter journey than the American Transcontinental, but long enough to cross six frontiers. Six times I completed a form stating the currency that I was importing. Six times I produced the currency that I was exporting. I paid for five visas and ran wildly along station platforms to change money for a drink, and returned to Mürren with a prize collection of unchangeable currencies. But I am grateful to those frontiers none the less. Even an occasional war is not too high a price to pay for the preservation of differences and for the postponement of the Esperanto Age.

Mountain railways and funiculars are not exempt from the law that mechanical progress is always balanced by spiritual regress. "Technological progress has merely provided us," as Aldous Huxley remarks, "with more efficient means of going backwards." Ski-ing, which was once a culture, is degenerating into a civilisation. The pioneers of Alpine ski-ing were recruited from those who loved mountains. They enjoyed ski-ing, but they regarded the long descent as a glorious extra, a bonus which the generous gods bestowed upon those who approached the secret shrine of the hills in their winter dress. Our chief reward was the freedom of the Alpine snows, a freedom to which our ski were the passport. To escape from the complexity of civilisation into the clean beauty and austere loneliness of a mountain world which had forgotten its busy summer traffic with man was all the recompense which we asked for the labour of the long ascent at a time when seal-skins were unknown. To have seen the unsullied snow of the Hahnenmoos, to have cut the first ski track up the Elsighorn, and to have watched the January moon silvering the Concordia before the Concordia was the first stop on a standard run from a railway station – such were the compensations of ski-ing in the Eocene Age.

A modern racer, in some phrase of airy denigration, contrasted the low standard of those who won their First Class Badge many years ago with the high standard of the modern "Gold." There has certainly been a remarkable increase in speed, particularly speed on hard snow, but the change has not been all gain. Progress in one direction has been balanced by regress in others. In the pioneer phase of our sport we did not judge ski-ers only by physical standards. Cross-country ski-ing, as we knew it, was an exacting test of the mind no less than the body. Snow scholarship was an integral element in the sport. We graduated as ski-ers by studying the snow surfaces which were our medium, and the expert of those days was not a speed king who knows the pet name of every bump on a hard-snow "standard," but a sound cross-country runner who could move safely among mountains, and who could ski at fair speed down unknown ground and over snows of varying texture. In those days ski-ing was a culture, for the study of snow is a branch of natural science. All noble sports demand from their followers an intimate knowledge of Nature in all her many moods.

Every great cultural cycle, as Spengler has shown, begins when a nomad tribe settles down as an agricultural community. It is the economy of the farm, the village and the small city which gives birth to great Art. Ten men, said Aristotle, are too few for a city, ten thousand are too many. It is from Nature, from Homer's "life-giving earth," that Art draws its inspiration, the inspiration which withers and dies in the giant cities of a dying civilisation.

Ski-ing has passed through the Spenglerian cycle. It began as a culture in contact with Nature. In the Gothic phase of our sport we ski-ed on snow moulded only by the natural agencies of sun and wind, frost and thaw. Ten men are too few for a ski-ing community, ten thousand are too many for ski-ing funiculars. In those days we ski-ers were as scattered as the primitive communities in which culture is born. To-day we struggle in *téléfériques* and funiculars as crowded as the slums of our megalopolitan civilisation, and the surface on which we ski is nearly as hard and quite as artificial as the city pavements which mask the kindly earth. "The wind whistles past, and only a mottled look on the snow betrays the secrets of its surface. And, until he can diagnose snow while travelling at high speed, until he can carry a compass in his head, and instinctively allow for the difference in texture, according to the orientation and the steepness of the slope, he will spend more time on his back than on his feet. For the ski-runner the snow is no inert mantle on the hills, the shroud which buries those dead pastures that are waiting for the resurrection of the spring. It is alive with a multiple personality. He learns to love the snow as a friend, and to wrestle with it as an enemy."

How it dates – this passage from *The Mountains of Youth!*

My reverie was interrupted by the King Boar.

". . . The course was in perfect condition, but unfortunately it snowed two days before the race. Luckily they had a battalion of Alpine troops available, so they turned them on to the course to stamp it out good and proper. But they were a bit slack, and poor Bill ran off into a patch of sticky stuff and cracked his ankle. You can't be too careful when there's this soft snow about."

I remembered an incident observed by Hugh Dowding. A young racer was hesitating at the top of the Männlichen run. The weather had just cleared after a snowstorm, and the racer prodded the offending powder with his stick. "Funny stuff, this," he murmured disapprovingly.

Yes; it is time that I rewrote my little book, *Alpine Ski-ing*.

"Funny stuff" . . . and yet as late as 1920 we still regarded hard snow as "funny stuff." Here is an extract from the preamble to the revised Second Class Test:

"For the first time the Committee require that a Second Class Runner must be a good runner on both hard and soft snow. This is an important advance, as up till now a candidate might win his Second Class Badge without being a good runner except in powder snow."

We took it for granted that a ski-er would feel at home on natural snow and be puzzled by artificial snow. We were still living in the Dawn Age of the Spenglerian cycle.

Somebody asked the King Boar if he knew Davos. He replied that he had spent two days there and had joined Bill Bracken's racing class. "Bracken spent the whole day fooling about in soft snow, so I chucked his class." I thought of Bill as I last saw him on the snows, linking long, graceful tempo turns in deep powder, and I marvelled that the beauty of his soft-snow technique had not conquered King Boar.

The train turned the corner near Wengernalp, disclosing a view which even picture postcards cannot stale.

"Is this your first visit to the Oberland?" Without a glance through the window at one of the most famous of Alpine views, King Boar replied: "Yes, I've never been here before. Old Sam's piloting me down to Grund. We hope to crash down in time to catch the first Bahn back and then work in a couple of Tschuggens, and come back by the Bumps." The train drew up at the Scheidegg. King Boar, anxious lest he should miss the Bahn at Grund, leaped to his feet, and trod heavily on the toes of a lady sitting beside him. He turned, but a faint look of dismay faded from his face, for the lady was only a foreigner – that is, a citizen of the country in which King Boar was ski-ing. My old interest in the evolutionary controversy revived as I watched him grasp the carriage rack with prehensile arms, and swing himself through the door. With swift movements this experienced Jungle-Crasher carved a passage for himself to the ski truck.

Leaving my own ski for the moment in the ski truck, I followed King Boar out of the station. I was curious to note his reactions to the view.

To the mountain-lover the Scheidegg is a shrine dedicated to the great shades who passed this way. Byron crossed the Scheidegg in the year after Waterloo. "Heard the avalanches falling every five minutes nearly—as if God was pelting the Devil down from Heaven with snowballs . . . we looked down the other side upon a boiling sea of cloud, dashing against the crags on which we stood." Byron "crashed down" to Grund on a mule, and visited the Grindelwald Glacier, "like a frozen hurricane"—a phrase more effective than its more polished version in "Manfred":

> The aspect of a tumbling tempest's foam
> Frozen in a moment;

crossed the Great Scheidegg to Meiringen, and returned to Interlaken, where a girl gave him some flowers and made a speech in German. "I do not know whether the speech was pretty, but as the girl was, I hope so."

Seldom have I seen the Scheidegg view to greater perfection. A recent snowstorm had cowled the Monk in Dominican white. The Jungfrau smiled through a bridal veil of diaphanous mist. The "frozen hurricanes" showed faintly through a dust of silver.

King Boar muttered angrily: "There's a lot of new snow about. Wonder if we'll make it? Hurry up, Sam."

And then Gravity, a great gentleman, bundled him out of view.

CHAPTER XXVIII

"Time is His Conquest"

He who has once been happy is for aye
  Out of destruction's reach. His fortune then
Holds nothing secret; and Eternity,
  Which is a mystery to other men,
Has like a woman given him its joy.
  Time is his conquest.

— Wilfrid Scawen Blunt

I DID not follow King Boar by the shortest route down to Grund, but meandered slowly down a hidden and secret valley which I have christened "For-ski-ers-only Glade," whose exact whereabouts I have no intention of revealing. I was staying with the British Ski Team at the Bear Hotel. The *téléférique* age had transformed my old friend Fritz Amacher into a liftman, and on my way to dress for dinner we exchanged a few sentimental sighs about the old days. "Thirty thousand feet of downhill ski-ing in a day, Fritz . . . that's what they can do at Schmitzenheim. We only managed thirty-five thousand feet during that week in 1918 which we spent together."

Fritz nodded and remarked that those days had been by far the best and happiest of his life. It was certainly a wonderful week. We began on Monday by climbing from Grund to the Scheidegg, 4,000 feet in soft snow – there was no train running. On Tuesday we climbed more than 5,000 feet to the Lauberhorn, on Wednesday 6,300 feet to the Schwarzhorn, on Thursday we climbed 6,000 feet to the Wildgerst, and ran down 8,000 feet to Meiringen, and after a day's rest traversed the Faulhorn, eschewing the indolent modern short cuts down the Faulegg ridge in favour of the longer route by Sägisalp. This involved 8,000 feet of climbing and 10,000 feet of the best and most varied ski-ing which I have ever enjoyed. We averaged 6,000 feet of climbing and about 7,000 feet of downhill ski-ing. We never returned by the route of the ascent, and our five days included the two finest traverses of the Alps from the point of view both of scenery and of snow. *Qui n'a pas vécu avant 1789*, said Talleyrand, *ne connait pas la douceur de la vie*, and it is no less true that he who has not ski-ed before the funicular revolution *ne connait pas la douceur du ski.*

On my way to dinner I made a suggestion to Fritz. "To-morrow the British team are going to vary their training by climbing the Wildgerst. We can go with them as far as Grindelalp, after which they will be glad to get rid of us, and we shan't be sorry to be alone."

I was up next morning before the dawn. Nearly twenty years had passed since we last came this way. Fritz was out of training and it was my first climb of the season. We were glad to find that we could still climb 3,500 feet in three hours.

We had had enough by the time we reached the ridge above Grindelalp, so we said good-bye to the racers, and emptied our sacks in search of beer. It was one of those perfect February days with a hint of spring in the air. The railway up the Chrisegg, which but for the war would have been opened in 1940, will be built some day, and this is all to the good. I have no quarrel with mountain railways as such. *La vérité*, as Renan says, *consiste dans les nuances.* The ideal mountain railways should carry us, as the Chrisegg will carry us, about 3,000 feet up a mountain whose summit is 6,000 feet above the valley. Cresta * ski-ers will not climb a yard above the summit station. They will, of course, ruin the Grindelalp, which will no doubt be polluted with standard courses, but this is not too great a price to pay for the fact that the elderly and those who are out of training will be able to reach the Faulhorn, Wildgerst and Schwarzhorn without undue difficulty. I have no fear lest the austere remoteness of the "Lake of the Witches" or the "Blue Glacier" just behind the Schwarzhorn will be invaded. In this matter of railways I am at one with Hilaire Belloc. "The railways are trenches that drain our modern marsh, for you have but to avoid railways, even by five miles, and you can get more peace than would fill a nosebag. All the world is my garden since they built railways, and gave me leave to keep off them."

The railway will come, Grindelalp will not be the same again, but, though I am reconciled to this loss, the golden hour which Fritz and I passed above the "still unravished bride of loveliness" was flavoured with the faint sadness of farewell. But it was a golden hour none the less. The great peaks across the valley were haunted by the memories of the past which we had shared together.

Fritz pointed with a cheerful chuckle to the Berglistock. "We were much less pleased," he said, "to get to the top than to get to the bottom." He was right, for we had reached the summit far too late on an afternoon in May. We knew that the descent would be desperately dangerous; we were tired and hot, and the half-hour that we spent on the sun-baked rocks was dedicated to glum foreboding.

Our premonitions fell short of fact. The line we were forced to follow on the descent changed from one rock ridge to another, and forced us to cross and recross the gullies which

* The term applied to ski-ers who spend their time memorising every bump of a "standard course," much as racers memorise every curve on the famous Cresta toboggan run at St. Moritz.

seam the face, gullies which were swept intermittently by a barrage of spring avalanches. Spring snow is wet and heavy, and few things are more difficult than to free oneself from the gluey embrace of even the smallest of spring snowslides. As, indeed, I know full well, for I once travelled five hundred feet towards a *Bergschrund*, sucked downwards by a pitiful streamlet of treacly slush. There is dignity in the thunder of an avalanche which awakens ten thousand echoes among the hills, but I have nothing but loathing for the silky venom of these malignant rivulets which will sneak a climber off his feet with no warning but a hiss, and deposit him with no sound but a flop into the crevasse which guards like a moat the passage from the glacier to the cliff. We were very lucky, for we had just scampered across the broadest of the *couloirs* before an avalanche fell, and a little lower I was beginning to pay out the rope while Fritz advanced, and once again the snow flooded down the gully which we were about to enter.

We guessed what was coming to us as we consumed a melancholy sandwich on the summit. The panorama from the Berglistock is noble and extensive, but the mountains, in which lurked great perils, had ceased to be our friends. I remember little of what we saw, for only one thing was in sharp focus, the white loop of the Grindelwald road to the Upper Glacier, defined against a blurred foreground of unfriendly rock and treacherous snow.

Roads have inspired many prophets from Isaiah to Hilaire Belloc, but there is a chapter in the history of roads which only a mountaineer could write, for only the mountaineer knows what roads mean to those who have escaped with full knowledge and consent from their gross and comfortable security. If the climber be not in peril, the white ribbon in the valley will reinforce his pride of conquest. He will remember with complacency the things from which he has escaped, the strident clamour of coachmen soliciting the custom of the idle, the moist platoons of the personally conducted guided by melancholy shepherds to grottoes hewn out of the complaining ice. He will be happy to contrast the cool aloofness of those whom the high mountains welcome with the perspiring gregariousness of those who belong to the valley. One day I shall write a book about the pleasures of Smugness, with long and rich quotations from my own writings, and a very special chapter on roads seen from above.

The valley road invites no such reassuring reflections when the pride of conquest is infected by fear. The slow-moving spots far below may be trippers, but they are trippers who will be sitting down to *Abendessen* at the time you may be attaching yourself by a rope to a rocky couch. In such moments of revolt you long for the unheroic pleasures of delicious flatness. And so there shall be a chapter on roads faintly showing in the dim starlight, roads sadly envied by unhappy men huddled together for warmth on some chilly ledge, roads bordered by focal points of snug and human warmth, lights which, as they go out one by one, flash a tantalising vision of happy indolence gratefully sinking with contented sighs into the warmest and most feathery of beds.

But pride returns when perils are past, and when we come down from the mountain we claim the road as our own. As we stroll down in the evening, while the twilight weaves its web of colour and shadow round the mountain of memories, we are glad to encounter the *Kurgäste* on their evening pilgrimage in search of an appetite. For we know that the road belongs to those who have the enterprise to leave it, to those who return redeemed by danger and ransomed by peril.

"And a highway shall be there, and a way, and it shall be called the way of holiness . . . and the redeemed shall walk there: and the ransomed of the Lord shall return, and come to Zion with songs."

Contrasts such as these enrich the mountains with that intensity of remembered emotion which is the chief reward of the climber.

"And what is there to distinguish virtue from dishonour or the valour of Cæsar from the softness of the Egyptian eunuch, that can make anything remarkable but the labour and the danger, the pain and the difficulty?" *

Our eyes followed the east ridge of the Berglistock down to the saddle of the Lauteraar. Many years ago four friends approached this pass from the south. Winter still resisted the sun in the long glacier valley of the Lauteraar, but as they thrust themselves through the cornice, and scrambled on to this window of the hills, they were welcomed by the sudden glory of the Grindelwald Valley in the incomparable livery of May. For an indolent hour they idled in the sun, and watched tobacco clouds drowsily curling up towards the windless sky, and listened to the chorus with which spring streams celebrate their deliverance from the silent frost.

"Perhaps the four of us," wrote one of these friends, "will get together for another May run when we get over to the 'other side.' We shall never get all the conditions right again in this life."

True enough, for the writer of this letter and one other of those who crossed the Lauteraar have now crossed another pass. *Où sont les neiges d'antan?* Gone with the spoor of one's ski, but the mountain that one has climbed holds something of one's past life on its crest. Like a kindly biographer, it retains what one would wish remembered, and rejects the trivialities of life, sifting the gold of great memories from the sand of littleness which filters back into the stream of oblivion. The steps carved out of the stubborn ice have vanished, but the mountains retain the imprint of friendships forged in their company. The memory of the dead passes into them, and their silence still echoes old songs and old laughter. Pleasure is of the moment, but the accidents of time and space, and the decay which awaits all mortal things, have no power to destroy the imperishable element in the happiness of the hills.

* Jeremy Taylor.

Chance rather than choice often determines our mountain partnerships, and I am grateful to the accident of fate which gave me Fritz as a companion during the years that we climbed together. He likes the mountains the way that I like them, and his pattern of mountain memories is much the same as mine. And therefore we do not need the mechanism of consecutive conversation to revive our common memories. A word or a phrase, a grunt or a chuckle, serves to "beget the golden time again." That, of course, if not the best kind of talk, is at least the best kind of verbal communication. As, indeed, Samuel Johnson realised. Surprisingly, for no man loved better than Johnson to overwhelm his friends in a spate of rhetoric. Like other good talkers, he had the defects of his qualities. He made people pay for the performances which he so generously provided; he had a passion for getting things quite clear, but he was more interested in making his own meaning clear to others than in understanding what others were vainly trying to make clear to him. Like other quick thinkers, he often knew what slow thinkers were trying to say long before they had said it, and he could never resist the temptation of completing their sentences for them as a preliminary to exposing the imbecility of what they had never been allowed to say. No man was more fortunate in his biographer. Boswell winced and wilted, but revelled in Johnson's mastery of the lash. He was immensely vain, and suffered agonies from the public humiliations which Johnson inflicted on him; but because he was a supreme artist, his creative genius forced him to record with immortal candour his moments of acutest abasement.

Once when Boswell so far forgot himself as to laugh at Johnson and not with Johnson, the old lion wheeled round in his chair and roared. He "instantly retaliated with such keen sarcastick wit, and such a variety of degrading images, of every one of which I was the object, that, though I can bear such attacks as well as most men, I yet found myself so much the sport of the company that I would gladly expunge from my mind every memory of this severe retort." Instead of expunging it from his mind, he ensured that his humiliation should be remembered by posterity. Once again the artist had triumphed over the man.

"May there not be very good conversation," Boswell asked, "without a contest of superiority?"

"Not animated conversation," replied Dr. Johnson.

But Johnson was not always aggressive. "That is the happiest conversation," he mused, "where there is no competition, no vanity, but a calm interchange of sentiments."

And I suspect that Johnson had not only a Boswell to roar at, but a Fritz Amacher to grunt at.

The hard crust refused to soften, so Fritz and I put on our ski and climbed for another hour. We chose the precise moment for the run when the snow was likely to be at its best, not only on the upper slopes where it was slightly softened, but also on the lower slopes where, with luck, it would not yet be slush. It was a charming run, for the snow varied according to orientation and gradient from powder through breakable crust and spring snow to the hardest and most unyielding of surfaces. It was a run which tested mind no less than legs. Snowcraft was necessary to avoid breakable crust and to select from the accident of hollow and ridge the perfect line which alone yielded pleasant ski-ing. Runs such as these are infinitely more amusing than sliding like a robot down standardised surfaces.

Below Grindelwald we halted. "In the old days, Fritz," I said, "we used to think ourselves pretty good ski-ers, but times have changed, and if this was a standard course we shouldn't win any badges for to-day's performance."

"No," said Fritz, "and *um so besser*. This is *Touren-Skifahren*. At the end of last season four visitors engaged me for a week to carry their lunches. And I wouldn't let them be lazy. So we spent all our time this side of the valley and we didn't ski wildly downhill like the *junge Leute. Sie gehen mit der Bahn hinauf und fahren wild hinunter und saufen im Bar und* *fahren wieder hinauf mit der Bahn.** And at the end they were very thankful to me, and I told them that it was you who had taught me when I was a boy to like this nice *Touren-Skifahren.* The way we ski gives us time to look round and see something of the mountains and not only the tips of our ski."

We met the shy approach of colour in the last fields above the road. A rash little crocus was sunning itself on a steep southern slope which had just discarded the last moist rags of snow. A little stream too long muted by the frost disputed the dominion of winter. Fritz sniffed the spring in the air and chuckled with joy.

From Grindelalp we had watched a lonely ski-er high up on the Chrisegg ridge, and as we ran down the last slopes to the road he joined us. If I see a stranger emerging from a mountain railway he may, for all I know, be a mountain-lover or a King Boar. But I had no doubts about this unknown ski-er, for he had scorned the allurements of the railway and had met the dawn on the undesecrated heights. And although I had never seen him before, I greeted him as a friend, for I knew that even if we were to differ on the things for which men fight, we should be linked by the strongest of bonds.

"I should not be alone," he began, "if my friends were not so lazy. They promised to come with me, but when I called them this morning they said: 'After all, we have paid for our *abonnement* on the railway and it would be a waste not to use our weekly ticket.' "

He told us that he was employed by a famous ski shop in Bern, and he added, with a reproachful glance at the Scheidegg: "*Die Leute sind verrückt. Sie fahren wild hinunter. Die Ski gehen kaput. Die Stöcke gehen kaput. Die Kanten gehen kaput. Gut fürs Geschäft. Immerhin verkaufe ich lieber Seehundsfelle.*" †

* "They ride up in the train, ski madly down, drink in the bar, and then take the train up again."

† "The people are mad. They ski madly downhill. The ski get broken, the sticks get broken, the edges get broken. It's all good for business, but I'd rather sell sealskins."

CHAPTER XXIX

"Despite of Wrinkles"

> So thou through windows of thine age shalt see
> Despite of wrinkles this thy golden time.
>
> – SHAKESPEARE

THE tactful but insistent knocking intruded itself into the texture of my dream. I clung desperately to the illusive vision, but it evaded me, and I awoke regretfully. Turning on the light, I blinked sulkily at the ceiling. Surely I had earned a long and lazy night after four days' consecutive ski-ing, in the last of which I had climbed some 6,000 feet in powder snow. I padded across the room and looked out of the window, hoping to discover some pretext for calling the expedition off, but the uncompromising stars robbed me of all excuse for laziness.

Lena, who still distributes tea and cakes to thirsty ski-ers at the Hotel Central, beamed over our breakfast as hot coffee dispelled the sluggish trail of sleep.

It had just turned five when Fritz and I stepped out into the street, lit by one disconsolate lamp. Passing between houses heavy with sleep, we emerged on to the starlit snows. As we tramped up the path to Hertenbühl the first hint of colour intruded on the darkness. The Wetterhorn was no longer a shadowy line, but was defined with sharp precision against the velvet darkness of the sky. We recovered our faith in the existence of the sun. The Alps might still be drowsy with sleep, but in the Near East it was day. The Golden Horn was glowing in the dawn, and colour would soon be stirring in the lagoons of Venice. As we climbed higher the stars went out one by one as if touched by an unseen hand, until only the morning star remained. We watched the last phase from a point near Grindelalp. The eastern sky was radiant with Dante's "*splendori antelucani.*" The little wind which goes before the dawn ruffled the silence and the mountains stirred with expectancy. Arrows of light began to radiate from an invisible focus behind the Wetterhorn. The sun slowly climbed above the ramparts of rock. The flat and lifeless snows at our feet, flecked with pearl-grey shadows, sparkled into ten thousand stars, and mind and body relaxed in the flood of colour and warmth.

One day the projected railway will be built and there will perhaps be a restaurant at the point where Fritz and I met the dawn, and ski-ers will see from their bedroom windows what Fritz and I saw when the sun came out of his eastern chamber and climbed into the sky behind the Wetterhorn. But will they? I think not. The dawns which one has earned by long hours of toil beneath the frosty stars are more wonderful than those which one watches in comfort from a bedroom window. There is a close connection between the ascetic and the æsthetic. It would puzzle a materialist to explain how frequently the reward of beauty is associated with the discipline of toil, as if Nature consciously reserves her noblest effects for those who take some trouble to earn them. There is no reason why powder snow should be lovelier than the beaten snow of a standard course, but you have to earn your powder snow by climbing, whereas you need only buy a ticket to discover beaten snow. A single ski track which is a symbol of a difficulty conquered is far more beautiful than the "tramlines" of a ski-er who has never mastered the technique of keeping his ski together. The sun's relation to the horizon is the same at sunset as at sunrise, but the dawn which the idle never see is lovelier than the sunset which the lazy can enjoy.

If beauty were determined solely by the laws of optics and by the angle of the sun, the last hour before the sunset should be as beautiful as the first hour after the dawn; but this is not the case, as, indeed, the Italian and Flemish primitives were well aware. The painters of the great ages loved the cool and fragrant beauty of the hour which follows the dawn. Art began to decline when artists stayed in bed.

Early risers are often intolerably smug, and Fritz and I certainly felt a glow of complacent satisfaction as we looked down on the sleeping valley far below. There is a quality in the cool little breezes which come with the dawn, and a cleansing virtue in the clean air of the early morning hills, which dissolves the last traces of sluggishness in one's blood. Down there in the valley, in a stuffy atmosphere of tumbled blankets, drowsy folks were blinking at the sunlight which was filtering through the curtains, but we were alert and eager for the unfinished adventure.

Once again we pointed our ski uphill, but without that dragging reluctance with which we had faced the few hundred feet above Grindelwald. Then we had been oppressed by the thought of the 6,300 vertical feet between us and the summit, but the 3,000 feet which we had climbed, so far from draining our strength, had recharged our energies. Fatigue is a function of the mind no less than of the body, and second wind is a psychological no less than a physical phenomenon. Our expenditure of physical effort had been partially offset by the lightening of the mental load with which we had started the ascent.

It would be easier to convert Cresta ski-ers into ski-tourers if we could persuade them that a long, steady climb is often less tiring than a short spurt. I enjoy all but the first half-hour of a 5,000-foot peak, but I never cease to resent the 50 feet which separates the top of the Allmendhubel funicular from the Allmendhubel summit. On such short sections the mind is impatient to reach the top; but as one leaves the valley for a big expedition one resigns oneself to the long hours which must pass before the summit is attained, and resignation is followed by enjoyment. For there is a subtle pleasure in the rhythm of a long-continued ascent, a rhythm which is obscured in the staccato of a short spurt. The experienced climber achieves a balanced movement in which ease and comfort are not sacrificed to speed, and which leaves the mind free to enjoy the beauty of slowly widening horizons.

Just below the Krinne Pass we paused once again and glanced back at the long valley up which we had just been climbing. The delicate silver point of the ascending zigzags of our tracks enriched the beauty of the soft glinting snow-fields seen against the low sun. The handiwork of man is not always an unwelcome addition to the handiwork of nature. Thirty years ago two ski-ers whom I had never met traversed the Oberland Glaciers from Meiringen, just before we crossed those same passes from the Lötschen Valley. In those days there was no Jungfrau Railway and the solitude of the Concordia Platz in January was seldom disturbed. We spent six days among glaciers, six days during which the tracks of our unknown ski-ers represented the one fragile link with the world of man. A faint aroma of human companionship still clung to their imprint on the snow. Some afterglow from the emotions which they had experienced still seemed to linger in the pattern of their downward curves. I have never, to my knowledge, met those ski-ers, and if we did meet we should meet as strangers; but when their tracks finally vanished in the shadows of the Grimsel Gorge we felt as though we were parting from friends with whom we had shared the ardours and endurance of a great adventure.

The beauty of ski tracks varies in inverse proportion to their number. An intersecting pattern of "tempo turns" on a canvas undefiled by beginners is among the loveliest of man's contributions to natural beauty. But the mass production of tracks defiles the delicate individuality of snow crystals, whose facets reflect the sun. Humanity, when it gate-crashes into nature's winter shrine, leaves its record in the surface of the standard course, but the lines etched by mountaineers into the remoter snows suggest one of those relationships in which intimacy is not made the excuse for unwarranted impositions on the good nature of a friend.

We left our ski on the Blue Glacier Pass, and scrambled on foot up to the Wildgerst cairn, which we reached six hours after leaving Grindelwald, and there we passed an idle hour of pure content, in the golden warmth of windless sunshine.

"The gods," says Aristotle, "may be honoured but not praised, for we praise things by reference to a standard, and the gods are beyond compare." And that is exactly what I feel about the Oberland; but as this chapter will be read not only by the faithful who need no proof, but by sceptics, I will try, for their sake, and not for mine, to justify my conviction that the North Wall of the Oberland is "beyond compare" for splendour of invention and variety of creative design. There are certain stock mountain types which are repeated indefinitely throughout the Alps. Limestone runs naturally to vertical "steps" and dolomitical towers, granite to spires and pyramids. A faint suggestion of mass production intrudes itself into one's enjoyment of ranges in which either granite or limestone predominates, but there are no mountains in the world in the least like the Wetterhorn, or the Eiger, or the Jungfrau. God made them and broke the mould.

The interplay of granite and limestone is perhaps one of the complex causes to which this range owes its variety of form. The Finsteraarhorn is pure Gothic. There is a suggestion of the basilica in the roof of the Dammastock, and of the classic entablature in the broad snow crest of the east face of the Mönch. The Jungfrau, on the other hand, is a masterpiece in the Baroque style. The "frozen hurricanes" of her hanging glaciers and the volutes of the Silberhorn and Schneehorn convey much the same impression of exultant movement that the Baroque architects conveyed in stone. And the Jungfrau, like the Salute at Venice, has the serene assurance which no Baroque exuberance can disturb.

Our reaction to mountain scenery is a complex of æsthetic emotion and personal associations. Whether the universe would continue to exist if there were no conscious beings to observe it is a question upon which philosophers have disagreed. Among the mountains these anthropocentric fantasies seem less improbable, for there are moods in which it is easy to believe that the Matterhorn and the Jungfrau are in some sense a creation of man's adoration, and that a mountain such as the Dent Blanche above Zermatt only emerged from the trance of time when it was first discovered by mountaineers. Other mountains, such as Mont Blanc and the Jungfrau, inspired poets long before they challenged mountaineers. Now, the Oberland is associated not only with the beginning of mountaineering, but also with the dawn of the Romantic movement. Byron and Goethe discovered the beauty of these peaks long before Mr. Justice Wills and Leslie Stephen began to climb them. "Leslie Stephen," writes Hugh Kingsmill, "found Byron's Swiss poetry cheap and insincere. As a hard-headed agnostic, suspicious of emotion not founded on fact, he resented no doubt such verse as:

The fish swam by the castle wall,
And they seemed joyous each and all.
The eagle rode the rising blast,
Methought he never flew so fast.

This eagle, flying past Chillon to the mountains of Ouida's Ischl, rode a purely romantic blast, and was visible only to romantic eyes. The orthodox climber, however, does not care for romance. His love of the mountains is based, like domestic love, on knowledge and understanding. It is reasoned, almost respectable. But the visions of Byron and of the German Romantics have the magic of first love, passionately adoring what is unknown and out of reach."

My brother does less than justice to Leslie Stephen, and his strictures apply, not to "orthodox climbers," but only to a minority whom I for one should not describe as orthodox. But his tribute to the Romantics is discerning, perhaps because it is based on "that knowledge and understanding" which he depreciates. He could have strengthened his case had he been familiar with the art produced during the Romantic revival. At a time when the Corsican was making trouble in the foothills, and the Russians were tramping across the Alpine passes, the eccentrics who thought mountains beautiful penetrated into the Oberland Valley and began to paint the Jungfrau and the Wetterhorn. Those old coloured aquatints – a process which seems to have disappeared – have a charm for me which no modern painting possesses, for these period pieces carry the mind back to the days when the mountains had not been climbed or explored.

Instead of attempting to prove that the Oberland is "beyond compare," I might have done better to quote Browning:

Here's my case. Of old I used to love him,

and leave it at that. Certainly that golden hour on the Wildgerst was untroubled by critical dissection of the mountains which were our delight. The serene winter sunshine evoked a mood of unquestioning adoration. The crests were edged by a ribbon of reflected light which mirrored the unseen snows on the invisible southern slope of the range, a bordering of silver-blue which softened the transition from the concrete line where the mountain ended to the infinite depths of the unfathomable sky. Ruskin, who was not only a superb master of rhetoric, but also an accurate scientific observer, noted this curious and most unusual effect in a famous passage describing the Alps from the south.

"Then, in the luminous air beyond and behind this blue horizon line, stand, as it were, the shadows of mountains, they themselves dark, for the southern slopes of the Alps of the Lago Maggiore and Bellinzona are all without snow; but the light of the unseen snowfields, lying level behind the visible peaks, is sent up with strange reflection upon the clouds; an everlasting light of calm Aurora in the north."

The Alps are, of course, lovelier in spring than in winter. I have seen the May dawn from the Wildgerst and the dull grey foreground of shadowed snow to the north served as a foil to the colour scale ranging from the green-blue of Brienz to the dark gentian of distant Lucerne; but even in January these foothills are pregnant with colour. The Alps are the sentinels of Italy, and her gracious influence softens their asperity. How different the view which we saw from the Wildgerst and the panorama from the Hardanger Jökul above Finse on the Oslo–Bergen line. Even in summer the ice-capped plateau is bleak and inhuman, for the glaciers lie heavy upon the unfertile rock below, a shroud covering a corpse; but the snows which mantle the Alpine foothills are a blanket below which the convalescent is regaining strength.

We scrambled down from the Wildgerst to the Blue Glacier Pass, where our ski awaited us. The physical process of putting on one's ski is the same whether one has climbed 6,000 feet or taken train to a railway station, but the mental reactions are very different.

The Cresta ski-er who enjoys perhaps a dozen downhill runs in a few hours knows nothing of the thrill of the unique moment in the ski-tourer's day, the moment for which the long hours of the climb provide the appropriate preparation. And the ski-er who has a pet name for every bump of his favourite standard course is a stranger to that moment of quickening suspense as the skis dive down the first slope of an unexplored run on untracked snow. Neither Fritz nor I had crossed the Wildgerst or compared notes with anybody who had. But I had studied the Wildgerst from the Great Scheidegg, and had noted that though the slopes between the Blue Glacier Pass and the valley face south, they are intersected by tributary ridges, on the short north slopes of which we might reasonably expect to find powder. My plan was to use these ridges to enjoy powder-snow ski-ing on a slope of sun-crusted snow. No such problems enrich the joys of Cresta ski-ing.

Finally, the very ski themselves seem a thousand times more animated when you buckle them on to your feet on some windy pass thousands of feet above the haunts of gregarious ski-ers. Fight your way through a crowd, disentangle your ski from a hundred others on a railway truck, and you will not find it easy to establish sympathetic co-operation with the inert and lifeless boards. But the ski which have been your companions for hours, the ski which have left a continuous furrow from the valley floor to a mountain crest, seem charged with dynamic energy. They react to your impatience and share your eagerness to be off.

Twenty years have passed since Fritz and I linked our turns down the snows of the Wildgerst, but "time which antiquates antiquity hath yet spared" the memory of our ski-ing partnership. I can still remember the resolve to *schuss* a steep slope leading to a cup-shaped hollow; the sudden terror as the ski dived through wind-driven patchy snow, the urge to lie down, the determination to stand, the struggle to force the ski together, the wind in one's ears which rose to tempest fury, the shock as the ski dived into the heavy snow of the outrun, the relief as their points appeared above the white smother, immense surprise as the uncontrollable demons hurrying through space suddenly sobered into the most docile of slaves, and the glory of the Christiania swing which brought the opening act to its triumphant conclusion. Fritz was a few seconds late in starting. I watched him as he came over the sky-line, and saw him sway as his ski struck the wind-touched powder. He fought for and regained control; he thrust out his leading ski to meet the shock of the outrun, swept past me and swung round with such speed that he faced the slope which he had descended. Fritz looked back at the line of beauty which he had created in the snow. And he saw that it was good. And like the morning stars at the dawn of creation he shouted for joy.

My next vivid memory is of a moment of acute suspense as my ski took control on the southern slope. I had waited too long before turning, and I knew that if I tried to turn in the crust I should be thrown violently outwards; and I was consoled to see that the slope below switched back and up on to the short northern face of the tributary ridge, and there with luck I should strike powder before being carried over the crest on to the next steep slope of sun-crusted snow. . . . Oh, the relief, as the crisp cutting sound of the crust yielded to the velvet touch and soft rustle of powder; but the speed was still uncomfortably high. Could I make the turn or should I be carried over the ridge? It was one of those days when everything goes right and every turn comes off. With a yard to spare my ski swung round to rest.

From the pass to the Schwarzwald we dropped 5,000 feet on the southern slopes, yet by exploiting the friendly aid of the accommodating ridges we had found 4,000 feet of powder-snow ski-ing on these great expanses of crust. Sometimes we followed with long, sinuous curves a winding ribbon of powder only a few yards in breadth, sometimes we could let our ski have their heads, secure in the knowledge that the powder would not change to crust before we could swing to rest. Ski-ing such as this is not for the mentally inert, for there was no point between the pass and the valley which did not call for quick judgement, which did not test the power to diagnose, while still on the move, the ever-changing surface of the snow. This is cross-country ski-ing at its best, a skilled craft, exacting in its demands and generous in its reward.

We paused for a few moments at the frontier between the open slopes and the first of the pines which decorate the last slopes leading down to the valley. The sombre cliffs of the Wetterhorn towered above us, enmeshed in the web of twilight. Every phase of this glorious day seems linked in memory with the changing aspects of the Wetterhorn, from the classic Grindelwald view to the triple-crested peaks which Lory painted from the meadows above Rosenlaui. At every halt our eyes instinctively turned towards our great companion. We had "learned his great language, caught his clear accents," and now as the shadows deepened we paid him the tribute of a grateful farewell.

The last few hundred feet of curving descent through a pattern of pine carried us from the colour and radiance of the high mountains into the kingdom of unchallenged winter. We had reached the sheltered and shadowed valley, where the firs sagged beneath their burden of snow, and where the river-bed was a stranger to the benediction of the sun. We called a short halt beside an inn whose rafters stooped towards and almost met the snow. A group of pines on a western hill suddenly burst into flames as the sun set behind their snow-laden branches.

Easy wood-running and open glades led from Schwarzwald

to Rosenlaui. The crystalline flaky snow rustled under our ski like autumn leaves. It is only in the most sheltered of valleys and in the neighbourhood of river-banks that one finds this most perfect of all forms of powder snow.

The last hint of daylight had vanished from the west as we started slowly along the plain between Rosenlaui and the steep cliff over which the Reichenbach falls to Meiringen. The thin trickle of the river edged its dispirited way round ice-fretted boulders and beneath smothers of snow, and its icy breath reached us in a frosty trail of mist which stung like a whip. It was bitterly cold. The night had broken that bridge of human associations which man laboriously builds between himself and the mountains. All sense of companionship had disappeared. These shadowy masses fading by slow gradations into the sharper darkness of the star-pointed night had recovered their inhuman aloofness. They had forgotten the brief episode of contact with man, and were dreaming, not of that mere yesterday when mammoths lumbered across the rivers of ice which flow down the valley of the Aar, but of that remoter abyss in past time when the first island summits of the Alps appeared above the silent waters of the central seas.

The darkness and solitude and the lonely stars began to oppress us. "*Le silence éternel de ces espaces infinis m'effraie.*" Then suddenly we turned a corner and the valley of Meiringen opened below us, and the inhabited hills sparkled with the cheerful constellations of human lights, evoking friendly pictures of snug interiors, and of the warm welcome which we knew would be awaiting us at the Bear at Meiringen. The Bear is one of those inns which still retain something of the atmosphere of romantic Switzerland. It is the sort of place in which Leslie Stephen or Byron would have felt at home.

The very phrase "cross-country ski-ing" implies travel. The perfect cross-country tour should not end under the same roof from which it started. Our mountain day had ended as all such days should end, not in a cocktail bar, but in a friendly kind of inn, where beer can be ordered "*vom Fass*," and wine can be bought, not by the *bottle*, but by the "*Dezi*."

The books I enjoy writing are the books which I am going to write – next year. Few things are pleasanter than the vague ruminations which end when the book is begun, and few things are more tedious than translating those ruminations into words. No author learns with experience. I began this chapter with high hopes, undeterred by previous failures. My memories of this memorable day were so vivid. . . . I knew exactly what I wanted to say before I began to say it. . . .

*Si nemo ex me quærat scio, si quærente explicari vellim nescio.**

* "If nobody asks me, I know. If I wish to explain, I do not know." – St. Augustine

CHAPTER XXX

Afterthoughts on the Spanish War

BATTLE in Spain" was written two years before the outbreak of the present war. Before this book is published Spain may have declared war on Great Britain.

General Franco incensed the Germans by declaring his neutrality during the Czech crisis of 1938. But the recent collapse of France and the presence of German troops on the Spanish frontier have greatly strengthened the pro-Nazi elements in the Phalangist Party, and the Spain which saved Catholicism in the Iberian Peninsula may yet fight as the ally of the Dictator who is determined to destroy Catholicism in Germany.

Life is a choice of sacrifices, and our effective choice is seldom between white and black, but between various shades of grey. There has been only one war in which all the good people were on one side, and all the bad on the other – the war which ended when the good angels drove the bad angels out of Heaven. The Republicans in the Spanish War, and the

Nazis in the present war, had just grievances to exploit; but the Nationalists in Spain were, and the Allies in the present war are, fighting the battle of Christian civilisation.

The effective choice in Spain was not between a Fascist dictatorship and parliamentary democracy, for Communism had destroyed democracy in Spain; but between a dictatorship under which Christianity could survive, and a dictatorship which had already eliminated organised religion from the territories under its control. The massacre of priests and the destruction of churches was the decisive factor which rallied to the support of General Franco convinced Liberals and Protestants, such as my father, and thousands of Catholics who had no belief in dictatorships, whether of the Right or of the Left, and who would have readily endorsed the verdict of the great French historian, Alexis de Tocqueville, on the consequences of unlimited power.

"Unlimited power," wrote de Tocqueville, "appears to me to be in itself an evil, and a dangerous thing, and the mind of man unequal to the disinterested practice of omnipotence. I think that God alone can exercise supreme and uncontrolled power, because His wisdom and justice are eternally proportionate to His might. But no power on earth is so worthy of honour for itself, or of reverential obedience to the rights which it represents, that I would consent to admit its uncontrolled and all-predominant authority. When I see the right and the means of absolute command are conferred on a people or upon an aristocracy or a democracy, a monarchy or a republic, I recognise the germ of tyranny."

The collapse of France is a good example of the vanity of prophesying. Of all those with whom I have discussed the European complex, one man alone predicted with confidence the French failure. In 1938 General Fuller told me that the Maginot Line would prove to be the tomb of France, a phrase which I have never forgotten and which I recalled more than once during recent months. An Italian friend of mine predicted in October, 1939, the sequence of events in 1940. "The French are all saying," he remarked, "that Gamelin is a great general. How do they know? It will be best to wait until next summer before handing out bouquets. It is not at all unlikely that Germany will overrun France, turning the Maginot Line either through Switzerland or Belgium. It is not pleasant for us to have eighty million Germans on the Brenner, and the Duce will do nothing to establish a German hegemony over Europe. If France collapses, we must join Germany; but I do not think that we shall intervene until the issue has been decided."

A friend of mine in close touch with the Fascist leaders told me that the Duce hated England, not because of sanctions, but because England has forced him under the heel of Hitler. "He may have to fight for Hitler," said my friend, "to prevent Hitler overrunning Italy."

Most of the professional prophets assumed that Russia would be on our side when the war broke out, and that Italy and Spain would lose no time in declaring war on France. Italy would not have declared war had not France collapsed, and nobody who failed to foresee the surrender of France can take credit for predicting events which would not have taken place had France resisted. I am writing these lines just after France has broken off diplomatic relations with Great Britain. We may be at war with France before this book is published. Nobody can be blamed for failing to predict a future in which France will certainly be the tool and may be the ally of Germany, or for failing to foretell the consequences of the French dereliction, consequences which may include a Spanish declaration of war on this country, and a new Civil War in Spain in which Britain will be fighting on the side of the rebels.

Had the Republicans won, the Spanish Government would have been subservient to Russia, whose agents, according to Mr. Gollancz, helped to bring about the French collapse. And even had a Republican Government, favourable to France, been in power, is there any reason to assume that they would have been less ready to bomb Gibraltar than the French? For the first plane to bomb Gibraltar was a French plane! I do not remember that any of our professional prophets predicted that. The truth is that once the Germans had reached the Pyrenees no Spanish Government would be in a position effectively to resist a German demand for an attack on Gibraltar.

The collapse of France has its lessons for England, lessons which will remain unheeded so long as we continue to explain the French *volte-face* as a Fascist counter-revolution. The Paris correspondent of the *Manchester Guardian* (June 27, 1940) pointed out that Pétain was whole-heartedly supported by the pacifist Left Wing elements, by Socialists and by the Radical Party, the backbone of the Third Republic.

II

In retrospect the Spanish War seems dwarfed by the scale of the present tragedy. Spanish Catholicism was at stake in Spain; but it is the future of Christianity in Europe which is in peril at the moment. And yet, in spite of the magnitude of the European tragedy, the Spanish War has its lessons for to-day, and the present trend of Spanish foreign policy has its moral for all those who are concerned for the future of Christianity.

It is relevant to consider the reasons for the Republican defeat, for we may still profit by drawing correct deductions from their failure.

The Republicans began the war with almost everything in their favour. They were in possession of all the great centres of industry. The gold reserves were in their hands. The fleet had rallied to their side. The Nationalist risings in Madrid and in Barcelona had failed. Franco had to begin the reconquest of Spain from Morocco, across Straits in control of a hostile fleet.

On the balance the Republicans received as much assistance from France and Russia as the Nationalists from Germany and Italy.

The Republicans lost because they sacrificed military to political considerations. The war was regarded as a means to an end, political revolution. Officers were appointed for political reasons. The army was "democratised," and the regular officers who remained loyal to the Republic were regarded with profound suspicion. Now there is no reason why officers, like priests, should not be recruited from every social stratum; but unless the officer, like the priest, feels himself to be the representative of a hierarchic tradition, set apart from other men, he will lack the confidence in himself and the power to impose respect which are essential in the ordeal of battle. Democratic formulas cannot be applied in war, which is in essence aristocratic, for leadership in war, to be effective, must be imposed from above, not dictated from below. There were many gallant officers in the Republican army, but there was no sense of hierarchic solidarity. Many a battalion surrendered strong positions and retreated because their officers had no confidence in the staying powers of battalions to the right or to the left.

Many of those who tried to build up the Republican army have since written books to explain their failure. There is widespread agreement that the Nationalists won because their morale was better, and because the Republican military effort was cramped and hampered by the political control of the Communists. I brought back with me to England a curious collection of pamphlets which I found in trenches captured from the Republicans, among them the notes for a speech delivered in English by a political commissar to an American battalion on the supreme importance of an orthodox interpretation of Dialectical Materialism, and a dreary little pamphlet on the alleged phallic origin of Christianity. "The rod of Moses was clearly a phallic symbol." "Poor devils," said General Fuller; "fancy serving out all this dull stuff! What they want is *La Vie Parisienne*."

Political considerations which hampered the military effort proved even more fatal to the industrial effort. The attempt to eliminate at one fell swoop the "profit motive" resulted not only in widespread inefficiency but also in universal corruption. The demand for a *levée en masse* and the indiscriminate arming of workers had a disastrous effect on production. It is much more amusing to lounge about with a rifle than to do an honest day's work. Thousands of oranges, the export of which would have procured foreign exchange, were left rotting on the quays because the men who should have been loading them found it more amusing to round up and shoot Fascist suspects.

The peasants, who were angered by the persecution of the Church and infuriated by the incompetence of bureaucratic control, lost heart. It was interesting to contrast the carefully cultivated fields in territory which had been under Nationalist control since the outbreak of the war with the ill-kempt disorder and neglect of the territory captured from the Republicans.

I met at Malta, in March, 1940, an Italian who had helped to organise the anti-Fascist brigades which fought in Spain on the Republican side. "The principal reason for the Republican defeat," he told me, "was the insensate savagery of the anarchists. The Spaniards are a cruel race, far more cruel than the Italians. We Italians do not want to kill or to be killed. If we have a revolution in Italy we shall shout a great deal and shoot very little. But in Barcelona they shot a great deal and were very silent. The Spanish anarchist exaggerates the vices of the Spaniard and has none of his virtues, excepting courage. He has no sense. I used to try to convince these fools that they would lose the war if they continued to burn churches and to murder priests. But they were pure fanatics beyond the reach of reason. The Republic needed the support of the peasants, and lost that support by its campaign against the Church, for the Spanish peasant is, and will always be, a Catholic."

The Republican leaders did not under-estimate the influence of Catholicism or the folly of the religious persecution, but they were impotent to restrain the anarchists and Communists. Very few of their supporters in England realised the decisive importance of the religious issue. English Liberals have always assumed that all foreigners are more interested in politics than in religion, and that the majority of foreigners ask for nothing better than to be governed by the nearest available equivalent to Mr. Gladstone or Mr. Asquith. The English, in general, irrespective of their political views, find it difficult to believe in the power of ideas which they find uncongenial, and in the existence of popular support for leaders such as Hitler, Mussolini or General Franco, whose views are so painfully un-English.

Progressive opinion in England assumed that Franco would have no friends in Spain except among priests and aristocrats, and that the people would instinctively rally to the support of a government which permitted the active persecution of the religion which was still the religion of the overwhelming majority of the Spanish people. Catholicism and Nationalism may be regrettable survivals from a reactionary age, destined to disappear in the enlightened world of to-morrow, but no sound estimate of contemporary Europe is possible which disregards the immense influence of these ancient loyalties.

It was no less shallow to assume that because General Franco accepted the help of Hitler, enemy of Catholicism, his claim to be defending Catholicism was a mere pretext. Nations fighting for existence have always accepted help, where help was available, irrespective of the religious or political views of their allies. England is a Christian country, but we made every effort to secure an alliance with, and should still be prepared to accept help from, Russia. And rightly so, for our objective is the destruction of Nazism, and we may legitimately play off one anti-Christian dictator against another. The criterion in such matters is the objective of the war – the destruction of Spanish Communism in Franco's case, and of German Nazism in our own.

It will be tragic if Spain is forced by the pressure of the

Germans on the Spanish frontier to fight on the side of the Power which the Vatican undoubtedly regards as the enemy of Christian civilisation. The Church in Spain is as hostile to Nazism as the Church in Italy, but the Spanish Church will be as impotent as the Italian Church to counteract Nazi influence, if the national interests impose subservience to German policy.

In Spain, as elsewhere, Nationalism is a stronger force than Christianity. B. is not necessarily weak because B. is weaker than A. Christianity was the greatest of all influences in the creation of European civilisation, but the influence of Christianity has declined since the Reformation, and the influence of Nationalism has increased.

Nationalism necessarily makes a more immediate appeal to ordinary people than religion. It is easier to love the familiar fields and hills of the home which you have seen than the Heaven which you have not seen; easier to hate the foreigner across the frontier than the legendary Devil.

Nationalism, though it exacts sacrifices in time of war, makes demands which men obey without difficulty and imposes views which men accept with ease; whereas the Church, where she is true to her mission, is always in conflict with unregenerate human nature. The Church recalls us to our duties; whereas Nationalism reminds us of our rights, *Lebensraum*, colonies and so forth. The Church preaches humility, whereas Nationalism urges us to feel proud of our nation and therefore of ourselves as citizens of that nation. The Church insists that we should love our neighbour; Nationalism, that we should be prepared to fight the neighbour across the frontier.

There are, as the Vatican radio recently reminded us, times when Christians must be prepared to fight for their country, and there is no necessary conflict between Nationalism and religion; but though the legitimacy of Nationalism is not in question it is regrettable that Nationalism should be so much stronger than religion.

Regrettable, but not in the least surprising. It is so easy to evoke the enthusiasm of the tribe in defence of its totems, so wearying to be eternally scolding people for doing the things which they want to do, and for leaving undone the things which they do not want to do. It is an uphill task, indeed, to be for ever reminding the rich that they should be charitable, the proud that they should be humble, and the sensual that they should be chaste. In spite of the inherent difficulties of her mission, the Church has raised the average standard of behaviour, has enriched the world with the example of saints, and has imposed a civilised veneer on unregenerate human nature. It is not, however, surprising that the Church usually fails where she comes into conflict with ingrained social customs such as the duel. The Church never ceased to condemn the duel, but men of honour continued to fight. The Church will never compromise on contraception, but Catholics in England and in the States average only one more baby per family than Protestants. The decline in the Catholic birth-rate is due partly to abstinence, partly to an increasing infertility in the urban populations, but also, and in a larger degree, to contraception.

Few things are more wearisome than this constant struggle against fallen human nature; and it is therefore not in the least surprising that ecclesiastics should seize every legitimate opportunity of encouraging people to do what they want to do, or that the Church should have identified herself, wherever possible, with the national or social aspirations of the people among whom she has laboured. In the feudal ages the Church supported feudalism. Why not? There was a great deal to be said for feudalism, as even Marx admits. In democratic countries the Church pays court to King Demos. Why not? There is a great deal to be said for democracy. And if democracy vanishes from Europe, the Church will have to come to terms with the new Cæsarism.

The Church's influence has never been greater than when the Church is allied with revolutionary Nationalism, as in Ireland or in the Spain of the Civil War or in Serbia during the Turkish domination. I cannot recall a single case in which a country has subordinated national to religious interests, but I remember many instances where religious have been subordinated to national interests.

The case for a church, universal and supra-national, is strengthened by the fact that the ordinary Christian is always at the mercy of his national loyalties. It is therefore essential that there should be one who can speak, not as an English, Italian, French or German bishop, but as the Father of the whole Christian family. And in these tragic days it is a source of pride and consolation for Englishmen to know that the Pope has made it clear that he hopes for a victory for our arms. The Vatican has always been well disposed towards Great Britain for two reasons: first, because there is no empire in which Catholic missionaries are treated with greater courtesy and consideration than in our own; second, because we preach and practise the principle of religious tolerance. In England, Catholics, like other people, have to contribute to the support of State schools, but Catholic schools are subsidised by the government. In the United States Catholics have to pay for the secular education of American youth, and receive no assistance from the government for their own schools. Catholic Malta, where I lectured in February, 1940, is an interesting example of British tolerance. A Maltese anti-clerical who feels a sudden impulse to break a clerical window can satisfy this complex for two pounds ten if he throws a stone through the Anglican Chaplain's window, but must pay five pounds if his target is the Archbishop's house.

After my lecture in Malta I received a letter from a Maltese Catholic on the familiar theme that this war is nothing but a struggle for power between rival imperialisms. My correspondent was characteristic of some Christians in neutral countries whose anti-British complex is more powerful than their love of the Church or their concern for the fate of Catholics in Poland, Bohemia or Germany. The mental processes of such people are controlled by inherited prejudices and uninfluenced by reason. Even if England were all that England's enemies represent her to be, what matters in this war is not England's past but Europe's future, for if we fail Christian civilisation will vanish from Europe. As indeed the Vatican realises. Three weeks after Italy had declared war, an American priest is reported in *The Times* of July 5, 1940, as having spoken as follows on the short-wave broadcast from the Vatican to the States:

"It is clear," he said, "that we have been allowing our unreasoned fear of what we call entangling alliances to obscure an obvious duty of charity towards the defenders of our own cause, which the Pope has called the cause of universal morality. The conscience of the isolationist is to-day ill at ease. He is faced with the inevitable consequences of his selfishness and is visibly afraid that his eleventh-hour offer of help to the afflicted branch of his family has come too late even to save himself.

"We shall speak to-night of the Christian attitude towards military service. We have sympathy with the pacifists, but they are wrong. No word in the Gospel or in Papal teaching suggests that justice should go undefended, or that it is not worth dying for. Conscientious objectors can be respected for their opinions, but their error does not excuse them from the responsibilities of patriotism. . . . The Church is no conscientious objector. Our Lord lived among soldiers and he never placed soldiers in a class with the Pharisees, the publicans, money-changers, or avaricious rich men. There is no suggestion in the Gospel that our Lord could not admit the hypothesis that two nations could be at war and one of them be in the right."

In conclusion let me repeat that I am not trying to prove that religion has very little influence, but merely that religion is far less influential than Nationalism. That devotion to the Church can influence men to support an unpopular cause is proved by the fact that millions of Catholics in democratic countries supported Franco. Of these Catholics the great majority would have sympathised with the Republicans had not the Republicans persecuted religion.

CHAPTER XXXI

Come What May

THE Persian soldier in Herodotus, who was following Xerxes to the disaster which he had foreseen, confides to a fellow-guest at the banquet that complete and impotent prescience — πολλὰ φρονέοντα μηδενὸς κρατέειν — is the bitterest pain that man can know.

I have recalled in this book the premonitions of war and ruin which haunted me during the Olympic Games at Garmisch, but because prescience was not complete, because one always continued to hope against hope, I continued, unlike the soldier in Herodotus, to enjoy the banquet of life. What was the use of worrying? Impotent prescience absolves one from the duty of continuing to play Cassandra. All one can do is to put one's views on record and leave it at that.

"There is a strange and disquieting parallel," I wrote in the summer of 1936,* "between the attitude of the untravelled Englishman to-day and the confident complacency of the men who were living in the last decade of the Roman Empire. The legend

* *Within That City*, pp. 217–222.

of the invincible Roman legions lasted right up to the sack of Rome, and the legend that England will always muddle through, losing every battle but the last, will survive until England awakens to find herself a small and unimportant island in the North Sea . . . the atmosphere of untroubled security peculiar to this country is particularly striking to those who live much abroad. The effect of this contrast, which is so marked on one's return, gradually fades as the soporific climate of English prosperity reasserts itself. One forgets, because one wishes to forget, that we are continuing to enjoy a far higher standard of comfort than our European neighbours, and that our neighbours, in their peevish way, are less reconciled than they were to the mysterious dispensations of a providence which has filled the English with good things and sent most of the Europeans empty away. Our own people are scarcely aware of the growing savagery of the world in which we live, and have no fear that our little island of goodwill and friendliness may one day be submerged by the rising tide of brutality. We enjoy wagging a moral finger at wicked Europeans, and still continue to hope that the collective security of Geneva will provide us with the security which less noble races are forced to seek in that conscription which is still unthinkable to the freedom-loving Englishman. We smile indulgently at the pacifists of the Oxford Union, and encourage dictators in their belief that we are too decadent 'to fight for King and Country,' and we reinforce this low estimate of our courage by peace ballots which may well have been among the deciding factors that provoked the Abyssinian war. Is the British Empire doomed to imminent destruction, or does our stock still contain hidden recuperative powers which may avert or at least postpone the inevitable end? It may be so, but the omens are not propitious:

> "*Nous n'irons plus au bois*
> *Les lauriers sont coupés. . . .*"

"Auricular confession," writes Goethe, "should never have been taken away from mankind." Autobiography is a modern and imperfect substitute, for most autobiographies would be classified as imperfect confessions. It is tempting to remind the reader of the occasions on which one was right, easy to forget how often one was wrong. Though the plight of England to-day seems to justify the pessimism of the predictions which I have just quoted, the splendid courage of our fighting men has proved that the English stock contains the recuperative powers which I had been inclined to doubt. Indeed, disasters of recent months, so far from weakening our resolution, have cured all save the wilfully blind of the illusions responsible for our present misfortunes.

II

Hitler has displayed great ingenuity in exploiting the weapon of fear. The soldier of to-day is exposed to giant tanks, dive-bombing, bombs fitted with screaming sirens, and so on, but war only becomes unendurable when men lose self-control and the self-respect which is born of self-control. Thousands of parents must have asked themselves, when the New Armies went into action, whether their sons would stand up to the grim ordeal of totalitarian war. My wife and I had a personal interest in this problem, for our second son, John, was in Flanders.

In times of great anxiety one returns to the classics, which never date. I reread the last act of "Macbeth" while our armies battled their way towards the coast:

Ross. Your son, my Lord, has paid a soldier's debt. . . .
Siward. Had he his hurts before?
Ross. Aye, on the front.
Siward. Why then, God's soldier be he!
Had I as many sons as I have hairs
I would not wish them to a fairer death.

From the moment that the army crossed the frontier into Belgium an impenetrable curtain separated them from their relations at home. We did not even know whether John was in Flanders or whether he was still in France. After the surrender of the Belgian army it seemed impossible that our own armies could escape, and then slowly the rumour of a miracle took shape. Husbands, brothers, and sons began to come back from Dunkirk. . . .

My son was a private in the Royal Warwickshires, which fought a series of desperate rearguard actions, and which was among the last of the battalions to leave Dunkirk. The days passed, and our hearts leaped with hope every time the telephone rang, and it was not always easy to reply as cordially as we could have wished to those whose only crime was that they were themselves and not John.

And then suddenly the voice came through for which we had been waiting: "Mummy, is that you? Yes, I'm absolutely all right. But we would none of us be here but for our Colonel. He deserved the V.C. six times over."

When we met John talked of the war in a curiously detached way, as if he were describing events of which he had been a remote spectator. "Life in Coventry," he said, "was so dull that even a street accident seemed interesting. I didn't believe that anything interesting could ever happen to me, and for a long time I felt that the war wasn't real, only a kind of a street accident on a big scale. Of course I had the wind up when the dive-bombers came over and the shelling began."

After he had left, Colonel Mole, his commanding officer, wrote to my wife, and said some very nice things about John's bravery at the Front. A copy of the letter was sent to John, who replied: "I am completely baffled by the Colonel's letter. Have you seen the film 'Freedom'?" And then followed two pages about films.

Private Lunn is introduced into this story not as an individual but as a type, a rank-and-file representative of the new armies who are hoping for a return match with the Nazis on the home ground. I have met civilians who have been mesmerised by

Hitler's success, and who seem to think of Germans as supermen, beyond the dominion of time and space, but such defeatist mysticism is unknown among those who have met the Germans on the field of battle, and who are serenely confident that they are more than a match for the Germans, provided that the odds against them are no heavier than the odds which our airmen have successfully defied.

From the other side of the Atlantic comes an echo of the confidence which inspired them, and inspires the New Armies to go forward from a glorious defeat to a still more glorious triumph.

"So long as the English tongue survives," writes the *New York Times* of June 1, 1940, "the word Dunkirk will be spoken with reverence. For in that harbour, in such a hell as never blazed on earth before, at the end of a lost battle, the rags and blemishes that have hidden the soul of democracy fell away. There, beaten but unconquered, in shining splendour, she faced the enemy.

"They sent away the wounded first. Men died so that others could escape. It was not so simple a thing as courage, which the Nazis had in plenty. It was not so simple a thing as discipline, which can be hammered into men by a drill sergeant. It was not the result of careful planning, for there could have been little. It was the common man of the free countries, rising in all his glory out of mill, office, factory, mine, farm, and ship, applying to war the lessons learned when he went down the shaft to bring out trapped comrades, when he hurled the lifeboat through the surf, when he endured poverty and hard work for his children's sake.

"This shining thing in the souls of free men Hitler cannot command, or attain, or conquer. He has crushed it, where he could, from German hearts.

"It is the great tradition of democracy. It is the future. It is victory."

The courage and confidence of the men who came back from

Dunkirk may have contributed to a curious change of mood. There was less faith in ultimate victory before Dunkirk than after the capitulation of France.

There is no tradition of defeat in this country, for we have never been successfully invaded since the Norman Conquest, and until the Germans broke through at Sedan, no Englishman doubted the great dogma of British invincibility which we have inherited from our ancestors. Invasion, refugees, annexation, Gestapo – these things might happen to the Czechs, Poles, Norwegians, Dutch, Belgians, and French, but they just could not happen here. And then doubt dawned, and Englishmen began to wonder whether our inviolability was in fact a law of Nature. Through my open window I can see the roses in my garden at Bickley. I remember a shell crater in an Ypres garden in 1915, a crater which was the only evidence of war and disorder in the Flemish neatness of a garden whose owner had only just fled from Ypres. I remember unexploded hand grenades between beds of violets in a garden at Pozuelos, just outside Madrid, and the angry bark of a machine gun on the other side of the wall. Ypres, Madrid – Bickley?

Will there be a shell-hole in our bed of roses, and a machine-gun in action in the road which passes our home? Why not? One of our greatest assets in this struggle is the conviction that a British defeat would be a monstrous reversal of nature, and a German invasion an intolerable impertinence. "What the dickens do you think you're doing here?" exclaimed an Englishwoman when a German airman landed in her back garden. And the German, having no reply to this indignant question, handed over his revolver without a murmur.

III

I retain a vivid memory of the Diamond Jubilee of 1897, and of the little old lady, a diminutive but formidable figure, who symbolised England riding on the crest of a splendid wave. I often ask myself whether I would have preferred to have lived and died in the complacent security of our Augustan Age or survived to see England defeated. As I do not believe that England will be defeated, I need not answer that question, but at least I can put on record the fact that I do not envy our complacent grandfathers, and that I would not buy their security by surrendering the experience of the weeks during which we faced the possibility of invasion and ruinous defeat.

Those who have lived through wars and revolutions and who have faced the possibility of defeat and slavery have an infinitely greater understanding of the past than those who have merely read of these things in the quiet security of protected existence. I remember reading Maupassant's vivid stories of the Franco-Prussian War while I was at Oxford. I was interested, but the mental climate of that period seemed curiously remote. But if I were to reread Maupassant to-day I should understand, for I have seen refugees flying from a German advance and have passed through a Paris under the shadow of imminent surrender. I learned a great deal from De Tocqueville and Carlyle about the French Revolution, but I learned more from the few weeks I spent in revolutionary Spain during the Civil War. A recurring pattern runs through history, a pattern which we most clearly perceive when we ourselves have relived the poignant experiences of the past. Our Victorian grandfathers believed that the age of Reason and inevitable progress had dawned, but we have learned that there can only be an uneasy truce in the unending struggle between those who fight for freedom and those who are determined to enslave the soul of man. In every age there will be men who counsel surrender, and men who will reply: "If Athens betrayed these things it would not be well." There will always be periods when the lamps of freedom go out one by one, and tyranny seems triumphant, and there will always be men who will draw the moral that it would have been better to have compromised with evil things than to have fought on, hoping for ultimate victory and risking defeat.

Athens, under the leadership of Demosthenes, tried to rally the Greek states against Philip of Macedonia and Athens was defeated at Chæronea. And there were many who attacked Demosthenes, and who insisted that Athens should have kept clear of entanglements and surrendered the leadership of the Greek states to Philip, just as there are many to-day who are beginning to whisper that we were foolish to guarantee Poland, or to seek to unite the free countries of Europe against the Nazi dictatorship. Let Demosthenes answer our modern faint-hearts in words which are for all time: "Even if the future had been revealed to all men, even then Athens could only have acted as she did if she remembered her ancestors or valued her good name in the ages to come. For the moment it seems as if she had failed, as man must always fail if God wills it. But had Athens, who claimed to be the leader of Greece, surrendered her position to Philip, she would have been dishonoured for betraying the common cause. Athens has never in all her history surrendered to an oppressor, however formidable, or bartered freedom for servile security. . . . Men of Athens, be very sure that you did well when you imperilled yourself for the safety and for the freedom of all. . . ."

The remote possibility that London may fall helps us to read something of our own anxiety into St. Jerome's cry of anguish when he heard that Rome had been sacked. "When I learned that the bright light of all the world had been extinguished, that the Roman Empire had lost its head, and that the whole universe had perished in one city, then, indeed, 'I became dumb and humbled myself and kept silent.' " He did not keep silent for long. Rome had fallen, but the world went on, and the old problems recurred in a new setting. St. Jerome soon recovered his old form, and continued with uneroded enthusiasm to impart the kind of advice which saints continue to give and which sinners continue to disregard. " 'Her sex,' you will say, 'is particularly suitable for household service.' Choose an old woman, then, choose one who is misshapen, choose one of proved continence in the Lord."

Advice which is, no doubt, equally sound in connection with other appointments than housekeeping.

It is consoling in times such as this to discover that even the unheroic possess reserves of courage upon which they can draw. I have described, earlier in this book, a Ski Championship at Innsbruck which degenerated into a rehearsal for war. Peter was competing, and I was partially responsible for that disastrous fiasco, and my hair, which was brown when I went to Innsbruck, was dusted with odd wisps of grey when I returned. Peter and his wife and child are in Malta, which is bombed almost daily, and no letters have come through since Italy declared war, but my hair is no greyer, and the possibility that Peter, Antoinette and David may be wiped out by a chance bomb at Malta, or my wife and I at Bickley, in no way spoils the pleasure of such pleasures as still come one's way, as, for instance, an evening with a very dear friend at a Sadler's Wells performance of "The Magic Flute." At times such as these one learns to catch happiness on the wing. "We are all," says Victor Hugo, "under sentence of death, with a kind of indefinite reprieve." But when we are young we believe ourselves to be immortal, and are less grateful than we might be for the beauty which dies.

> And since to look at things in bloom
> Fifty springs are little room,
> About the woodlands I will go
> To see the cherry hung with snow.

We are less exacting than the "Shropshire Lad." Fifty days was "room" enough to glory in the loveliest spring in human memory – the spring of 1940 – with which Nature did her best to compensate for the folly of man.

The Napoleon of Notting Hill no longer reads like a Chestertonian fantasy. How I wish that Mr. Chesterton could have lived to see men organising the difficult defence of Beaconsfield! How he would have chuckled with delight at notices in Hyde Park, "To the Trenches." In the old days romance began for me when I set foot on foreign soil, but I have rediscovered romance in England at war. May can be beautiful not only on Maggiore, but in Regent's Park.

That happiness and understanding must be paid for in the coin of pain and suffering is a truth which mystics never cease to proclaim, a doctrine whose validity even the unmystical majority can verify in times such as these. For surely our love of England is far deeper and more understanding to-day than the rococo patriotisms of the Kipling age? We have recaptured the vision of the England that faced Napoleon:

> Another year! Another deadly blow!
> Another mighty Empire overthrown!
> And we are left, or shall be left, alone;
> The last that dare to struggle with the Foe.
> 'Tis well! From this day forward we shall know
> That in ourselves our safety must be sought;
> That by our own right hands it must be wrought,
> That we must stand unpropped, or be laid low.
> O Dastard whom such foretaste doth not cheer!
> We shall exult . . .

Exult . . . Wordsworth was right. It is more inspiring to have a mere walking-on part in the supreme drama of England's battle for the freedom of Europe than to play lead in the complacent comedy of the Victorian Age. The old barrier between men of action and men of thought disappears in times such as these, for even the philosopher must bestir himself if a bomb falls near his study. "The person that has acted fears," writes Emerson, "the person that looks on is formidable." Is De Valera then less formidable than Hitler? Even Emerson could not have written such nonsense had he lived through these last weeks in Europe.

To-day the enemy holds the coast-line from the Arctic Circle to the Spanish frontier. The hopes of millions of the enslaved, in Bohemia, Poland, Norway, Holland, Belgium, France, Austria and Germany, are centred on our island fortress.

Come what may, I am glad to have lived on into these difficult but glorious days, and for the rest –

Adhuc confitebor illi.

May 1st, 1938 – July 20th, 1940